The Native American
in American Literature

Recent Titles in
Bibliographies and Indexes in American Literature

The Native American in American Literature

A Selectively Annotated Bibliography

Compiled by **Roger O. Rock**

Bibliographies and Indexes in American Literature, Number 3

Greenwood Press

Westport, Connecticut • London, England

Library of Congress Cataloging in Publication Data

Rock, Roger O.
The Native American in American literature.

(Bibliographies and indexes in American literature,
ISSN 0742-6860 ; no. 3)
1. American literature—History and criticism—
Bibliography.   2. Indians in literature—Bibliography.
3. American literature—Indian authors—History and
criticism—Bibliography.   4. American literature—
Indian authors—Bibliography.   5. Indians of North
America—Bibliography.   I. Title.   II. Series.
Z1229.I52R64   1985   016.81′09′3520397   84-27972
[PS173.I6]
ISBN 0-313-24550-9 (lib. bdg.)

Library of Congress Catalog Card Number: 84-27972
ISBN: 0-313-24550-9
ISSN: 0742-6860

First published in 1985

Greenwood Press
A division of Congressional Information Service, Inc.
88 Post Road West, Westport, Connecticut 06881

Printed in the United States of America

10 9 8 7 6 5 4 3 2 1

For Mom and Dad,
and Luella Roller,
my ninth grade English teacher

Contents

Preface

This work is intended to serve as a starting point for students of the American Indian in literature or of American Indian literature. Researchers, teachers planning curricula, and librarians at all levels will find it especially useful.

Several years ago, when I was a graduate student trying to write a critical paper on the role of the Indian in American fiction, my first trips to the library turned up few references to the Native American in literature and even fewer references to Native American literature. However, I soon discovered that the problem was not that there wasn't such information--indeed, there turned out to be a large and ever-increasing supply of it--but that little bibliographical control had been exercised over it. I set out to do something about that and, happily for all of us trying to do research in the field, so have several others.

It is to the good fortune of all of us that none of us recently producing a bibliography seems to have greatly duplicated the work of any other. There is some overlap from one bibliography to the next, but in every case the focus of the work is different, and the nature of the annotations (if any) is unique.

There is no comprehensive bibliography on the American Indian in literature, but there have been some recent listings of Native American literature that can be considered nearly so. Bibliographies dealing specifically with Native American literature--that is, with works by Indian authors--are discussed generally in the introduction to the "Native American Literature" section of this book. Of those bibliographies that, like this one, deal with several aspects of literature by and about Indians, only two really have much in common with this one, and there are some important differences. (The numbers in parenthesis are the entry numbers of the listings in this collection.)

Jack Marken's The American Indian: Language and Literature (180) offers nearly 3,700 listings of books and articles in sixteen categories but with emphasis on works by Indians. Marken lists about 100 bibliographies and some works on literature, including nearly 200 critical discuss-

-ions, but the bibliography is not annotated. Anna Lee Stensland's Literature by and about the American Indian (265) is thoroughly annotated but is clearly aimed at meeting the needs of teachers from kindergarten through high school, cites books primarily, and offers few critical texts.

Several other works are much more general and have relatively little to do with literature. One of the most recent of these is Dwight Smith's Indians of the United States and Canada: A Bibliography, Volume II (254). It offers more than 3,000 titles but fewer than 50 involve literature. A favorite of historical researchers that has been recently updated is Francis Paul Prucha's A Bibliographical Guide to the History of Indian-White Relations in the United States (232). There are more than 9,000 citations in this work, but only 126 are concerned with Indians in literature.

This bibliography is intended to augment rather than to compete with works such as those mentioned above and those noted in the "Native American Literature" section. It is perhaps the most eclectic collection available that focuses on literature, drawing upon the resources of universities, high schools, museums, public and private libraries, government agencies, and individuals. It has taken advantage of the bibliographies compiled by anthropologists, literature students, theology students, folklorists, psychologists, linguists, historians, and students of proba- bly a dozen other disciplines. Included here are books, catalogs, pamphlets, scholarly journal and popular magazine articles, theses, dissertations, and microforms. I have drawn the line only at nonprint media and foreign language sources, which are not included.

The "Bibliographies" section contains 307 citations, 99 of them annotated; the "Indian in Literature" section, 395 items, 128 annotated; and the "Native American Literature" section 897 titles, 290 annotated.

Although I endeavored to acquire and read all the works noted, I was not totally successful in this. Works not personally seen are not annotated unless I was able to find several separate secondary sources to coincide on certain points of description. In any case, annotations for the most part simply describe the contents as they pertain to the Indian in literature, and they were considered unnecessary where the title "says it all." The need for annotations is probably obviated to some extent by the sub- ject index. In a very few cases only incomplete bibliographical data was obtainable, but this, too, was passed on--better a slim lead than none at all, I figured.

I did not set out to examine general reference books, literary histories, general critical works, such as books on American literature or western American literature, or works dealing with genres of literature, even though portions of such works must inevitably deal with the Indian's role in literature as a character. However, whenever such works with significant portions were discovered, I did include them. The reader is reminded that the contents of this bibliography certainly do not represent the sum of what has been written on the Indian in literature.

My search for materials on the Indian in literature en-
compassed a period of a little over six years. Because I
was and am a full-time high school English teacher with many
extracurricular duties, my work on this project was
relegated to evenings, weekends, and what free time existed
during the summer months. It was accomplished on my own
time and without any grant or scholarship. During summers I
used the on-campus resources of the Eastern Montana College
Library in Billings and the Mansfield Library at the
University of Montana in Missoula. Because of my location
in the remote northeast corner of the state, however, I did
most of my work through the local public library. However,
I don't think the circumstances of my work make it less
thorough; if anything, the opposite is true. Library and
data base searches take time. I had time to wait on these
things; moreover, I had time to explore works I obtained.
Additionally, telephones and computers have given outpost
libraries virtually the same access to information that any
university library has, albeit not convenient access to
large reference collections. I had access to the resources
of the Montana State Library and the libraries of Montana's
federations as well as to the computer databases of the
Pacific Northwest Bibliographic Center (PNBC) and its
successor, the Washington Library Network (WLN). The WLN is
a computer system linking the resources of a hundred
libraries in Washington, Oregon, Idaho, Montana, Alaska, and
British Columbia. The database currently has information
for more than 2,500,000 bibliographic records which include
books, periodicals, films, and other library resources.

Acknowledgments

I owe a special debt of gratitude to the librarians who have helped me over the years, most especially to Mary Moore, Director of the Glasgow (Montana) City-County Library and Coordinator of the Golden Plains Library Federation; to her successor, Shirley Krotz; and to the following employees of the Glasgow Library: Kathy Ellerton, Inter-Library Loan Librarian; Betty Jo Reigel, Inter-Library Loan Librarian and morale-booster; Donna Boots, Acquisitions Librarian and Critic; Karen Ortman, Inter-Library Loan and Outreach Librarian; Cindy Winter, Assistant Inter-Library Loan Librarian; Jeanne McCreadie, circulation; Phyllis Maxson, Jane Stewart and Rose Corey.

The librarians of the Montana State Library (Helena), the Pacific Northwest Bibliographic Center (Seattle), and the Washington Library Network (Seattle) were also most helpful; I regret I cannot thank them all by name, but they did their work for me largely anonymously.

I must also thank the Nashua (Montana) School Board of Trustees and the school administrators, Don Gilbertson, who was superintendent when I started the project, and Robert Barnes, who was superintendent when I finished it, for allowing me use of school equipment and the school library.

Introduction: Beginning Literary Research on Native Americans

Research on American Indians poses some unusual problems for students of literature. Mainstream critical works in American literature that consider the literary treatment of the American Indian more frequently deal with the Indian as a subtopic than as a major focus of study, so one must learn to pay more attention to chapter headings than to book titles. Then, too, much of the scholarship involving Native American literature (Indian authors), and to some extent the treatment of Indians in literature, has not been accomplished by students of literature but by linguists, cultural anthropologists, educators, folklorists, historians and others whose domains fall outside the humanities. Consequently, conventional sources often have little pertinent information in them, while sources outside the discipline may offer a great deal of it.

The situation, of course, is changing. Indian literature is beginning to move toward the niche it deserves in American arts and letters, and Indian treatment in literature is being reappraised in the light of modern literary open-mindedness. But the works of the past remain a tangle. This bibliography and the others recommended in the preface and in the introduction to the "Native American Literature" section should steer researchers through most of the problems, but for those who want to "light out for Indian territory" on their own, here are some bits of wisdom on doing research on Indians in literature that were acquired the hard way.

Two of the most important names any researcher must know for doing any kind of research are Wilson and Bowker, publishers respectively of <u>The Reader's Guide to Periodical Literature</u> (1900--) and <u>Books in Print</u> (1956--), which generally are the first two stops on any quest for basic information. "Indians, Bibliographies," "Indians in Literature," "Indian Literature," "Indian Legends," and "Indians, Folklore," are among relevant subject headings in both references. Not only do these books list virtually everything published for common consumption, but even the smallest of libraries is likely to have them.

Unfortunately, the earlier versions of these reference books did not cover the wide territory that those of the last several years do, which causes a kind of inverted pyramid effect when going backwards through them: The further back you go, the less you find. A predecessor of Reader's Guide was William F. Poole's Index to Periodical Literature, 1802-1906 (rev. ed., Boston: Houghton Mifflin, 1893-1908), which indexed more than 400 periodicals by subject but not by author. The Cumulative Book Index (Wilson, 1928-1968) was a library standard before Books in Print took over, and some libraries have complete sets. (They have an insulation value of about R45 and are often kept on the coldest wall of the basement.) The Bibliographic Index: A Cumulative Bibliography of Bibliograhies (Wilson, 1934--) is another starting point, as is Bowker's American Book Publishing Record Annual, but for these one will probably have to visit a larger public library or a university. The same is true for the Library of Congress catalogs, the Social Sciences and Humanities Index (Wilson, 1907--), Dissertation Abstracts (Ann Arbor, Michigan: University Microfilms, 1938--), and other indexes of scholarly writings, chief among which are the Popular Periodicals Index and the Essay and General Literature Index in the humanities and Abstracts in Anthropology and Historical Abstracts in the social sciences.

Special mention also needs to be made of a very convenient source of information on a variety of subjects relating to education. This is the Educational Resources Information Center (ERIC), a federally funded national information system sponsored by the U. S. Office of Education, which is accessible in most libraries. The ERIC Clearinghouse on Rural Education and Small Schools (CRESS) collects materials related to rural education and small schools, and American Indian, Mexican American, migrant and outdoor education for input into the national ERIC system. There are numerous bibliographies, as well as other types of books and articles, on the American Indian published by ERIC and/or ERIC/CRESS. Most of these are available in microfiche from depositories scattered across the country and in both microfiche and hard copy from ERIC Document Reproduction Service (EDRS), Customer Service, P.O. Box 190, Arlington, VA 22210. Current prices of ERIC materials are available from EDRS, but ERIC despositories should have them. Items listed in this book which are usually available in microfiche are marked with ERIC's order number, a six digit number preceded by the letters ED. Some items have an ED number but are not available from EDRS. In addition, ERIC compiles the Current Index to Journals in Education (CIJE), a monthly index which provides citations from more than 500 major educational publications. Research in Education is ERIC's monthly abstract journal announcing recently completed research and research-related reports in education. The ERIC resources plus the Education Index (Wilson, 1929--), which classifies more than 150 magazines, among them College English and English Journal, pretty well cover any research in the field of education that might relate to the Indian in literature.

Two especially useful periodicals that are indexed an-
nually by their publishers are <u>American Literature</u> (Durham,
NC: Duke University Press), and <u>Western American Literature</u>
(Logan, Utah: Western American Literature Association).
These two professional journals publish critical articles
and reviews pertinent to their areas of concern, and
occasionally this involves the Indian as author or
character.

Bibliographies of American literature abound. Some are
broad, sweeping collections, others very specific; some
claim to be "comprehensive," others to be "selective." An
example of the big collections is Charles Evans', <u>American</u>
<u>Bibliography: A Chronological Dictionary of All Books. . .</u>,
which consists of 12 volumes and chronologically catalogs
35,854 titles of works printed in America. It was privately
printed for the author by Columbia Press from 1903-1904 and
was reprinted in 1941-1942 and again in 1959 by Peter Smith
of New York. Other examples are <u>American Bibliography 1801-</u>
<u>1819</u> by Ralph R. Shaw and Richard H. Shoemaker, which was
brought out in 22 volumes by Scarecrow Press in 1963, and
Bradford M. Fullerton's <u>A Selective Bibliography of Ameri-</u>
<u>can Literature, 1775-1900</u> (New York: William Payson, 1932;
New York: Dial Press, 1936).

Some American literature bibliographies pursue courses
that I would call--for lack of a better word--obliquely
related to the course of this book; that is, not quite
parallel: The subjects are closely related but separated by
the thin, but opaque, partitions of academic discipline.
The best example of this I can think of is the two volumes
on western American literature by Richard Etulain: <u>Western</u>
<u>American Literature: A Bibliography of Interpretive Books</u>
<u>and Articles</u> (Vermillion, South Dakota: Dakota Press, 1972)
and <u>A Bibliographical Guide to the Study of Western American</u>
<u>Literature</u> (Lincoln: University of Nebraska Press, 1982).
Etulain lists many books on the frontier, western
literature, regional literature, pioneers, and so on that
contain pertinent material on Indian literature and Indians
in literature. (For more detailed descriptions of Etulain's
works, see the entries in the "Bibliographies" section.) But
whether or not books like Etulain's have any Indian
material, or how much they have, is often never clear
because such contents are rarely described. Etulain has, in
his latest work, isolated 129 titles that specifically deal
with Indians, but the relevance of the bulk of his
collection to Indian studies is uncertain. The most
practical approach to such collections would seem to be from
a broad-based general subject cross-reference list; that is,
for example, if one were interested in the treatment of
Indian women in literature, one might single out works on
women in literature, frontier women, frontier life, frontier
letters and diaries, the western hero, and the frontier in
American literature in ascending order of desperation. When
works, like Etulain's, were known to contain relevant
listings they were included in this collection, but
obviously most could not be adequately explored.
Researchers should be on the lookout for these kinds of

books and bear in mind that--even though such works may make
no mention of Indians in the title or elsewhere--they could
be full of useful material.
     The Guide to American Literature and Its Backgrounds
since 1890 by Howard Mumford Jones and Richard M. Ludwig, 3d
ed., rev. (Cambridge, Massachusetts: Harvard University
Press, 1964) tries to present to the reader "in
understandable order" the "intellectual and sociological
(political) events and literary productivity" of the period.
This work exemplifies that cross between bibliography and
history--called a literary history--that typifies a variety
of the more specific studies. Presence of the words
"guide," or "literary history" in the title are good
indicators that this is what you are getting. Part II of
the Jones-Ludwig book, however, is a list of American titles
since 1890.   But one can pore over many such compendiums
without learning much about Indians in literature. Clarence
Gohdes's Bibliographical Guide to the Study of Literature of
the United States (Durham, North Carolina: Duke University
Press, 1959) is divided into 35 sections, each cataloging a
different category of literary resource material. Section
31, "Literature on or by Racial or other Minorities," lists
only seven works on Indians. However, other sections, such
as "Selected Studies of Regional Literature," might prove
useful.
     Literary History of the United States: History, edited
by Robert E. Spiller, Willard Thorpe, Thomas H. Johnson,
Henry Seidel Canby, Richard M. Ludwig, and William M. Gibson
(4th ed. rev.   New York: Macmillan Co., Inc., 1974), with
contributions from some 53 other literary scholars, is a
work that represents trends in American thought perhaps more
accurately than most because it is the product of
collaboration and because it has evolved through four
editions since 1947.   Unlike many such works, this one
contains a chapter (by Stith Thompson) on American Indian
literature, "The Indian Heritage." The article is a concise
discussion of the nature of the oral literature of the Indians that might serve as an introduction to Indian literature, and the bibliography at the end of the book does
suggest some additional reading. More importantly,
probably, Literary History of the United States: History
does not ignore treatment of the Indian in works by authors
who feature him as a character; thus, someone researching
the role of the Indian in literature might gain some broad
understanding from this work and perhaps even some insight
into the evolution of the Indian in literature.
     Two other types of reference material that can prove to
be invaluable or to be total wastes of time are local lists
and lists of unpublished material. In either case, if the
list is out of date, there is a good chance the material it
documents is unavailable; in fact, even where cited in a
recent bibliography, it is likely that the list itself is
unavailable. Unless pertinence of such a list is evident by
its title or by its description, the material it contains
may very well be irrelevant. Norma Olin Ireland's Local Indexes in American Libraries: a Union List of Unpublished In-

dexes (Boston: Faxon, 1947) is a case in point. In its 221
pages of listings it shows only one Illinois high school
library and one Texas junior high as having anything on Indians. However, even though out of date, such lists as
Ireland's have an incidental value: if a school or library
ever kept a list, it may have a current one. This is particularly true for museums and college libraries with large
Native-American-related holdings.

The works that follow do not represent all of what has
been written, nor are they necessarily the best that has
been written. They are simply all that could be found under
the circumstances and in the time allotted.

A word of caution to users of works listed in this one:
Annotations by the bibliographers cited here tend to fall
into two categories, descriptive or evaluative, or into
some blend of the two. To the student of literature, descriptive notes by an anthropologist, depending on his
purposes, aren't always illuminating. However, descriptive
notes—even those by anthropologists—seem to be generally
of more help than the evaluative ones. Evaluative ones,
under the pretext of criticism, tend to fall into two
categories: those which comment on the craftsmanship of the
work and those which are essentially judgments of the
writer's point of view; the former type are of some use, the
latter not much. However, in the main, judgmental notes
would seem to be concerned with the degree to which Indians
are portrayed accurately in the listed work. Accuracy of
portrayal, is, perhaps, a valid criterion for evaluation,
but methods employed in ascertaining accuracy seem sometimes
to be less than scientific. Simply because a list has been
read and approved by Indians, for example, does not make it
an accurate list. But the promoters of some collections
seem to trade on this fact. Many of the booklists for
children or teachers fall into this category. Teachers
should be aware, I think, that cultural authenticity, while
desirable, is no measure of literary merit—if it were,
Faulkner and Cooper and Longfellow would have to be culled
from the curriculum—and that shortcomings which novels and
stories have in their portrayal of Indians do not
necessarily render them useless, although awareness of such
failings is essential if the work is to be used effectively.
Conversely, many "recommended" books are not particularly
good examples of literature. Another failing of
"recommended" lists is that many of the titles omitted from
them because they didn't measure up culturally will end up
in the classroom anyway but most likely without the teacher
being aware that there is anything wrong with them.
Fortunately, some critical lists use literary merit as a
standard and accuracy of portrayal as a point of criticism.

The Native American
in American Literature

Bibliographies

0001. Abler, Thomas S., and Weaver, Sally, M. <u>A Canadian Indian Bibliography, 1960-1970</u>. Toronto: University of Toronto Press, 1974.

> Annotated. Lists material of scholarly interest on Candadian Indians and Metis. Prepared by anthropologists and lawyers, but is multi-disciplinary. All abstracts in English. Deals with only Canadian aspects of Indians on both sides of border. Some Eskimo materials. Some unpublished materials and theses. Case law digest that is a part of it tries to bring together all case law relating to Canadian Indians since July 1867.

0002. Abraham, Pauline. "Bibliography: Indians of North America, Mexican Americans, Negroes--Civil Rights. An Annotated List." Bethesda,MD: EDRS, ED 092 301, May 1974.

> Books, fiction and nonfiction, for use in junior and senior high schools. Annotations point up strengths and weaknesses of each book in author's estimation. Approximately 70 citations in each of the three sections.

0003. "Access to Indian Information." <u>American Library</u>, 4 (January 1973) : 28-29.

> Tells about advent of <u>Index to Literature on the American Indian, 1970.</u>

0004. Altick, Richard D., and Wright, Andrew. <u>Selective Bibliography for the Study of English and American Literature</u>. 2nd ed. New York: Macmillan, 1963.

0005. American Association of School Librarians, Committee on the Treatment of Minorities in Library Books and Other Instructional Materials. "Multi-Ethnic Media:

Selected Bibliographies." <u>School Libraries</u> in installments Winter 1970, Summer 1970, Spring 1971, Summer 1971, Summer 1972; also <u>School Library Journal</u> April 1973.

> According to David Cohen, coordinator of the American Library Association Office for Library Service to the Disadvantaged's Task Force on Ethnic Materials Information Exchange Social Responsibilities Roundtable, "all of the material" from these magazine listings "has been reexamined and items that are no longer available or have been superseded have been dropped" and the remainder included in his book (see Cohen).

0006. <u>American Indian Education, A Selected Bibliography.</u>
    Bethesda, MD: EDRS, ED 030 780, 1969.

> This bibliography and the six supplements (numbered below) that followed it were designed "to provide cumulative coverage of American Indian education throughout currently available issues of <u>Research in Education</u> and <u>Current Index to Journals in Education.</u>" Indexed. Annotated in typical ERIC fashion with descriptors (terms which aid in identifying the relevance of the work), descriptive note (which is sometimes a half-page long), and a citation of the journal from which the item was taken. Many relevant works--including bibliographies, anthologies, and critical works-- from these collections are cited in this bibliography.
>   <u>Supplement No. 1</u>, ED 044 213, October 1970.
>   <u>Supplement No. 2</u>, ED 058 980, September 1971.
>   <u>Supplement No. 3</u>, ED 075 121, March 1973.
>   <u>Supplement No. 4</u>, ED 086 378, February 1974.
>   <u>Supplement No. 5</u>, ED 100 547, February 1975.
>   <u>Supplement No. 6</u>, ED 107 427, June 1975.

0007. <u>American Indian Index, No.1, 1953</u>. Chicago: J.A. Heubner, 1953.

> Analyzes U.S. Bureau of American Ethnology <u>Bulletin</u>. Lists legends, myths, music, mythology. Mimeo.

0008. <u>American Indians, an Annotated Bibliography of Recommended Resource Materials. Elementary Grades.</u>
    Bethesda, MD: EDRS, ED 056 798, 1971.

36 p.   Prepared by Indians representing many tribes and reservations throughout California. Annotated. Purpose is to provide teachers with a recommended list of appropriate materials on Indian culture, heritage, and history. Contains 257 citations of elementary school library books published between 1884 and 1971. Also lists films, recordings, workbooks, and teachers guides. Entries show grade level.

0009. American Indians: An Annotated Bibliography of Selected Library Resources. Bethesda, MD: EDRS, ED 040 004, 1970.

171 p.   Compiled by participants in the Library Services Institute for Minnesota Indians, this annotated bibliography evaluates reference materials from an Indian point of view. Over 500 entries classed by educational level. Includes books, pamphlets, periodicals, films, filmstrips, slides, and records. Most published since 1960.

0010. "American Indians." Booklist 69 (September 15, 1972) : 176-181.

For educators. Titles: 10 primary (K-3), 14 intermediate (4-6), and 10 upper (7-9). Also lists films, film strips, recordings, periodicals. Directory of sources.

0011. American Indian Library Task Force. Alternatives in Print, A Catalog of Social Change Publications, 1st and 2nd editions. Columbus: Ohio State University Library, 1972.

372 p.   Editions 3-5 were published by New Glide Publications, San Francisco. The fifth edition is edited by Noah Levin and was published in 1977-78. Many citations of works published outside the mainstream, some representing "counterculture," some representing racial, ethnic or other minorities. Editions examined were indexed by name of group (publisher) and subject.

0012. American Library Association, Research and Adult Services Division. "Selective Bibliography of Bibliographies of Indian Materials for Adults." American Library 4 (February 1973) : 115-117.

Briefly critically annotated by Will and Lee Antell, both scholars and both Chippewa Indians. Items listed "rated" as "good," "fair," "superior," "poor," "acceptable," or "unacceptable." Criteria used to arrive at these distinctions are not described. Materials are also marked "general" or "scholarly."

0013. Anderson, Barbara Louise. "The Southwestern Indian in Contemporary American Literature 1920-1955; an Annotated Booklist for Adolescent Readers." Professional Paper, School of Library Science. Emporia, Kansas: Emporia State University, 1955.

67 p.   Emporia State University Library said this was unavailable for loan. They didn't say why.

0014. Anderson, John Q., Gaston, Edwin W., Jr., and Lee, James W., eds. Southwestern American Literature: A Bibliography. Athens: Ohio University Press, 1979; Athens: The Swallow Press, 1979.

0015. Anderson, Sue Ellen, compiler. North American Indians: An Annotated Resource Guide for the Elementary Teacher. Center for Indian Education. Farmer College of Education. Arizona State University. Tempe, Arizona; Bethesda, MD: EDRS, ED 085 156, 1972.

0016. "An Annotated Bibliography of Books for Librarians Serving Children of Indian Ancestry." Bethesda, MD: EDRS, ED 041 655, March 18, 1968.

13 p. 79 entries. History, fiction, biography, teacher reference. Most show grade level.

0017. An Annotated Bibliography of Young People's Books on American Indians. Indian Education Curriculum Bulletin No. 12. Bethesda, MD: EDRS, ED 070 547, January 1973.

62 p. Approximately 367 books published between 1931-1972. Several by Indian authors. Graded primary-grade 12. Books chosen for accuracy and fair treatment of Indian. Fiction and non-fiction.

0018. An Annotated Bibliography of Young People's Fiction on American Indians. Curriculum Bulletin No. 11. Office of Education Programs. U. S. Bureau of Indian Affairs. Washington, D.C., 1972.

55 p. Books listed by tribes. Approximately 100 books. Annotated.

0019. Antell, Will and Lee. _American Indians: An Annotated Bibliography of Selected Library Resources._ Institute for Minnesota Indians: University of Minnesota Library Services, 1970.

>   Descriptive annotations. Prepared for Minnesota elementary and high school use.

0020. Aoki, Haruo. _Nez Perce Texts_ Publications in Linguistics, Vol. 90. Berkeley: University of California Press, 1979.

0021. Arizona Library Extension Service, Department of Library and Archives. "Books about Indians by Indians." Phoenix: Arizona Library Extension Service, Department of Library and Archives, 1973.

>   2 p. Arizona and New Mexico authors.

0022. Association on American Indian Affairs. _A Preliminary Bibliography of Selected Children's Books about American Indians._ New York: Association on American Indian Affairs, 1969.

>   14 p. 63 books judged by American Indians to be realistic and unpatronizing. Grouped by age level, primary-high school. Books listed published in 1950's and '60's. Annotated.

0023. Baird, Newton D., and Greenwood, Robert. _An Annotated Bibliography of California Fiction 1664-1970._ Georgetown, CA: Talisman Literary Research, 1971.

0024. Basler, Roy Prentice. _A Guide to the Study of the United States of America: Representative Books Reflecting the Development of American Life and Thought._ Washington, D.C.: Library of Congress, 1960.

>   Chapter One deals with "Literature (1607-1955)," Chapter Seven with "The American Indians." Chapter Seven examines general works; archaeology and prehistory; tribes and tribal groups; religion, art and folklore; the white advance; and the twentieth century. A supplement covering the period 1956-1965 was published in 1976.

0025. Bataille, Gretchen M. "American Indian Literature: A Selected Bibliography for Iowa Schools." Iowa State Department of Public Instruction. Bethesda, MD: ED 170 100, August 1978.

0026. Bataille, Gretchen M., and Silet, Charles L. P.
"The Indian in American Film: A Checklist of
Published Materials on Popular Images of the Indian in
the American Film." Journal of Popular Film 5 (No. 2,
1976): 171-182.

0027. Beder, E. F. "Kingston to Newson to Balke; or
Bibliographical Adventures among the Indians."
Bulletin of the New York Public Library XLVI (June
1942) : 525-530.

0028. Beidler, Peter G. and Egge, Marion F. The American
Indian in Short Fiction: An Annotated Bibliography.
Metuchen, N.J.: Scarecrow Press, 1979.

0029. Bellon, Elmer C. "An Annotated Bibliography of
Children's Literature about California." MA Thesis.
Sacaramento: California State University, 1968.

0030. Berry, Brewton. The Education of American Indians:
A Survey of the Literature. Washington, D.C.: U. S.
Government Printing Office, 1969.

            121 p. See note immediately below.

0031. Berry, Brewton. Foundation of Americans, Indians: A
Survey of the Literature. Columbus: The Research
Foundation of Ohio State University, 1968.

            It is not clear whether this item and
      the one immediately above refer to two works
      by the same author or to one work that is
      listed under two different titles; however, I
      believe the latter to be the case. George
      Spindler reviews the one above in American
      Anthropologist 73 (April 1971) : 388-389.

0032. "Bibliography of Native American Prose Prior to the
Twentieth Century." Indian Historian, 13 (September
1980) : 23-25.

0033. "Bibliography of Recommended Readings." in Vol. 10,
Makers of America--Emergent Minorities, 1955-1970, pp
189-197.   Chicago: Encyclopedia   Britannica
Educational Corp., 1971.

            Fiction and non-fiction involving many
      races, nationalities, in America.

0034. Blacke, Irwin R. The Old West in Fiction. New York:
Obolensky, 1961.

0035. Blaine, Martha R. Pawnees: A Critical Bibliography.
The Newberry Library Center for the History of the
American Indian Bibliographical Series. Bloomington:
Indiana University Press, 1981.

0036. Blanck, J. "News from the Rare Book Sellers: Catalog of Indian Captivities and Massacres: Description of almost Four Hundred Books, pamphlets and broadsides." Publisher's Weekly 143 (March 27, 1943) : 1374-1375.

Article discusses recent catalog acquired by Edward Eberstadt and Sons of New York.

0037. Blank, Ruth. "What Shall Our Children Read? A Selected Bibliography of American Indian Literature for Young People." Bethesda, MD: ED 214 695, February 9, 1981.

Annotated. 178 titles 1953-1980.

0038. Books about Indians. rev. 5th ed. New York: Museum of the American Indian, 1977.

0039. "Books about Indians and Reference Materials." Boise: Idaho State Department of Education; Bethesda, MD: EDRS, ED 030 531, 1968.

Over 500 entries. Books, films, filmstrips. Superceded by ED 052 887. See below.

0040. "Books about Indians and Reference Materials." Bethesda, MD: EDRS, ED 052 887, 1971.

177 p. Over 1500 books published between 1911-1971 cited by publisher. Many annotated. Usually only author's last name cited and date. Seems to be aimed at schools. Supercedes ED 030 531.

0041. Braber, Lee and Dean, Jacquelyn M. "A Semi-Annotated Bibliography: The Wabanakis." Boston Indian Council, Inc., Jamaica Plain, Massachusetts. Bethesda, MD: ED 226 894, 1982.

0042. Brandon, William. "American Indian Literature." Indian Historian 4 (February 1971) : 53-55.

This bibliographic essay might serve as an introduction to the student of American Indian literature for it mentions many signficant collections of American Indian writings across a wide range of cultures and time periods. Brandon's thesis is that "it is beginning to be clear that there is emerging here, although still only partly visible, one of the world's great literatures." The "here" to which he refers is the "collections of legends, rituals, songs, tales, poems,

myth-cycles, gathered from end to end of the
hemisphere by explorers, soldiers, teachers,
native American scribes and chroniclers,
missionaries, traders, vagabonds, ethnogra-
phers, over the past four and a half centuries."

0043. Bridgford, Clay.   "Teaching about Minorities: An
Annotated Bibliography on Blacks, Chicanos and
Indians." Prepared for a Conference on Teaching about
Minorities, Rocky Mountain Social Studies Council,
Denver, Colorado, April 1971; Bethesda, MD: EDRS, ED
049 970, April 1971.

     For the K-9 social studies teacher and
student of ethnic studies. Some references
to fiction and poetry, several to bibliographies; both print and non-print media cited.

0044. Bright, William.   Bibliography of the Languages of
Native California: Including Closely Related Languages
of the Adjacent Areas. Native American Bibliography
Series No. 3. Metuchen, N.J.: Scarecrow Press, 1982.

0045. Brinton, Daniel G. Aboriginal American Authors and
Their Productions. Philadelphia: D. G. Brinton, 1883;
Chicago: Checagou Reprints, 1970 (500 copies).

     Also listed as: Aboriginal American
Authors and Their Productions, Especially
Those in the Native Languages. In this work,
Brinton discusses many samples of ancient
Indian literature by Mayan, Aztec and North
American Indian authors as well as recent (as
of 1882) examples.

0046. Brinton, Daniel G. Library of Aboriginal American
Literature New York: AMS Press, n.d.

     Reprinted from 1882 edition.   Not
examined, so relationship to the work cited
immediately above, if any, is unclear.

0047. Bristol, Roger Pattrell, The American Bibliography
of Charles Evans, Vol. 14. Worcester, MA: The
American Antiquarian Society, 1959.

0048. Broderick, D. "Hi, Ho, Silver and All That." Library
Journal 96 (September 15, 1971) : 2852-2853.

     Suggests nonfiction background reading
for librarians prepatory to choosing
children's books on Indians. Cites works by
Dee Brown, Edgar Cohn, Vine Deloria, Clair
Huffaker, Stan Steiner, Dale Van Every and
others.

0049. Bromberg,   Eric.   "A Bibliography of Theses and
      Dissertations Concerning the Pacific Northwest and
      Alaska,   1949-1957."   Oregon   Historical   Society
      Quarterly. 59 (March 1958) : 27-84; supplement 65
      (December 1964) : 362-391.

            Masters   theses   and   Ph.D. dissertations
      in field of social sciences which pertain to
      Alaska   or   Northwest (Washington,   Oregon,
      Montana,   Idaho and British Columbia).   Social
      sciences includes English, drama forestry,
      agriculture.   Classified by subject field,
      author's last name. Index.

0050. Brugge,   David M. Navajo Bibliography. Window Rock,
      AZ: Navajoland Publications, Navajo Tribal Museum,
      1967.

            Lists books, articles together alphabeti-
      cally by title. Fiction-nonfiction not distin-
      guished.   According   to   the   author, "no
      attempt at selectivity has been made, but all
      available reference to the Navajo people and
      their environment, regardless of source, have
      been included. These include historical, eth-
      nographic, biographical, technical, popular,
      and fictional works as well as archival mate-
      rials,   newspaper   accounts,   articles from
      journals and magazines, books, pamphlets, man-
      uscripts, and technical papers from both gov-
      ernment and Navajo tribal files."

0051. Brumble,   David H., III. An Annotated Bibliography of
      American   Indian   and Eskimo Autobiographies. Lincoln:
      University of Nebraska Press, 1981.

            177 p.   More   than   500   narratives, of
      which more than 100 are book-length.

0052. Brumble, David H. "A Supplement to An Annotated
      Bibliography   of   American   Indian   and   Eskimo
      Autobiographies."   Western American Literature 17:3
      (November 1982): 243-260.

0053. Buck, June M. "Indian Literature for Junior and
      Senior High Schools." Phoenix, AZ: Division of Indian
      Education, State Department of Public Instruction,
      1968; Bethesda, MD: EDRS, ED 042 531, 1968.

            25 p. 52 fiction entries from 1940-66, 8
      citations of poems, plays or other creative
      writing from 1961-67, 23 entries of myths,
      legends,   folktales 1947-67, 32 nonfiction
      entries   1959-67,   52 biographical entries
      1947-63. Bibliography of sources is appended.

0054. Butler, Ruth Lapham. The Newberry Library: A
Checklist of Manuscripts in the Edward E. Ayer
Collection. Chicago: Newberry Library, 1937.

> Annotated list of some 2,000
> manuscripts. One of seven sections list is
> divided into is Native American languages.

0055. Byler, Mary Gloyne. American Indian Authors for
Young Readers: A Selected Bibliography. New York:
Association on American Indian Affairs, 1973;
Bethesda, MD EDRS, ED 086 420, 1973.

> 26 p. Author examined over 600
> children's books in preparing this
> bibliography and rejected two out of three
> because of offensive contents. She reviews
> some of the rejects in an essay prefacing the
> bibliography, explains why they were
> offensive and explores many of the ways in
> which white authors have distorted the facts
> about the American Indian or produced
> misconceptions by some other means. Byler is
> Cherokee, is (or was) editor of Indian
> Affairs Newsletter of the Association on
> American Indian Affairs. Her book is
> available for purchase from Interbook.

0056. Byler, Mary Gloyne. "Image of the American Indian
Projected by Non-Indian Writers." Excerpt from
American Indian Authors for Young Readers: A Selected
Bibliography in Library Journal 99 (February 15, 1974)
: 546-549.

> Byler rakes a number of authors over the
> coals in this issue; one of them replies (see
> Monjo) in Library Journal 99 (May 15, 1974) :
> 1454-1455.

0057. Carlson, Ruth Kearney. Emerging Humanity:
Multi-Ethnic Literature for Children and Adolescents.
Dubuque, Iowa: William C. Brown, 1972.

> 246 p. Also lists professional and
> adult books. Each chapter prefaced with
> suggestions for using list in a teaching
> situation. Chapter 7 introduction is an
> essay, "At the Edge of Two Worlds: The Indian
> Way and the Way of the White Man." Booklist
> is not annotated. Books in Print does not
> show the publisher. Address on the title
> page is: William C. Brown Publishers, 1355
> Locust Street, Dubuque, Iowa 52003.

0058. Cashman,   Marc,   ed.   <u>Bibliography   of   American   Ethnology</u> St. Paul, MN: Todd Publishing, Inc., 1976.

    Partially   annotated.   Lists   several thousand   books   on   topics   of   folklore, mythology, and literature among others.

0059. <u>Catalog   of   the   Library   Belonging   to Mr. Thomas W. Field.</u>   New   York: Bangs,   Merwin   and   Co.,   1875. Supplement, New York: Shelley, 1875.

    <u>Catalog</u>   376   p.;   supplement   59 p.   (See Field,   Thomas).   Library contacted said this was   non-circulating   but could be photocopied or microfilmed.

0060. Center   for   the   Study   of   Man,   Smithsonian Institution,   Washington,   D.C..   "Current North American Indian   Periodicals."   <u>Social Education</u> 36 (May 1972) : 494-500.

    Gives   name,   sponsoring agency, address, frequency   of   publication, subscription rate, description.

0061. Cheda,   Sherril.   <u>The   First   Americans: A   Reading Guide.</u>   Reprint   from   <u>Ontario Library Review</u>, December 1970 : 223-229.

    Copies   were   once   available from PLS, 4 New   Street,   Toronto.   Categories include art, biography,   contemporary   fiction   and nonfiction,   easy   readers, education, Eskimos, general   historical,   laws,   treaties, aboriginal   rights,   legends.   Both Canadian and   American   authors.   Cheda   is   or   was a librarian   at   the   Indian-Eskimo   Association in Toronto.

0062. Clancy,   James   Thomas.   "Native American References: A   Cross-indexed   Bibliography   of   Seventeenth Century American   Imprints   Pertaining to the American Indian." <u>Proceedings   of   the   American   Antiquarian   Society</u> 83 (October 1973) : 287-341.

    Lists   "every   known   seventeenth-century book,   pamphlet,   and   broadside   published in America   found   to   pertain   to   Native Americans."   Covers   the   years   1639-1700; Intended   to be   the   first part of a work which would   cover   the   entire   period   1639-1800. Divided   into three sections.   In section one, all   listings   are   arranged chronologically. Section   two is an ethnological index arranged by   tribe.   Section   three   is a geographical index arranged by states.

0063. Coan, Otis W. and Lillard, Richard G. <u>America in
       Fiction: An Annotated List of Novels that Interpret
       Aspects of Life in the United States, Canada and
       Mexico</u>. 5th ed. Palo Alto, CA: Pacific Books, 1967.

0064. Cohen, David, cord., Task Force on Ethnic Materials
       Information   Exchange   Social   Responsibilities
       Roundtable.   <u>Multi-Ethnic   Media: Selected
       Bibliographies in Print.</u> Chicago: Office for the
       Library Service to the Disadvantaged, American Library
       Association, 1975.

              Part one is bibliographic essays, part
         two bibliographies, part three sources of
         information.   Notes   for   39 of the 224
         citations state they have something to do
         with Indians.

0065. Cole, Joan E. "A Bibliography of Juvenile Holdings
       in the Library of Congress E11-99: America (General),
       North America, Aboriginal America, Indians of North
       America; F2251-2659: Columbia, Venezuela, The Guianas,
       Brazil."   MS   Thesis.   Washington, D.C.: Catholic
       University of America, 1962.

0066. Cooperative Children's Book Center. "Materials on
       Indians   of North America: An Annotated List for
       Children." Bethesda, MD: EDRS, ED 039 991, May 1970.

              15 p.   Compiled and arranged by broad
         cultural area. 86 citations.

0067. Correll, J. Lee; Watson, Edith L.; and Brugge, David
       M. <u>Navajo Bibliography with Subject Index.</u> Revised
       edition.   Research   Report No. 2, Research Section,
       Parks and Recreation, The Navajo Tribe, Window Rock,
       AZ, 1969; Bethesda, MD: EDRS, ED 050 862, 1969.

              398 p.   Approximately 5,640 references
         all relating to Navajo. Includes popular and
         fictional works, articles from magazines and
         journals.   In alphabetical order and arranged
         chronologically. No notes.

0068. Costo, Rupert, ed.; Henry, Jeanette, writer.
       <u>Textbooks and the American Indian.</u> San Francisco:
       Indian Historian Press, 1970.

              The work of 32 Indian scholars and many
         others, including non-Indians. More than 300
         books examined in study, all at the time in
         use in classrooms from the primary grades
         through high school. Evaluators were looking
         for stereotypes, distortions, misinformation,
         omissions, scope, depth and other aspects of

the texts that might impair their
effectiveness. According to the author and
editor, "not one could be approved as a
dependable source of knowledge about the
history and culture of the Indian people in
America."

0069. Crossman, Mary. "AMERINDIANS." Stockton, CA: The
    Public Library of Stockton and San Joaquin County,
    1970.

        17 p. Classifies 22 general books; 72
    on individual tribes; 15 on government
    regulations; 20 art, folklore and literature;
    14 music, dance and games; 10 religion; 4
    foods; 26 notable Indians; 10 Indian
    languages; 10 recordings. Only gives
    author's last name, book title and library
    call numbers. No pubisher, place or date.

0070. Curtis, Mary Barnett. "Bibliography of the Five
    Civilized Tribes." Magazine of Bibliographies 1 (March
    1973) : 8-37.

0071. Dankey, James P., ed.; Hady, Maureen E., comp.
    Native American Periodicals and Newspapers, 1828-1982:
    Bibliography, Publishing Record and Holdings.
    Westport, CT: Greenwood Press, 1984.

        Comprehensive record and holdings list
    of extant issues of 1,164 historic and
    contemporary periodicals, including literary,
    political, and historical journals as well as
    general newspapers and feature magazines.
    Main alphabetical listing contains all title
    variants. Data includes standard publishing
    information, relevant cataloging numbers,
    index sources and location sources for actual
    copies and microform holdings. All data cited
    was acquired from issue-by-issue examination
    of copies in various collections. Indexes to
    subjects, editors, publishing organizations,
    keywords and subtitles; geographical index
    arranged alphabetically by state, city and
    title; chronological index of publications.

0072. Davidson, Levette J. A Guide to American Folklore
    Denver: n.p., 1951; Westport, CT: Greenwood Press,
    n.d.

0073. Davidson, Levette J. Rocky Mountain Life in
    Literature: A Descriptive Bibliography. Denver:
    University of Denver Book Store, 1936.

0074. Davidson, Levette J. and Bostwick, Prudence. The
       Literature of the Rocky Mountain West 1803-1903.
       Caldwell, Idaho: Caxton, 1939.

0075. Davis, Dixie M., comp. "Bibliography of Resources on
       the American Indian for Students and Teachers in the
       Elementary School." Bethesda, MD: EDRS, ED 074 005,
       February 1967.

              37 p. Includes fiction, myths, legends,
       poetry. Coded to show level.

0076. Day Care and Child Development Council of America.
       "Multi-Ethnic Reading and Audio Materials for Young
       Children: Annotated Bibliography." Washington, D.C.:
       Day Care and Child Development Council of America,
       1972; Bethesda, MD: EDRS, ED 073 202, 1972.

              For young children in day care programs
       and homes. Four sections: Spanish, Indian,
       Black, and reference sources.

0077. Denver Public Libraries. Indian Heritage. Denver:
       Denver Public Libraries, n.d.; Bethesda, MD: EDRS, ED
       036 342, n.d.

              Annotated. Selected holdings of the
       libraries. Annotations include call numbers.
       Adult and children's selections.

0078. Deutsch, Herman J. "The West in Paperbacks." Pacific
       Northwest Quarterly, 54 (1963) 113-123.

0079. DeWaal, Ronald B. "Colorado State University Western
       American Literature Collection." Mountain-Plains
       Library Quarterly 12 (Summer 1967) : 29.

              Article announces the beginning of
       Western American Literature, the Western
       American Literature Association's quarterly
       journal, and the CSU libraries special
       collection on Western American literature.
       "It is anticipated," says DeWaal, "that it
       will ultimately become the most comprehensive
       collection of its kind in the country." At
       the time of DeWaal's writing, the collection
       was at 5,000 volumes and growing. It includes
       imaginative literature written during the
       19th and 20th centuries about the U.S. west
       of the Mississippi, including Alaska, Western
       Canada and Northern Mexico. "Every effort,"
       DeWaal said, is being made "to acquire first
       editions, limited editions, and autographed
       editions."

0080. Dickinson, A. T., Jr. American Historical Fiction.
2nd edition. New York: Scarecrow Press, 1963.

        1,909 novels classified into periods of
American history, briefly annotated. Index
references treatment of the Indian in the
categories of Indian captives, captives
adopted by Indians, Indian life and customs,
Indian territory, Indian uprising in
Minnesota, and Indian wars. Also treated
specifically are Indians in California and
the Northwest.

0081. Dillingham, Peter. "The Literature of the American
Indian." English Journal 62 (January 1973) : 37—41.

        Brief discussion of contemporary Indian
prose and poetry available (and accessible)
to high school students.

0082. Division of Educational Research and Services. Guide
for Native American Resource Materials. Missoula:
Division of Educational Research and Services,
University of Montana, September 1976.

        97 p. This book, which made at least
one previous appearance in 1973, would seem
to be primarily aimed at the needs of Montana
educators; however, it has application to any
study of Indian culture. Section I lists by
tribe and in alphabetical order books
pertaining to Native American tribes
presently residing in Montana. Section II is
an annotated list of available children's
literature on Native Americans which shows
tribe and age level work is aimed at.
Section III lists current North American
Indian periodicals with a description of
each. Section IV is a partial list of books
dealing with the American Indian influence on
American civilization. This last area is
subdivided into 15 subsections, one of which
is "Influence on Literature."

0083. Dobyns, Henry F. Native American Historical
Demography: A Critical Bibliography. The Newberry
Library Center for the History of the American Indian
Bibliographical Series, Francis Jennings, ed.
Bloomington: Indiana University Press, 1976.

0084. Dobyns, Henry F., and Euler, Robert C. Indians of
the Southwest: A Critical Bibliography. The Newberry
Library Center for the History of the American Indian
Bibliographical Series, Francis Jennings ed.
Bloomington: Indiana University Press, 1981.

0085. Dockstader, Frederick J., and Alice W. <u>The American
Indian in Graduate Studies: A Bibliography of Theses
and Dissertations.</u> Contributions from the Museum of
the American Indian Heye Foundation, Vol. 25, Part 1,
New York: Museum of the American Indian, Heye
Foundation, 1973; Vol. 25, Part 2, New York: Museum of
the American Indian, Heye Foundation, 1974.

Part 1 is a reprint of the 1957 edition.
Part 2 contains the index for both parts.
Part 1 lists 3,659 titles from 1890-1955;
Part 2 lists 3,787 titles from 1955-1970. In
their preface to the supplement, the
Dockstaders state, "we do believe that the
present work now covers some 90 percent of the
studies which include the subject of the
American Indian."

0086. Donelson, Kenneth, ed. "Southwestern Literature and
Culture in the English Classroom." <u>Arizona English
Bulletin</u> 13 (April 1971) : 1-118; Bethesda, MD: EDRS,
ED 052 180, April 1971.

Folklore, customs, literature, reading
lists.

0087. Dorris, Michael. "Native American Literature in an
Ethnohistorical Context." <u>College English</u> 41, No. 2
(October 1979) : 147-162.

Linguistic and cultural diversity of
Indians is contrasted with the continuing
sameness of European culture. Talks about
the ambiguity of the term "Native American
Literature," discusses the importance of
understanding the cultural context in which a
literature is created and functions, and
reviews works by Europeans and contemporary
works by Native American writers. A
bibliography lists bibliographies, works on
history and culture, language, non-Indian
views of Native Americans, literary history
and criticism, general anthologies, oral
literature and traditional materials,
contemporary literature, and periodicals.

0088. Douglas, Frederick H. <u>A Guide to Articles on the
American Indians in Serial Publications</u>, Part 1.
Denver: Art Museum, Department of Indian Art, 1934.

332 p. Many listings of Indian myths,
legends, and folktales.

0089. Downs, Robert B. <u>American Library Resources: A
Bibliographical Guide.</u> Chicago: American Library
Association, 1951.

428 p. Lists printed library catalogs, union lists of books and periodicals, descriptions of special collections, surveys of library holdings, calendars of archives and manuscripts, and catalogs of exhibitions, as well as a few unpublished bibliographies, chiefly theses and dissertations. Classified broadly by the Dewey Decimal System. Supplements cover the periods 1950-1961 and 1961-1970.

0090. Drake, Samuel Gardner. <u>Catalogue of the Private Library of Samuel G. Drake of Boston: Chiefly Relating to the Antiquities, History, and Biography of America, and in an Especial Manner to the Indians, Collected and Used by Him Preparing His Works upon the Aborigines of America.</u> Boston: S. G. Drake, 1845.

0091. Dumont, Robert V. "Information Source: Education for American Indians." Bethesda, MD: EDRS, ED 050 855, December 1969.

17 p.

0092. Dunkley, Grace. "Literature that Transcends Cultural Differences." Bethesda, MD: EDRS, ED 093 562, May 1974.

8 p.

0093. Durham, Philip. "A General Classification of 1,531 Dime Novels." <u>Huntington Library Quarterly</u> 17 (1954) : 287-291.

The remnants of the Dr. Frank P. O'Brien collection of dime novels--which belong to the Huntington Library--are listed under 17 classifications. Those grouped under the category, "Indian Tales," make up about four percent of the whole, but Indians figure in a large number of the books in a variety of categories.

0094. Eastman, Mary H. <u>Index to Fairy Tales, Myths and Legends.</u> 2nd ed. Rev. Boston: F. W. Faxon, 1926. Supplement, 1937.

0095. Eberstadt and Sons. <u>Indian Captivities and Massacres; Being the Contemporary Record of Caucasian Contact and Conflict with the Native American; Books, Pamphlets, and Broadsides Offered for Sale.</u> New York: Eberstadt and Sons, 1943.

70 p.

0096. Erisman,   Fred   and   Etulain,   Richard,   eds.   Fifty
    Western   Writers: A   Bio-Bibliographical   Sourcebook.
    Westport, CT: Greenwood Press, 1982.

        Contains   biographical,   bibliographical
    and   critical   information   on 50 writers past
    and   present   whose   subject   was   or   is   the
    American West.

0097. Etulain,   Richard   W.   Bibliographical   Guide to the
    Study   of   Western   American   Literature.   Lincoln:
    University of Nebraska Press, 1982.

        According   to   the   "Preface,"   this
    bibliography   "updates,   enlarges,   and
    reorganizes Western   American   Literature: A
    Bibliography   of   Interpretive   Books   and
    Articles.   Vermillion,   South Dakota: Dakota
    Press,   1972."   (See   below.)   A   significant
    change   is   the   inclusion   of   material
    specifically   about   Indians.   It   lists
    bibliographies,   anthologies,   general   works,
    special   topics--which   includes   a   section
    entitled   "Indian   Literature   and   Indians in
    Western   Literature"   (129 entries)--and works
    on   individual authors, some Native Americans,
    born   in   the   trans-Mississippi   West   or who
    spent   large   portions   of   their lives there.
    The   value   of   Etulain's guide to students of
    Indian   literature   and   Indians in literature
    remains   that   it   indexes   works   on   the
    frontier,   western   American   literature,
    western   authors, and other topics of American
    literature   which   probably   involve   Indians,
    although   their   apparent   focus would exclude
    them   from   lists   of   books devoted to Indian
    literature   or   Indians   in   literature.
    Emphasis   is on writers of fiction and poetry.
    317   pages.   Not   annotated   except   for
    infrequent   one-liners which describe contents
    not   suggested   by the title or offer opinions
    on the work. Author index.

0098. Etulain,   Richard. Western   American   Literature: A
    Bibliography   of   Interpretive   Books   and   Articles.
    Vermillion: Dakota Press, 1972.

        Divided   into   five   major   sections:
    bibliographies   listing   research   on   western
    American   literature, anthologies of western
    literature,   general   works   (books,   theses,
    dissertations,   articles),   research   dealing
    with   three   major   topics--the   Beats,   local
    color,   and regionalism, the Western (focusing
    on   the   formula   western and western movies),
    and works on individual authors, a few of

them Native Americans. While portions of many works listed most likely involve Indian literature or Indians in literature, there is nothing listed on these topics specifically. Research listed is concerned mainly with authors born or living most of their lives in the trans-Mississippi West or writing about the West. Emphasis is on writers of fiction and poetry. 137 pages. Not annotated. (Updated and expanded in 1982--See above.)

0099. Ewers, J. C. "The American Indian in Current Books." _Natural History_ 70 (November 1961) : 4-9.

Reviews of anthropologically oriented books.

0100. Fay, George E. _Bibliography of the Indians of Wisconsin_. Misc. Series No. 2. Oskosh: Museum of Anthropology, Wisconsin State University, 1965.

0101. Fenton, W. L. _American Indian and White Relations to 1830. Needs and Opportunities for Study_. Chapel Hill: University of North Carolina Press, 1957.

Pertinent sections feature titles relating to literature, songs, art, biography, and autobiography, captivities and the Indian in literature and thought. Indexed.

0102. Fernald, Louise. _Bibliography of Books on Montana and the West_. Missoula: University of Montana Library, n.d.

18   8 1/2 X 11 pages. Author and title. UM holdings arranged according to subject.

0103. Field, Thomas W. _An Essay Towards an Indian Bibliography--Being a Catalog of Books Relating to the History, Antiquities, Languages, Customs, Religion, Wars, Literature, and Origin of the American Indian in the Library of Thomas W. Field with Bibliographical and Historical Notes, and Synopses of the Contents of Some of the Works Least Known_. New York: Scribner, Armstrong, and Co., 1873; reprint ed., Columbus, Ohio: Long's College Book Co., 1951; reprint ed., Detroit: Gale Research Publications, 1967.

0104. "The First American." _Synergy_. A Publication of the Bay Area Reference Center (BARC), San Francisco Public Library, Jan-Feb 1970, entire issue.

Published as part of a joint reference project of the San Francisco Public Library and the North Bay Cooperative System. Offers

12 entries of (then) recent books by and
about Native Americans. Annotated. Very
brief.

0105. Fitzgerald, Bonnie. "Bibliography of Literature and
Cross-Cultural Values." Bethesda, MD: EDRS, ED 082
220, 1973.

17 p. Indian fiction, Indian legends.
Age levels provided.

0106. "Focus on Minorities: A Multicultural Booklist for
Children in the Primary and Intermediate Grades. . ."
New York: Thomas Y. Crowell, Spring 1972.

31 p.

0107. Fogelson, Raymond D. The Cherokees: A Critical
Bibliography. The Newberry Library Center for the
History of the American Indian Bibliographical Series.
Bloomington: Indiana University Press, 1978.

0108. Ford, Richard I. "Books in Review: The Indian in
America's Closet." Natural History, 79 (June-July
1970) : 78, 80, 82-84.

Briefly describes a number of books
published recent to date of article which
give an understanding of the American Indian
from a variety of perspectives. Includes,
fiction and non-fiction, but mainly the
latter; some anthologies of Indian writings,
poetry, tales.

0109. Foster, George E. Literature of the Cherokees.
Ithaca, New York: Office of the Democrat, 1889.

0110. Freeman, John, and Smith, Murphy D. A Guide to
Manuscripts Relating to the American Indian the
Library of the American Philosophical Society.
Philadelphia: The American Philosophical Society,
1966.

491 p. Primarily anthropological.
Nothing on literature. Two articles on
Indian-white relations, an article by Ella
Deloria on Sioux education, Deloria on Sioux
legends, piece on Teton forms in Riggs'
Santee dictionary.

0111. Fuson, Elgie M. Native Americans: A Bibliography for
Young People. Bibliographic Series 7. Sacramento:
Sacramento State College, 1970; Bethesda, MD: EDRS, ED
059 000, 1970.

Cites material published between 1905-1969 available in the curriculum library and the young people's collection of the Sacramento State College Library. 58 fiction, 152 nonfiction, 20 textbooks, 45 curriculum guides usable K-8. Shows grade level for each.

0112.   Gast, David K. "Minority Americans in Children's Literature." Elementary English, 44 (January 1967) : 12-23.

0113.   Getchell, Alice McClure. "Bibliography of Oregon Indian Myths." Oregon State Library, 1924. Reprinted with additions from Oregon Sunday Journal, July 27, 1924.

0114.   Gibson, A. M. "Sources for Research on the American Indian." Ethnohistory 7, No. 2 (Spring 1960):121-136.

Lists research centers with large holdings on Indians as well as collections of government. Also lists other aids to research.

0115.   Gibson, G. D. "A Bibliography of Anthropological Bibliographies, the Americas." Current Anthropology, 1 (1960) : 51-57.

0116.   Gibson, Michael. "The Western: A Selective Bibliography." Journal of Popular Culture. n.v., n.d. : 743/101-748/106.

"Items directly related to the popular or formula western through 1972."

0117.   Gill, George A. North American Indians, a Comprehensive Annotated Bibliography for the Secondary Teacher. Tempe: Arizona State University Press, 1973.

123 p.

0118.   Gill, George A., ed. A Reference Resource Guide of the American Indian. Tempe: Center for Indian Education, College of Education, Arizona State University, 1974.

Lists places to get information: libraries, book publishers, record publishers, college programs, foundations.

0119.   Gilliland, Hap. Indian Children's Books. Billings, MT: Montana Council for Indian Education, 1980.

Annotated, with evaluations by Indian educators and others--"highly recommended, recommended, acceptable, questionable, very

questionable"--and indication of suitable
grade levels. Chapter 2 deals with problems
in using available children's books about
Indians, such as inaccuracies and omissions,
and gives suggestions for teachers on
selection and use of books about Indian life
and culture. Approximately 1,652 entries
published between 1826-1978. Chapter 4 lists
books by tribe, region and subject. Chapter
5 lists publishers.

0120. Goodwyn, Frank. "The Frontier in American Fiction."
Inter-American Review of Bibliography, 10 (1960) :
356-369.

0121. "Good Words: Notable Books on the American Indian."
Bethesda, MD: EDRS, ED 060 699, April 1973.

11 p. Bibliography compiled by nine
students of Indian ancestry at the University
of South Dakota Library-Media Institute.
Consists of 50 titles published betweeen 1967
and 1971. Emphasis on books about plains
Indians and on realistic, honest, authentic
images of American Indians.

0122. Graustein, Jean McCarthy, and Jaglinski, Carol L.,
comps., An Annotated Bibliography of Young People's
Fiction on American Indians. Bureau of Indian Affairs
Curriculum Bulletin No. 11, January 1972; Bethesda, MD:
EDRS, ED 060 699, 1972.

61 p. Lists 250 works of fiction
written between 1933 and 1969 for children.
Annotations list tribes and suggest grade
level. Indexed by tribe.

0123. Green, Michael D. The Creeks: A Critical
Bibliography. Newberry Library Center for the History
of the American Indian Bibliographical Series.
Bloomington: Indiana University Press, 1980.

0124. Grumbach, D. "Fine Print: The Year of the Indian."
New Republic, 170 (May 18, 1974) : 31-32.

Journalism.

0125. Grumet, Robert S. Native Americans of the Northwest
Coast: A Critical Bibliography. Newberry Library for
the History of the American Indian Bibliographical
Series. Bloomington: Indiana University Press, 1980.

0126. Hamilton, Wynette; Snyder, Lucy; and Seal, Robert,
eds. "Bibliography, Research and News: Recent

Articles." American Indian Quarterly 2 (1975-1976):
386-401;   3   (1977):   70-88,   175-190,   271-291; 3
(1977-1978): 386-401.

0127. Harkins, Arthur M., comp. Modern Native Americans:
A Selective Bibliography. Bethesda, MD: EDRS, ED 054
890, July 1971.

> 131 p. Approximately 1,500 citations of
> works on Native Americans published between
> 1927-1970. Includes books, journal articles,
> original research. Not annotated. Basically
> sociological; very little on literature.

0128. Haslam, Gerald. "Who Speaks for the Earth?"
English Journal 63 (January 1973):42-48.

> Selected bibliography of Indian, western
> American and nature literature.

0129. Haywood, Charles A. A Bibliography of North American
Folklore and Folksong, Vol. 2: The American Indian
North of Mexico, Including the Eskimos. 2nd revised
ed. New York: Dover Publications, Inc., 1961.

> This started out as Haywood's Ph.D.
> thesis at Columbia in 1951. It was published
> in 1951 by Greenberg of New York. Items in
> Book II are classified by region (e.g. the
> northern woodland area) and subdivided into
> three groups: folklore, music, and tribes.
> The first chapter is concerned with
> bibliographies. Recordings are also indexed.
> Some entries are annotated. Items are in
> alphabetical order. The book is indexed.

0130. Heizer, Robert F. The Indians of California: A
Critical Bibliography. Newberry Library Center for
the History of the American Indian Bibliographical
Series. Bloomington: Indiana University Press, 1976.

0131. Heizer, Robert, and Elsasser, Albert B. California
Indians: An Annotated Bibliography. Reference Library
of Social Science, Vol. 48. New York: Garland
Publishing, Inc., 1977.

0132. Helm, June. The Indians of the Subarctic: A Critical
Bibliography. Newberry Library Center for the History
of the American Indian Bibliographical Series.
Bloomington: Indiana University Press, 1976.

0133. Henry, Jeanette, ed. Index to Literature on the
American Indian: 1970. San Francisco: Indian
Historian Press, 1972

> This bibliography was published anew for
> each of four years, the title remaining the

same except for the date. The years are 1970
(cited above), 1971, 1972, 1973. Both the
1970 and 1971 volumes were published in 1972;
the 1972 volume was published in 1974, and
The 1973 volume was published in 1975.
Virtually all aspects of Indian life past and
present are represented in literary
treatments of all descriptions cited here in
the form of books, and articles and stories
from popular magazines as well as journals
for the year of the title. The citations are
not annotated and the volumes are not indexed.
However, a list of subject headings
(presented at the front of each book) is used
to classify entries alphabetically. Entries
so classified are merged with author entries
in this alphabetical treatment.

0134. Henry, Jeanette. Organizing and Maintaining a Native
American Reference Library. Bethesda, MD: EDRS, ED
058 982, 1970.

14 p. Suggests books to be in such a
library, places to look for more books,
criteria to consider in book selection, and
practical information on how to run the
library.

0135. Hertzberg, Hazel W. "Issues in Teaching about
American Indians." Social Education, 36 (May 1972) :
481-485.

0136. Hewlett, Leroy, ed. Indians of Oregon: A
Bibliography of Materials in the Oregon State Library.
Bethesda, MD: EDRS, ED 058 999, 1969.

131 p. Some references to legends, folk
tales, myths, and Indian stories. Some
bibliographies. Some references to Indians
of other areas.

0137. Hill, Charles H. "A Summer Reading Program with
American Indians." Journal of American Indian
Education, 9 (May 1970) : 10-14.

0138. Hirschfelder, Arlene B. American Indian Authors: A
Bibliography of Contemporary and Historical Literature
Written or Narrated by Native Americans New York:
Association on American Indian Affairs, 1969.

Hirschfelder decries the custom of
promoting books "under the names of the
investigators or editors who record or revise
material written or narrated by Indians
rather than under the names of the . . .
Indians" and lists all selections under the
names of Indian sources or under "anonymous."

Names of editors, translators, recorders, and
so on, are also given however.

0139. Hirschfelder,   Arlene   B.   <u>American Indian Authors: A
Representative Bibliography</u>. New York: Association on
American   Indian   Affairs, 1970; Bethesda, MD: EDRS, ED
048 965, 1970.

> 45 p.   Approximately 160 books by
> Indians written between 1860-1970 annotated
> descriptively.   Tribes entered alhabetically,
> authors   entered   under   tribes.   Contains
> section on anthologies of oral and written
> literature   and   a   list   of   periodicals
> published by Indian tribes and organizations.

0140. Hirschfelder,   Arlene   B.   <u>American Indian and Eskimo
Authors: A Comprehensive Bibliography</u>.   New York:
Association on American Indian Affairs, 1973.

> An   annotated list of 400 then current
> and out of print books by Indian and Eskimo
> authors listed by author's name. Book was
> available for purchase from Interbook, Inc.,
> 545 Eighth Ave., New York, NY 10018.

0141. Hirschfelder,   Arlene   B. <u>American Indian Stereotypes
in the World of Children: A Reader and Bibliography</u>.
Metuchen, N.J.: The Scarecrow Press, Inc., 1982.

> 312 p. Part I is the reader: children's
> perceptions   of   stereotypes   of   Indians,
> emergence of plains Indians as symbol of
> North   American   Indians,   introduction   to
> Indian authors for young people, treatment of
> Indians   in   textbooks,   toys with Indian
> imagery,   "Indian"   programs   for   kids,
> nicknames, mascots.   Part II is an annotated
> bibliography.   Section one contains books and
> articles on stereotyping of Native Americans.
> Section   two lists "corrective materials."
> Detailed notes, objective and descriptive,
> summarize each work.

0142. Hirschfelder,   Arlene B. "Bibliography of Sources and
Materials for Teaching about American Indians." <u>Social
Education</u> 36 (May 1972) : 488-493.

> Annotated.   Books for elementary and
> secondary use.   Reprints were available from
> the Association on American Indian Affairs.

0143. Hirschfelder,   Arlene   B.; Byler, Mary Gloyne; and
Dorris, Michael A. <u>Guide to Research on North American</u>

<u>Indians</u>.   Chicago: American   Library   Association,
1983.

        The   opening   line   of   the   "Preface"
declares, "This bibliography is intended to
serve   as   a basic guide to the literature for
general   readers,   students,   and   scholars
interested   in   the   study   of   American
Indians--Native Americans." From the mass of
material written on Indians, some 1,100 books,
articles   and   other   written   materials in 27
fields of study are listed and described in
this   volume.   According   to   the   authors,
"Lengthy   annotations   identify   the   tribal
territories, time frame and point of view of
each   work."   All   selections   are in English.
Some works on Canadian, Mexican and South and
Central   American   Indians   are   included.
Twenty-seven chapters, each dealing with a
specific   subject area, are grouped under four
broad   subject   headings: "Introductory
Material,"   "History and Historical Sources,"
"Economic and Social Aspects," and "Religion,
Arts   and   Literature."   In the last category,
one   chapter   each is devoted to "Religion and
Philosophy,"   "Music   and Dance," "Education,"
"Arts,"   "Science,"   "Law," and "Literature."
This   last   chapter   cites   45 books and
articles, six of them bibliographies.   It
should   be pointed out that each chapter ends
with   a   description   of several pertinent
bibliographies   and   that the opening two
chapters,   "General   Sources" and "General
Studies,"   do   not   contain   all   of   the
bibliographies this volume indexes. The book
contains   both   a   subject   index and an
author-title index.

0144. Hodge, Frederick Webb, ed. <u>Handbook of Indians North</u>
     <u>of Mexico</u>. Smithsonian Institution Bureau of American
     Ethnology Bulletin No. 30. Washingon, D.C.: Government
     Printing Office, 1907-10 2 volumes.

        2193   p.   Reaches   back   to 1870's.
Articles deal with all aspects of Indian life
and customs.

0145. Hodge, Frederick Webb. "Indian Books for Children."
     <u>Saturday Review of Literature</u>, 8 (August 8, 1931) :
     44.

0146. Hodge, William A. <u>A Bibliography of Contemporary</u>
     <u>North   American   Indians: Selected   and Partially</u>
     <u>Annotated   with Study Guide</u>. New York: Interland
     Publishing, Inc., 1976.

Wide-ranging list: bibliographies, history, anthropology, contemporary images, culture, social organization, population dynamics, reservations, languages, migration patterns, city living, economics, education, politics, social control, music, dance, religion, health, government documents, newspapers, arts and crafts, museums, maps. Indexed.

0147. Hoebel, E. Adamson. The Plains Indians: A Critical Bibliography. Newberry Library Center for the History of the American Indian Bibliographical Series. Bloomington: Indiana University Press, 1977.

0148. Hoover, Herbert T. The Sioux: A Critical Bibliography. Newberry Library Center for the History of the American Indian Bibliographical Series. Bloomington: Indiana University Press, 1980.

0149. Huntington Free Library and Reading Room. Dictionary Catalog of the American Indian Collection. Boston: G.K. Hall and Co., 1977.

0150. "Index to Bibliographies Held by Project Media." Bethesda, MD: EDRS, ED 097 901, 1974.

20 p. Annotated list cites bibliographies and catalogs which deal with American Indians. Commercial film catalogs, periodicals and instructional materials lists included. All catalogs have a short descriptive sentence or paragraph. Lists films and a/v materials designed for K-12 that are (or were) available for rental.

0151. Indian Bibliography of the Bureau of Indian Affairs Instructional Service Center. First edition, with addendum. Bethesda, MD: EDRS, ED 059 815, 1970.

48 p. Portion of BIA library about, for and by American Indians. Some 600 documents 1893-1970. Many annotations.

0152. Ireland, Norma O. Index to Fairy Tales, 1949-1972. Westwood, MA: F. W. Faxon, 1973.

0153. Iverson, Peter. The Navajos: A Critical Bibliography. Newberry Library Center for the History of the American Indian Bibliographical Series. Bloomington: Indiana University Press, 1976.

0154. Jacobsen, Angeline. Contemporary Native American Literature: A Selected and Partially Annotated Bibliography. Metuchen, NJ: Scarecrow Press, Inc., 1977.

Despite the title's assertion that this
is a "selected" bibliography, it is still,
perhaps, the most comprehensive listing of
contemporary Native American authors,
particularly poets, available. It mainly
gathers works written and published between
1960 and 1976, but reaches back for earlier
works by contemporary writers and relaxes the
time limits to include myths and legends.
The list includes writings by Esikmos and
Canadian and Mexican as well as American
Indians. It lists over 2,000 works, 1,649 of
them poems. Other selections include "Native
American Spiritual Heritage, including a
Selection of Traditional Narratives;"
"Autobiography, Biography and Letters &
Personal Narratives;" "Fiction;" "Present Day
Realities Which Recall Memories of an Earlier
and Better Time: Interviews, Letters,
Stories and other Prose Selections;" "Humor
and Satire;" "Collections Analyzed;" "Sources:
Bibliographies, Indexes;" and "Periodicals
Analyzed." There is a title and first line
index to single poems and an author index.
Entries are arranged alphabetically by
author's last name.

0155. Jody, Marilyn. "Alaska in the American Literary
Imagination: A Literary History of Frontier Alaska
with a Bibliographical Guide to the Study of Alaskan
Literature." Ph. D. dissertation. Bloomington:
Indiana University, 1969.

0156. Jones, Dorothy M. and Wood, John R. "An Aleut
Bibliography." Alaska University. Bethesda, MD: ED
180 716, 1975.

0157. Jones, Margaret Ann. "Treatment of the West in
Selected Magazine Articles and Stories, 1901-1910, an
Annotated Bibliography." MA Thesis. Laramie:
University of Wyoming, 1955.

0158. Kaiser, Ernest. "American Indians and Mexican
Americans: A Selected Bibliography." Freedomways 9
(Fall 1969) : 298-327.

Partially annotated. Annotations are
descriptive, some fairly extensive summaries.
Books and articles chosen presumably for
their accurate depictions. In the
introduction, author is critical of generally
poor representation of Indians and Mexicans
in most books.

0159. Keating, Charlotte M. Building Bridges of

Understanding Between   Cultures.   Tucson: Palo   Verde
Publishing Co., 1971.

       Covers   black   Americans,   Indians,
Eskimos,   Spanish-speaking   Americans,   Asian
Americans.   Nationality   and   religious
groupings. Annotated.

0160. Kelly, Eraece B., ed. Searching for America. NCTE
Task   Force   on   Racism   and   Bias   in   the Teaching of
English. Urbana, Illinois: NCTE, 1972.

0161. Kidwell, Clara S., and Roberts, Charles. The
Choctaws: A Critical Bibliography.   The Newberry
Library Center for the History of the American Indian
Bibliographical   Series.   Bloomington: Indiana
University Press, 1981.

0162. Kimball, Richard Roy. "Beginnings of Literature
based   on   the   American   Frontier, a Descriptive
Bibliography." MA Thesis. Los Angeles: University of
Southern California, 1950.

       About   14   pages on Indians. Among other
types   of   literature,   this   thesis   lists
narratives   of   Indian   captivities, including
fictional   ones;   books   on Indian wars and on
Indian   lore   (mostly   history and biography);
and   works of fiction, including novels, short
stories,   tall   tales, poetry, and drama (some
of which feature Indians) through 1841.

0163. Klein, Barry, ed. Reference Encyclopedia of the
American Indian. 3rd ed. Rye, NY: Todd Publications,
1978.

       Bibliography   is descriptively annotated.
Subject   index refers to books in bibliography
by   title;   titles   are listed alphabetically.
Citations   are   also   indexed   by publisher.
Indians in literature section lists 11 titles.
Bulk   of   the   Reference Encyclopedia   is
concerned   with   lists: government agencies,
associations,   museums,   monuments and parks,
libraries,   reservations,   tribal   councils,
urban   Indian   centers,   schools,   college
courses,   audio-visual   aids,   audio-visual
distributors, magazines and periodicals, and
government   publications.   First   edition
appeared, edited by Bernard Klein and Daniel
Icolari, in 1967, published in New York by B.
Klein and Co. Klein and Co. issued a second
edition, revised, in 1970. Volume 2 of all
editions so far has been an Indian Who's Who.

0164. Klose, Nelson. Concise Study Guide to the American
Frontier. Lincoln: University of Nebraska Press, 1964.

Over   600   titles,   23   headings
(classifications)   of   specialized   studies
relating to frontier history.

0165. Kluckhohn,   Clyde,   and   Spencer,   Katherine.   A
Bibliography of the Navaho Indians. New York: J. J.
Augustin, 1940.

0166. Koehler, Lyle. "Native Women of the Americas: A
Bibliography." Frontiers: A Journal of Women's Studies
6:3 (Fall 1981): 73-101.

0167. Laird, W. David. Hopi Bibliography: Comprehensive
and Annotated. Tucson: University of Arizona Press,
1977.

0168. Lass-Woodfin, Mary J., ed. Books on American Indians
and Eskimos. Chicago: American Library Association,
1977.

0169. Lauber, John Francis. "A Selected Bibliography of
Books about the Pacific Northwest 1942-1952." MA
Thesis. Seattle: University of Washington, 1953.

43 p.

0170. Leisy,   Ernest.   The   American   Historical   Novel.
Norman: University of Oklahoma Press, 1950.

Chronological   survey   of   historical
novels   focuses   on   historical   events   and
novels based on them. Section I deals with
colonial America; Section II, the American
revolution and its aftermath; Section III,
the westward movement; Section IV, the civil
war and reconstruction; Section V, national
expansion. The last section has subsections
on the midwest, far west, and southwest.

0171. Lewis,   Robert   W.   and   DeFlyer,   Joseph E. "English
367: American Indian Literature." Study Guide for
Three Hour Correspondence Course, University of North
Dakota, Grand Forks, ND. Bethesda, MD: ED 228 022,
1982.

0172. Littlefield, Daniel F., and Parins, James W. A
Bibliography of Native American Writers, 1772-1924.
Native American Bibliography Series, No. 2. Jack W.
Marken, ed. Metuchen, NJ: Scarecrow Press, Inc.,
1981.

Lists   more   than   4,000   entries   by
American Indian authors from colonial times
until the American Indian was granted
citizenship. Includes translations, but
excludes material by Indians written down by
non-Indians. Entries are coded to indicate

whether address, collection or compilation,
drama, edition, fiction, letter, myth or
legend, nonfiction prose, poetry, sermon, or
translation into English. Part I is a list
of writers according to their tribal
affiliation. Part II lists writers known only
by their pen names. Part III gives
biographical notes about the authors.
Overall organization is alphabetical by
author's last name, but works for each writer
are listed chronologically. Entries are not
annotated, but authors are indexed by tribal
affiliation and there is a subject index. 343
pages.

0173. Littlefield, Daniel F. and Parins, James W. American
Indian and Alaska Native Newspapers and Periodicals
1826-1924. Historical Guides to the World's
Periodicals and Newspapers Series. Westport, CT:
Greenwood Press, 1983.

Lists newspapers and periodicals edited
or published by Native Americans and Alaska
Natives. Gives publishing history of, and
narrative profiles of the periodicals,
including some non-native publications that
focus on contemporary Indian and Eskimo
affairs. Relevant bibliographies are listed
for each, as well as location and index
sources. Appendixes list publications by
chronology, geography, and tribal emphasis.
Cross-references of variant titles are
provided in both table of contents and text.
A supplemental list provides information on
inaccessible titles. Subject index.

0174. Ludewig, Hermann E. The Literature of American
Aboriginal Languages, with Additions and Corrections
by William Turner. London: Trubner, 1858.

258 p.

0175. McGaghy, Dawn, comp. "The American Indian: A Selected
Bibliography." Bowling Green, Ohio: Bowling Green
State University Library, 1970.

12 p. Designed as a basic list "for the
reader whose knowledge of the Indian in
American history is slight," this
bibliography focuses on Indian-white
relations. It lists general reference works
and bibliographies, histories of Indian-white
relations and general histories, tribal
studies, and books on "the new Indian."

0176. MacKay, Mercedes B. and Moher, Thomas M., comps. South Dakota Indian Bibliography. Pierre, South Dakota: South Dakota State Library Commission, 1967.

        52 p. Annotated. Arranged by broad subject areas.

0177. McKaye, Vara L. "A Critical Bibliography of Certain Types of the Literature of New Mexico." MA Thesis. Albuquerque: University of New Mexico, 1930.

        Some consideration of Indians.

0178. McKenzie, Joanna. "Come Walk in My Moccasins--Building Understanding through Books." California Council for the Social Studies Review 12 (1972-73) : 37-42.

0179. Major, Mabel, and Pearce, T. M. Southwest Heritage: A Literary History and Bibliography. 3rd ed. Albuquerque: University of New Mexico Press, 1972.

        778 p. Describes poetry and prose of southwestern Indians, narratives of Spanish settlers and explorers, tall tales, ballads, poetry and fiction of anglo-Americans. Part I: "Literature before the Anglo-Americans to 1800;" Part II: "Literature of the Anglo-American Adventurers and Settlers, 1800-1918;" Part III: "Literature from C. 1918-1948;" Part IV: "Literature from 1948-1970." EDRS sources show ED number for this--ED 089 345--but indicate that the book is not available from EDRS.

0180. Marken, Jack W. The American Indian: Language and Literature. Arlington Heights, IL: AHM Publishing Corp., 1978.

        205 p. Index. Not annotated, but offers nearly 3,700 listings in 16 broad categories, each of which is subclassified. Cites books and articles from more than 300 journals. Section I is a list of 103 bibliographies; Section III, General Literature, is subclassified into collections and anthologies, Indian authors, discussions of types of Indian literature and general articles, and criticism and discussion of Indian literature, incuding works about Indians by non-Indians. After the general language section, Section IV, broad classifications are based on geographical/cultural regions, each of these subclassified under the headings general literature and general language, and entries under each of the latter classified according

to tribe. Anna Lee Stensland calls this "the
most nearly complete bibliography available
on the languages and literature of the
American Indian." Emphasis in it is on
productions by Indians, and consequently,
according to the author in his preface, omits
"most of the literature by non-Indians." But
he does include 184 critical discussions of
that literature. Books thought by the author
to be important are marked with an asterisk,
and those available in paperback with a
dagger.

0181. Marken, Jack W. <u>The Indians and Eskimos of North</u>
<u>America: A Bibliography of Books in Print through</u>
<u>1972</u>. Vermillion, South Dakota: Dakota Press, 1973.

200 p. Omits most fiction. Lists 24
bibliographies,   19   handbooks,   62
autobiographies, 268 collections of myths and
legends, and 2,537 titles in a catch-all
category called "All Other." Organized
alphabetically according to author. Also
cites reprints in American Archaeology and
Ethnology available from Kraus Reprint Co. A
limited subject index (only 28 categories)
refers to works cited by number.

0182. Marken, Jack W. "Some Recent Resources in Indian
Literature." <u>American Indian Quarterly</u> 2 (Autumn
1975): 282-289.

0183. Marken, Jack W., and Hoover, Herbert T. <u>Bibliography</u>
<u>of the Sioux</u>. Native American Bibliography Series,
Number 1. Metuchen, N.J.: Scarecrow Press, 1980.

388 p. Name index. Subject index.
Some 3,367 citations classified under 33
headings including "Captivity Literature,"
"Fiction and Other Works," "Indian Authors,"
"Literature--Collections and Stories," "Types
of Literature and Criticism," and "Theses and
Dissertations." About half of the entries
are annotated. Some annotations are
descriptive, some evaluative.

0184. Martinez, Cecilia and Heathman, J. E., computers.
<u>American Indian Education: A Selected Bibliography</u>
Educational Resources Information Center/Center for
Research and Social System. University Park: New
Mexico State University, 1969.

0185. Melody, Michael E. <u>The Apaches: A Critical</u>
<u>Bibliography</u>. Newberry Library Center for the History
of the American Indian Bibliograhical Series.
Bloomington: Indiana University Press, 1977.

0186. Meyers,   Robert   A.   <u>Amerindians   of the Lesser</u>
       <u>Antilles: A Bibliography</u>.   Bibliography Series. New
       Haven: Human Relations Area File Press, 1981.

0187. Michigan   Education   Association.<u>A Selected Annotated</u>
       <u>Bibliography of Material Relating to Racism, Blacks,</u>
       <u>Chicanos,   Native   Americans,   and Multi-ethnicity</u>.
       Volume I. Bethesda, MD: EDRS, ED 069 445, 1971.

               75 p.   Primary focus is on material
       which   the MEA felt to be "most representative
       of   the   realities   that   relate   to   the
       involvement   and   contributions of Blacks,
       Chicanos,   and   Native   Americans and the
       climate   of   the   times   during which such
       involvementand contributions occurred."   294
       entries,   including   novels.   Also includes
       nonprint resources such as films.

0188. Michigan   State University Libraries.   "Finding North
       American   Indian   Materials in the Michigan State
       University Libraries."   East   Lansing: Michigan State
       University Libraries, 1972.

               Gives   general references.   Lists several
       bibliographies.   Gives   introductory reading
       list.

0189. Mickinock,   Rey.   "Plight of the Native American."
       <u>Library Journal</u> 96 (September 15, 1971) : 2848-2851.

               A   bibliographical   essay dealing with
       factual   innacuracies   in books about Indians,
       both fiction and non-fiction.

0190. Minneapolis   Public   Library.   "The American Indian."
       Minneapolis: Minneapolis Public Library, 1969.

               20 p.

0191. The   Minnesota Historical Society. "Chippewa and
       Dakota   Indians: A Subject Catalog of Books, Pamphlets,
       Periodicals,   and   Manuscripts   in   the   Minnesota
       Historical   Society."   St.   Paul: Minnesota Historical
       Society, 1969.

               131 p.

0192. Mithun,   Marianne, and Woodbury, Hanni, eds. <u>Northern</u>
       <u>Iroquoian Texts</u>.   International Journal of American
       Linguistics Native American Texts Series: Monograph
       Number 4.   Chicago: University of Chicago Press, 1980.

               168 p.

0193. Momaday, Natachee Scott. <u>American Indian Authors</u>.
       Boston: Houghton Mifflin, 1972.

0194. Montana Department of Public Education. <u>The Indian
       in   the Classroom</u>. Helena: Montana Department of
       Public Education, 1972.

                    311 p. A guide for teachers of Indian
              students. Contains writings on Indian
              education, excerpts from literary works.
              Bibliography comprises about two thirds of
              book. Lists books about Indians and
              publishers, Indian records and record
              companies, Indian films in the Montana
              audio-visual library, addresses for film
              study guides, Indian educational films in
              print, film distributors, sources of rental
              films, Indian newspapers. Books, records,
              and films sections subclassified. Most
              titles annotated.

0195. Moorehead, Warren K. <u>American Indian in the U.S.,
       Period 1850-1914</u> Facsimile ed. Freeport, NY: Books
       for Libraries, Inc., 1970.

0196. Morgan, Betty M. "An Investigation of Children's
       Books Containing Characters from Selected Minority
       Groups Based on Specified Criteria." Ph.D.
       Dissertation. Carbondale: Southern Illinois
       University, 1973.

                    306 p. Pages 71-94 on American Indians.
              Briefly discusses various "concepts" of
              Indians, development of stereotypes,
              portrayal in literature.

0197. Muir, Gertrude H. "Indians of the Southwest in
       Fiction: A Bibliography." <u>Western Review</u> (Winter 1967)
       : 60-64.

0198. "Multi-Media Resource List: Eskimos and Indians, 1970
       supplement." Bethesda, MD: EDRS, ED 046 864, 1970.

                    12 p. This is supplement to ED 040 916.
              Cites 24 items relating to Eskimos, Indians
              of Canada, myths and legends, biography and
              fiction; lists seven publications of the
              Indian Eskimo Association of Canada; gives
              descriptive information on 12 periodicals;
              describes 34 films; describes miscellaneous
              charts, posters, maps and picture sets.

0199. Murdock, George P. <u>Ethnographic Bibliography of
       North America</u>. New Haven: Human Relations Area Files
       Press, 1960.

393 p. Over 17,000 books and journal
articles arranged by tribes alphabetically
within 16 geographical areas.

0200. Murdock,   George   P.   and   O'Leary,   Timothy J.
Ethnographic Bibliography of North America. 2nd ed. 5
vols. New Haven: Human Relations Area Files Press,
1975.

Approximately   40,000   entries   through
1972.   Not annotated. Volume 1 is a general
bibliography.   Others are keyed to geographic
regions.

0201. National   Indian   Education   Association. Index to
Bibliographies and Resource Materials. Minneapolis,
MN: National Indian Education Association, 1975.

0202. National   Indian Training Center. Indian Bibliography
2nd   edition. Brigham City, Utah: National Indian
Training Center, 1972.

Autobiographies,   traditional narratives,
poetry.

0203. National Library of Canada. Indian-Inuit Authors: An
Annotated Bibliography.   Ottowa: Information Canada,
1974.

108 p.   Comprehensive and wide-ranging:
poetry,   songs,   articles,   addresses,
conference   reports,   studies,   theses,
language, texts. Indexed.

0204. Naumer,   Janet   Noll.   "American   Indians: A
Bibliography   of   Sources."   American   Libraries 1
(October 1970) : 861-864.

Essay   listing   reference   works   and
bibliographies,   pamphlets,   periodicals,
non-print   materials,   photos,   slides,
transparencies, and recordings.

0205. Neuman,   Robert   W.,   and Simmons, Lanier A. "A
Bibliography Relative to Indians of the State of
Louisiana." Anthropological Study No. 4 November 1969.
Bethesda, MD: EDRS, ED 046 550, November 1969.

0206. Newberry Library--Chicago.   Dictionary Catalog of
the Edward E. Ayer Collection of Americana and
American Indians. 16 vols.   Boston: G. K. Hall and
Co., 1961.

0207. Newberry Library--Chicago.   Dictionary Catalog of
the Edward E. Ayer Collection of Americana and
American Indians, First Supplement. 3 vols. Boston:
G. K. Hall and Co., 1970.

0208. Newberry Library. <u>Narratives of Captivity among the</u>
<u>Indians   of   North   America.   A List of Books and</u>
<u>Manuscripts   on   the   Subject   in   the   Edward E. Ayer</u>
<u>Collection of the Newberry Library</u>. Newberry Library,
Publication   3.   Chicago: Newberry   Library,   1912;
supplement No. 1 comp. by Clara A. Smith. Chicago:
Newberry Library, 1928.

> 1912 edition has 120 p.; 1928 supplement
> 49.   The first list contains 1,339 titles,
> the   supplement,   143,   including different
> editions of some of the narratives of the
> first list. The supplement also contains the
> narrated experiences of 78 captives who were
> not named in the first list.

0209. Newman,   Killian,   ed. "A Preliminary Bibliography of
Selected   Children's Books about American Indians." New
York: Association of American Indian Affairs, 1969.

> 17 p. 63 books categorized by age group.

0210. New Mexico State University. "Manual for Providing
Library Services to Indians and Mexican Americans."
Las Cruces: New Mexico State University, March 1971;
Bethesda, MD: EDRS, ED 047 872, March 1971.

> 60 p.   Prepared by participants at the
> "Institute   to   Train   School   and Public
> Librarians to Work in Communities with Large
> Numbers of Mexican Americans and/or Indians
> June 8-July 3, 1970." Includes criteria for
> selecting books, lists of bibliographies on
> Indians and Mexican Americans. Each entry
> coded for interest and level.

0211. New   York   Museum of the American Indian, Heye
Foundation. <u>Books about Indians,</u> New York: New York
Museum   of   the American Indian, Heye Foundation,
November, 1977.

> 60 p.   Books from many publishers
> offered for sale on a retail basis from the
> museum shop.   This catalog may be purchased
> (for a nominal fee--$1.00 for the 1977 book)
> from the museum.   Books are catagorized by
> geographic and cultural region.   Each is
> briefly described.

0212. New   York   Museum of the American Indian, Heye
Foundation. <u>List of Publications</u>. 17th ed. Indian
Notes and Monographs No. 49. New York: New York
Museum of the American Indian, Heye Foundation, June
1975.

> This 39 page list is probably superceded

by now. Its focus is primarily
archaeological and anthropological. The 1975
edition shows nothing specifically dealing
with Indians in literature, Indian legends or
Indian authors.

0213. Nichols, Margaret S., and O'Neill, Margaret N.
Multi-Cultural Resources for Preschool through Second
Grade: In the Areas of Black, Spanish-speaking,
Asian-American, and Native American Cultures.
Stanford, CA: Multicultural Resources, 1972.

40 p. Was available from the publisher,
Box 2945, Stanford, CA 94305.

0214. Nickerson, Gifford S. Native Americans in Doctoral
Dissertations, 1971-75: A Classified and Indexed
Research Bibliography. Monticello, IL: Council of
Planning Libraries, 1977.

0215. Oaks, Priscilla. Minority Studies: A Selective
Annotated Bibliography. Boston: G. K. Hall, 1976.

0216. O'Leary, Timothy J. Ethnographic Bibliography of
South America. New Haven: Human Relations Area Files
Press, 1963.

387 p.

0217. Olsen, Diane. "Indians in Literature, A Selected,
Annotated Bibliography for Children." Minneapolis:
University of Minnesota, 1964; Bethesda, MD: EDRS, ED
014 353, 1964.

16 p. Biography, fictionalized
biography, lore and legend, stories and
novels, general information and background.

0218. Osborn, Lynn. "A Bibliography of North American
Indian Speech and Spoken Language." Bethesda, MD:
EDRS, ED 044 223, December 1968.

57 p.

0219. Palerm, Angel. "Original Americans." Americas 9
(December 1957) : 34-36.

A Review of five cultural anthropology
books including J. S. Slotkin's The Peyote
Religion: A Study in Indian-White Relations.

0220. Palfrey, T. H. and Coleman, H. E. Guide to
Bibliographies of Theses, U. S. and Canada. 2nd ed.
Chicago: American Library Association, 1940; 3rd
edition, Chicago: American Library Association, 1950.

Partial   annotations   make   this still of
some   use in finding early 20th century works.
Part   I   lists   general   lists;   Part II gives
lists   in   special   fields;   Part   III   is
institutional lists.

0221. Parsons,   Phyllis R.   "The Trans-Mississippi West in
Selected   Popular   Magazine   Literature   1820-1870:   An
Annotated   Bibliography."   MA   Thesis.   Laramie:
University of Wyoming, 1950.

82   p.   Part   I,   "The Call of the West;"
Part   II,"Avenues   of   Transportation   to   the
West;"   Part   III,"New Frontiers of the West;"
Part   IV,"New   Homes in the West;"   Part V,"The
New   Man of the West;"   Part VI,"The Wilderness
Conquered."   Part   III   contains   subcategory,
"The   Indians:"   50   titles wherein, according
to the author,   it is clear that "the policy of
extermination.   .   .   was   more   deliberately
advocated   for   the   man   than   for   the
(buffalo)."

0222. Perkins,   David and Tanis, Norman E. Native Americans
of North   America: A Bibliography Based on Collections
in   the   Libraries   of   California   State   University,
Northridge.   Metuchen, N.J.: Scarecrow Press, 1975.

Literature,   music,   religion.   Not
annotated.

0223. Peterson,   Richard   K.   "Indians   in   American
Literature."   Bulletin of Bibliography   30   (1973):
42-47.

0224. Peyer,   Bernd C.   "A Bibliography of Native American
Prose   Prior   to the 20th Century."   Wassaja/The Indian
Historian 13 (September 1980):   23-25.

0225. Phinney,   Archie.   Nez   Perce   Texts.   Columbia
University   Contributions   to Anthropology Series, Vol.
25.   New York: AMS Press, n.d. (reprint of 1934 ed.).

0226. Pilling,   James.   Bibliography   of   the   Siouan
Languages.   Washington,   D.C.:   Government   Printing
Office, 1887.

87 p.

0227. Pilling,   James.   Bibliography   of   the   Algonquin
Languages.   U.S. Bureau of Ethnology, Bulletin No. 13.
Washington, D.C.: Government Printing Office, 1891.

614 p.

0228. 72.   Pilling,   James C. Bibliography of the Chinookan
Languages.   1893; Seattle: Shorey Publications, 1970.

0229. Pilling, James C. Bibliographies of the Languages of the North American Indians. 1887-1894; reprint parts in 3 vols. New York: AMS Press, Inc., 1970.

0230. Porter, Frank W., III. Indians in Maryland and Delaware: A Critical Bibliography. Baltimore: Maryland Historical Society, 1979; Newberry Center for the History of the American Indian Bibliographical Series. Bloomington: Indiana University Press, 1979.

0231. Prichard, Nancy S. "A Selected Bibliography of American Ethnic Writing and Supplement." Bethesda, MD: EDRS, ED 041 921, October 1969.

　　　49 p. Afro-Americans, American Indians, Hispanic Americans, Oriental Americans. Covers fiction, poetry, drama, nonfiction including biography and autobiography, art, and folklore. Lists music, films, records, periodicals, anthologies, bibliographies, criticism, history. Little on the Indian in literature.

0232. Prucha, Francis Paul. A Bibliographical Guide to the History of Indian-White Relations in the United States. Chicago: University of Chicago Press, 1977.

　　　454 p. More than 9,000 items of predominately historical interest are listed in 17 chapters: "Materials in the National Archives," "Documents of the Federal Government," "Guides to Manuscripts," and "Guides to Other Sources" (which includes periodical indexes, newspapers, library catalogs, reports on special collections, and so on) make up Part One, Guides to Sources. Part Two, Classified Bibliography of Published Works, includes the chapters "Indian Affairs/Indian Policy," "The Indian Department," "Treaties and Councils," "Land and the Indians," "Military Relations,"Trade and Traders," "Missions and Missionaries," "Legal Relations," "Indian Education," "Indian Health," "Social and Economic Developments," "Indians and Indian Groups," and "Special Topics." The last chapter, "Special Topics," contains sections on "Indians in Literature" (126 titles), "Indians in Movies" (9 titles), and "Indian Writings" (14 titles). Prucha notes in his preface that, since "each work is entered in the bibliography only once, use of the index is necessary to locate all items that touch on a given topic." Use of the index, however, turned up only two additional titles pertinent to Indian literature and

three relative to the image of the Indian in literature. According to Prucha, the bibliography contains items published through 1974, although a few works published later were included.

0233. Prucha, Francis P. Indian-White Relations in the United States: A Bibliography of Works Published 1975-1980. Lincoln: University of Nebraska Press, 1982.

An up-dating of the bibliography immediately above. The classification in this book, according to Prucha, "is fundamentally the same as in the original volume." However, the number of subheadings has been reduced and some new ones have been added. Emphasis is still on history. Lists 61 titles pertaining to Indians in Literature and 27 relating to Indian writings. In all, Prucha adds 3,400 new titles to his first collection. Each is cited just once.

0234. Randle, Martha C. "The Waugh Collection of Iroquois Folktales." Publications of the American Philosophical Society, 97 (1953) : 611-633.

0235. Ray, Roger B. The Indians of Maine and the Atlantic Provinces: A Bibliographic Guide. Morris, Gerald E., ed. Maine History Bibliographical Series. Portland, ME: Maine Historical Society, 1977.

0236. Revai, Loretta Z. "An Annotated Bibliography of Selected Books about American Indians for Elementary through High School Students." Bethesda, MD: EDRS, ED 065 642, July 1972.

69 p.

0237. Rickards, Montana Hopkins. "Literature for the Native American (The American Indian)." Speech given at the annual convention of National Council of Teachers of English (NCTE) November 1970. Bethesda, MD: EDRS, ED 054 143, November 1970.

23 p. 82-item bibliography.

0238. Ronda, James P., and Axtell, James. Indian Missions: A Critical Bibliography Newberry Library Center for the History of the American Indian Bibliographical Series. Bloomington: Indiana University Press, 1978.

Items suitable for use by high school students are noted. Information on both missionary accounts of Indians and (later) Native American response to missionaries.

0239. Rose, W., et al., comps. "Books by Iroquois Authors (Mohawk, Seneca, Cayuga, Tuscarora, Oneida and Onondaga)." _American Indian Quarterly_ 6 (Fall—Winter 1982): 358-376.

0240. Rundell, Walter, Jr. "Interpretations of the American West: A Descriptive Bibliography." _Arizona and the West_ 3 (1961) : 69-88, 148-168.

0241. Ruoff, A. LaVonne. "History in _Winter in the Blood_: Background and Bibliography." _American Indian Quarterly_ 4 (No. 2, 1978): 169-172.

0242. Rusk, Ralph L. _The Literature of the Middle Western Frontier_. 2 vols. New York: Columbia University Press, 1925; reprint edition New York: Ungar, 1963.

> Vol. I, chapter 1 involves "cultural beginnings," "romantic and cynical views of the west. . . literature as a mirror of frontier civilization. . . ." Chapter 2, "Travel and Observation," includes narratives of captivities among the Indians. Chapter 6 deals with fiction, "the western point of view," chapter 7 with poetry, chapter 8 with drama. Volume II contains bibliographies.

0243. Sabin, Joseph. _Dictionary of Books Relating to America from its Discovery to the Present Time_. 29 vols. New York: Bibliographical Society of America, 1928-1936.

> This has been reprinted at least once and apparently the title varies. One variation of the title is _Bibliotheca Americana. A Dictionary of Books Relating to America, from its Discovery to the Present Time_. Another is _Bibliotheca Americana. A Dictionary of Books Relating to America_.

0244. Sanders, Lyle (Continued by Genevieve Porterfield). _A Guide to the Literature of the Southwest_. Albuquerque: University of New Mexico Press, 1942--.

0245. Sanders, Ronald. "Red Power at the Bookstore." _Midstream_ 18:6 (1972): 49-67.

0246. Sayre, Robert F. "A Bibliography and Anthology of American Indian Literature." _College English_ 35 (March 1974) : 706.

> A review of Jack Marken's _The Indians and Eskimos of North America: a Bibliography of Books in Print through 1972_ and of Thomas G. Sanders' and Walter W. Peek's _Literature of the American Indian_.

0247. Schoolcraft,   Henry Rowe. <u>A Bibliographical Catalogue</u>
<u>of Books, Translations of the Scriptures, and Other</u>
<u>Publications in the Indian Tongues of the United</u>
<u>States</u>. Washington: C. Alexander, 1849.

28 p.

0248. Schuster,   Helen   H.   <u>The   Yakimas: A   Critical</u>
<u>Bibliography</u>. Newberry Library Center for the History
of   the   American   Indian   Bibliographical   Series.
Bloomington: Indiana University Press, 1982.

0249. "A   Selected   Bibliography   of   American   Indian
Literatures." Association of Departments of English
(New York) <u>Bulletin</u> No. 75 (Summer 1983): 47-48.

0250. Shaul,   Lawana   Jean.   "Treatment of the West in
Selected Magazine Fiction, 1870-1900: An Annotated
Bibliography."   MA Thesis.   Laramie: University of
Wyoming, 1954.

123 p.   Examines the stories published
during   the   period   in   7 magazines and
classifies them into 7 categories, one of
which is "Indians and Soldiers." Contains a
list of authors and stories arranged by state
and character or "character types." Treats
Indian characters among others. The Chapter
on "subject matter and treatment" also
comments on attitudes about Indians prevalent
during   the   period   and   evident in the
literature.

0251. Sheldon,   Dorothy L. and Sitter, Victoria J. <u>A</u>
<u>Selective Bibliography of American Indian Literature,</u>
<u>History, and Culture</u>.   The General College Studies,
University of Minnesota, Vol 15, No. 3, 1968;
Bethesda, MD: EDRS, ED 030 526, 1968.

Examines   160 books published between
1825 and 1967. Six content areas: literature
by Indians or from their oral tradition;
autobiography and biography; fiction with
Indian subject; art; history; general texts on
anthropology and culture.

0252. Sleeth, Irene. <u>William Faulkner: A Bibliography of</u>
<u>Criticism</u> Denver: Alan Swallow, 1962.

Technically,   this   probably   doesn't
belong in this collection; however, it does
list   works   which   are   concerned   with
Faulkner's fictional treatment of Indians,
and it is typical of a kind of bibliography
that   is useful in specific applications.
There are also bibliographies available on

J.F. Cooper, Washington Irving, Nathaniel Hawthorne, and many other American writers whose works featured American Indians.

0253. Smith, Dwight L. Indians of the United States and Canada: A Bibliography. Clio Bibliography Series, No. 3. Santa Barbara, CA: American Bibliographical Center--Clio Press, December 1973.

> 450 p. Indexed. Entries are taken from the data bank of the abstracts publication, America: History and Life." It offers 1,687 annotated citations on scholarship in the historical and social sciences from 1954 through 1972. The collection is grouped chronologically, by culture area and by tribe. Tribes are subclassified, abstracts arranged by author.

0254. Smith, Dwight L. Indians of the United States and Canada: A Bibliography, Vol. II. Clio Bibliograhpy Series, No. 9. Santa Barbara, CA: American Bibliographical Center--Clio Press, 1983.

> 345 p. Extensive subject index (takes up pages 225-345) is a change from the first volume. Volume II utilizes the American Bibliographical Center's Subject Profile Index (ABC SPIndex). This index lists works under both general and specific headings with cross-references. The index makes 45 references to literature specifically, but also lists works under the headings "Biography, Drama, Fiction, Humor, Journalism, Language, Novels, Poetry, Satire, and Symbolism in Literature." In all, Volume II contains 3,218 abstracts on American Indian history and culture. A continuation of Volume I, this list numbers items consecutively with it beginning with number 1688. As in Volume I, listings are organized generally by culture area with general listings given first in each area section; works are then arranged by tribe within each culture area. As in the first volume, items in this one were chosen from the data base of America: History and Life, in this case volumes 10-15 (1973-1978), and the America: History and Life Supplement to Volumes 1-10 (1964-1973).

0255. Smith, Jessie Carnie. "Minorities in the United States: Guide to Resources." Bethesda, MD: EDRS, ED 080 133, 1973.

0256. Smith,   William   F.,   Jr.   "American   Indian
       Autobiographies."   American Indian Quarterly 2 (1975):
       237-245.

0257. Smith, William F., Jr. "American Indian Literature."
       English Journal 63 (January 1974) : 68-72.

              Annotated listing of books by Indian
       authors.   Not lengthy, but each item is
       described and critically evaluated. Contains
       6 anthologies, 6 biographies, 4 collections
       of   poetry,   6 collections of traditional
       narratives (myths, tales and legends).

0258. Smollar,   Eleanor,   ed.   "Reading is Fundamental's
       Guide   to   Book   Selection,   with   Supplement 1."
       Washington,D.C.:   Reading   is   Fundamental,   1970;
       Bethesda, MD: EDRS, ED 045 248, 1970.

              106 p.   Guide to purchasing books at
       elementary level.   Lists approximately 600
       titles   with   descriptive   annotations.
       Separate lists for each ethnic group
       classified according to reading level:
       elementary, teenage, adult.

0259. Smollar,   Eleanor,   ed.   "Reading is Fundamental's
       Guide   to Book Selection, Supplement 2." Washington,
       D.C.: Reading is Fundamental, 1971; Bethesda, MD:
       EDRS, ED 062 095, 1971.

              List   includes   folktales,   history,
       science fiction, biography, and general
       fiction.

0260. South   Dakota State Library Commission. "South Dakota
       Indian   Bibliography." Pierre, South Dakota: South
       Dakota State Library Commission, 1972; Bethesda, MD:
       EDRS, ED 072 915, 1972.

0261. Spiller, Robert E., and Blackburn, Philip C. A
       Descriptive Bibliography of the Writings of James
       Fenimore Cooper. New York: R. R. Bowker, Co., 1934.

0262. Spofford, Ainsworth.   "Rare Books Relating to the
       American Indian." American Anthropologist 3, 1No. 2
       (1901):270-285.

              Bibliographies,   explorers   accounts,
       histories, missionary narratives, captivity
       narratives, linguistic studies.

0263. Stensland, Anna Lee. "American Indian Culture:
       Promises, Problems, and Possibilities." English
       Journal 60 (December 1971) : 1195-1200.

Discusses a number of books (prose and poetry, fiction and nonfiction) suitable for use in the classroom.

0264. Stensland, Anna Lee. "American Indian Culture and the Reading Program." _Journal of Reading_ 15 (October 1971) : 22-26.

Books for reluctant readers.

0265. Stensland, Anna Lee. _Literature by and about the American Indian: An Annotated Bibliography for Junior and Senior High School Students_. New edition. Urbana, IL: National Council of Teachers of English (NCTE), 1979.

The _first edition_ of this work--same author, same title, same publisher-- appeared in 1973 and consisted of 208 pages, of which roughly 124 were devoted to an an annotated bibliography. Brief essays in the first edition discussed the value of Indian literature, Indian stereotypes in literature, and criteria for selection of books included in the bibliography.The bibliography section was divided into several categories: "Myth, Legend, Oratory, and Poetry;" "Fiction," for junior high students, and for high school students and adults; "Drama;" "Biography and Autobiography," for junior high and high school; "History;" "Anthropology and Archaeology;" "Modern life and problems;" "Music, Arts and Crafts;" and "Aids for the Teacher." Then followed "Study Guides for Selected Books," "Biographies of American Indian Authors," "Basic Books for a Collection," "Sources of Additional Materials," a "Directory of Publishers," an "Author Index," and a "Title Index." The _new edition_ consists of 382 pages, and most of the additional material seems to be in the form of added titles and descriptions. The first version did not list elementary level books, for example, and the second does, selected and evaluated by Aune M. Fadum, Assistant Professor of Elementary Education at the University of Minnesota, Duluth. However, Stensland says that generally, "as many as possible of the worthwhile books published since 1973 have been added, and the number of titles published prior to that has been enlarged." The format of the new edition is also somewhat different than its predecessor. The new book consists of two sections plus a directory of publishers and author and title indexes. Section I, "Teaching the Literature

of the American Indian," consists of three
subsections: the "Introduction," "Aids for
the Teacher," and "Biographies of Selected
American Indian Authors." The introduction
consists of four subsections: "Important
Themes in Indian Literature," "Indian
Stereotypes in Literature," "Indian Literature
of the Mid-Seventies," and "References," a
short bibliography of works apparently
consulted in the writing of the introduction.
"Aids for the Teacher" offers "Guides to
Curriculum Planning," "A Basic Library of
Indian Literature," and "Sources of
Additional Materials," libraries,
associations, museums, schools, and so on.
Section II, "Bibliography," is organized
pretty much along the lines of the first
version with the exception of introductory
matter. "Introduction to the Bibliography"
explains the criteria for selection of items
in it and offers and explanation of how to
use the bibliography. Each of the book
lists--"Myth, Legend, Oratory, and Poetry;"
"Fiction;" "Biography and Autobiography;"
"History;" "Traditional Life and Culture;"
"Modern Life and Problems;" and "Music, Arts,
and Crafts"--lists materials progressively
under the appropriate headings: "Elementary,"
"Junior High," and "Senior High and Adult."

0266. Stewart, Omer C. Indians of the Great Basin: A
Critical Bibliography. Newberry Library Center for
the History of the American Indian Bibliographical
Series. Bloomington: Indiana University Press, 1982.

0267. Stuver, Marie Tyler. "An Approach to Bibliographic
Control of Materials Relating to Indians of the United
States." Master's Project. Provo, Utah: Brigham Young
University, 1973; Bethesda, MD: EDRS, ED 096 949,
August 1973.

    A proposal on how to cope with the
proliferation of materials on the American
Indian. Describes some bibliographies useful
in acquiring Indian materials.

0268. Superintendent of Schools, Los Angeles County
Office. "Portraits: Literature of Minorities: An
Annotated Bibliography of Literature by and about Four
Ethnic Groups in the United States for Grades 7-12."
Los Angeles: Superintendent of Schools, Los Angeles
County Office, June 1970; Bethesda, MD: EDRS, ED 042
771, June 1970.

    70 p. Literature on Blacks, North
American Indians, Mexicans, Asians, organized

according to literary type: novels, short
stories, poetry, drama, folktales, legends,
biographies, autobiographies, essays,
letters, speeches, anthologies. Gives
detailed information and evaluations on
theme, literary quality, and emotional level
of materials. Separate bibliography for
teachers.

0269. Superintendent of Schools, Los Angeles County
Office. "A supplement to Portraits: Literature of
Minorities." Los Angeles: Superintendent of Schools,
Los Angeles County Office, June 1972; Bethesda, MD:
EDRS, ED 065 887, June 1972.

71 p.

0270. Sylvestre, Guy. Indian-Inuit Authors: An Annotated
Bibliography. Ottowa: Information Canada, 1974.

0271. Tacoma Public Library. "A Selected Sample of Books
by and about American Indians with Special Emphasis on
the Pacific Northwest." Tacoma, WA: Tacoma Public
Library and Tacoma Community College Library, 1970.

13 p. Biography and autobiography,
culture (language, myths, arts), early
history, treaties, laws, fiction. Gives call
numbers for the two libraries involved in
compilation. Does not show publisher or
number of pages. Not annotated.

0272. Tanner, Helen H. The Ojibwas: A Critical
Bibliography. Newberry Library Center for the History
of the American Indian Bibliographical Series.
Bloomington: Indiana University Press, 1976.

0273. Ten Kate, Herman F. C. "The Indian in Literature."
The Indian Historian 3 (Summer 1970) : 23-32.

A condensed translation of reviews from
Dutch magazines appearing in 1919 and 1920
which were reprinted in the Smithsonian
Report in 1921, this bibliographic essay
discusses scientifically accurate novels and
juvenile fiction about North and South
American Indians.

0274. Thornton, Russell, and Grasmick, Mary K.
Bibliography of Social Science Research and Writings
on American Indians. Center for Urban and Regional
Affairs, Publication No. 79-1. Minneapolis:
University of Minnesota, 1979.

Mostly history, although other
disciplines covered include sociology,

geography, political science, economics and American and ethnic studies. Not annotated.

0275. Thornton, Russell. <u>Urbanization of the American Indians: A Critical Bibliography</u>. The Newberry Library Center for the History of the American Indian Bibliographical Series. Bloomington: Indiana University Press, 1982.

0276. Tooker, Elisabeth. <u>Indians of the Northeast: A Critical Bibliography</u>. The Newberry Library Center for the History of the American Indian Bibliographical Series. Bloomington: Indiana University Press, 1978.

0277. Torrans, Thomas. "General Works on the American Indian, A Descriptive Bibliography." <u>Arizona and the West</u>. 2 (1960) : 79-103.

0278. Townley, Charles, comp. "American Indians: A Selective Guide to the Resources of the UCSB Library." Santa Barbara, CA: University of California at Santa Barbara Library, 1971.

      42 p.

0279. Trout, Lawana. "Pick of the Paperbacks: Experimental Approaches to Oral Tradition Literature." <u>English Journal</u> 64 (April 1975) : 94-97.

      Discusses how the study of Indian poetry might inspire creative writing projects in the classroom. Mentions a number of sources of poems and other types of literature.

0280. Tyler, S. Lyman. <u>The Ute People: A Bibliographical Check List</u> Indian Affairs No. 3. Bethesda, MD: EDRS, ED 059 004, 1964.

      Primarily historical. Includes bibliographies and guides.

0281. Tyson, Edwin L., comp. "American Indians: A Bibliography of Books in San Jose City College Library." San Jose, CA: San Jose City College Library, 1969.

      15 p. Primarily general historical and anthropological writings, although it includes a few books of legends, a few novels, a few critical works.

0282. Ullom, Judith. <u>Folklore of the North American Indians: An Annotated Bibliography</u>. Washington, D.C.: Government Printing Office, 1969.

      Groups myths, legends, and stories by

separately   in   each   area.   Annotations
describe collector and tales in volume.

0283. U.   S.   Bureau   of   Indian   Affairs.   "Indian
Bibliography."   Washington, D.C.: U. S. Bureau of
Indian Affairs, 1970.

0284. U.S. Bureau of Indian Affairs. Indians: Legends and
Myths. Washington, D.C.: Government Printing Office,
1975.

    4 p. 29 titles of books.

0285. United   States Bureau of Naval Personnel. Indian and
Mexican   Americans; A Selective Annotated Bibliography.
Bethesda, MD: EDRS.   ED 078 863, 1972.

    48 p. 200 references. Includes myths.

0286. United   States   Interior   Department,   Indian Affairs
Bureau.   Indians: References   for Young Students.
Washington, D.C.: Government Printing Office, 1973.

    13 p.

0287. United   States   Interior   Department,   Indian Affairs
Bureau.   Suggested   Reading   List,   Assiniboin.
Washington, D.C.: Government Printing Office, 1973.

    2 p.

0288. University of Idaho Library and Center of Native
American Development. Native American Materials in the
University of Idaho Library. Moscow: University of
Idaho   Library   and   Center   of   Native   American
Development, 1972.

    299 p. University of Idaho Library said
this was noncirculating and would not share
it.

0289. University Microfilms International. North American
Indians: A Dissertation Index. Ann Arbor, Michigan:
University Microfilms International, 1977.

    169   p.   Lists doctoral dissertations
written between 1904 and 1976 concerning all
American Indian groups within the North
American continent. Divided into two parts, a
keyword index (an arrangement of titles in
alphabetical sequence by a significant word
in   the   title) and an author index.
Information for ordering microfilm and paper
copies   is   included; most titles are
available.   While   this   volume makes no
mention of the fact, it apparently replaces a

previous volume, <u>North American Indians; A</u>
<u>Catalog of Over One Thousand Items; Books,</u>
<u>Reprints, Microfilm and Microfiche</u>, which was
published by University Microfilms in 1971.
A copy of the latter volume was not obtained,
so a comparison could not be made.

0290. Unrau, William E. <u>The Emigrant Indians of Kansas; A</u>
<u>Critical Bibliography</u>. The Newberry Library Center
for the History of the American Indian Bibliographical
Series. Bloomington: Indiana University Press, 1980.

Notes works suitable for high school
students.

0291. Vail, Robert W. G. "A Bibliography of North American
Frontier Literature, 1542-1800." <u>The Voice of the Old</u>
<u>Frontier</u> Philadelphia: University of Pennsylvania
Press, 1949: 84-492; reprint edition, New York:
Octagon Books, 1970.

0292. Vanderhoof, Jack Warner. <u>A Bibliography of Novels</u>
<u>Related to American Frontier and Colonial History</u>
Troy, New York: Whitston Publishing Co, Inc., 1971.

Annotations present place, time, content
and/or theme of the work. Novels written
during period which don't have to do with
frontier or colonial history are not included
unless their authors have previously written
such books.

0293. Wagner, Henry R. <u>The Plains and the Rockies; A</u>
<u>Bibliography of Original Narratives of Travel and</u>
<u>Adventure, 1800-1865.</u> 3rd ed. rev. by Charles E. Camp.
Columbus, Ohio: Long's College Book Store, 1953.

601 p. Notes on primarily factual
accounts.

0294. Walker, Carol. <u>Bibliography of the Luiseno Indians</u>.
Romona, CA: Acoma Books, 1976.

0295. Washington State University Library. "Doing Research
on Native Americans." Pullman, Washington: Washington
State University Library, 1971.

31 p. Part I is a bibliography for the
Native American Studies program. It was
compiled by the staff at Washington State
University Library at Pullman in 1971 (Part
II wasn't published when my copy came out.).
It is annotated and gives WSU call numbers.
It includes children's books, arts, crafts,
language and literature, and Indian-white
relations and encounters.

0296. Weatherford, Elizabeth and Seubert, Emelia, eds.
       <u>Native Americans on Film and Video</u>. New York: Museum
       of the American Indian, 1982.

               152 p.

0297. Weinman, Paul L. <u>A Bibliography of the Iroquoian
       Literature: Partially Annotated</u>.   Bulletin 411.
       Albany: New York State Museum and Science Service,
       1969.

0298. Weslager, C. A. <u>The Delawares: A Critical
       Bibliography</u> The Newberry Library Center for the
       History of the American Indian Bibliographical Series.
       Bloomington: Indiana University Press, 1978.

               Notes works suitable for high school
           students.

0299. "We Talk, You Listen: A Selected Bibliography."
       <u>Personnel and Guidance Journal</u> 50 (October 1971) :
       145-146.

               Designed to assist counselors. Refers
           to works on Mexicans, Puerto Ricans; 18
           references to Native Americans.

0300. Whiteford, Andrew Hunter. "North American Indians:
       1492-1969." <u>Choice</u> n.v. (February 1970) : 1709-1719.

               Article is part of a column, "In the
           Balance." Author Whiteford is director of the
           Logan Museum of Anthropology at Beloit
           College. The article describes some basic
           types of interest in the Indian and
           classifies some books which may respond to
           them. An extensive list despite the few
           pages, primarily historical and
           anthropological, but with selections on Indian
           literature, crafts, pictures, biography and
           personal narratives. Some descriptive notes.

0301. Whiteside, Don. <u>Aboriginal People: A Selected
       Bibliography Concerning Canada's First People</u>.
       Ottawa: National Indian Brotherhood, 1973.

               Indexed by author and subject. Indian
           authors noted.

0302. Willis, Cecelia A., and Eunice, Travis M., comps.
       <u>Significant Literature by and About Native Americans</u>.
       Bethesda, MD: EDRS, ED 071 837, February 1973.

               126 p.

0303. Winther, Oscar Osborn. <u>A Classified Bibliography of</u>
the Periodical Literature of the Trans-Mississippi
<u>West, 1811-1957</u>.   Bloomington,   Indiana: Indiana
University Press, 1961.

626 p. Lists 9,244 items, classified by
subject, primarily concerned with history.
Includes all items in <u>The Trans-Mississippi</u>
<u>West: A Guide to its Periodical Literature</u>
(Indiana University Press, 1942) and adds
pertinent items 1938-1957 as well as
citations from regional journals appearing
since 1938.

0304. Winther, Oscar Osborn, and Van Orman, Richard. <u>A</u>
<u>Classified Bibliography of the Periodical Literature</u>
<u>of the Trans-Mississippi West: A Supplement, 1957-1967</u>
Bloomington: Indiana University Press, 1970.

Adds 4,500 items to the collection.

0305. Wolf, Carolyn E. and Folk, Karen K. <u>Indians of North</u>
<u>and South America: A Bibliography Based on the</u>
<u>Collection at the Willard E. Yager Library-Museum</u>
<u>Hartwick College, Oneonta, New York.</u> Metuchen, New
Jersey: Scarecrow Press, 1977.

0306. Wolff, Hans. "Bibliography of Bibliographies of
North American Indian Languages Still Spoken."
<u>International Journal of American Linguistics</u>, 13
(1947) : 268-273.

0307. Woodress, James L. <u>Doctoral Dissertations in</u>
<u>American Literataure, 1891-1955.</u> Durham, North
Carolina: Duke University Press, 1957.

The Indian in Literature

This section lists works which comment upon or otherwise relate to the treatment of the Indian as a character in American literature. The focus is on prose fiction; however, some works which discuss the Indian in poetry and drama have been included, as well as some which comment on the Indian's role in the movies and on television. A few of the works listed are concerned with the Indian's portrayal in nonfiction. Since the emphasis here is on works essentially concerned with literary matters, in cases where the majority of a work was concerned with sociology or history, for example, the work was not listed.

0308. Abel, Midge B. "American Indian Life as Portrayed in Children's Literature." Elementary English, 50 (February 1973) : 202-208.

> Analysis of children's books about tribal life, published since 1960, for reading levels 1 through 3. Emphasis on factual books about Indians and Indian life, but some discussion of fiction and Indian legends. Includes bibliography.

0309. Abbott, Hazel Belle. "And What of the Indian? His Literature and His Treatment in our Dramatic Literature." MA Thesis. New York: Columbia University, 1924.

0310. Adler, J. "Melville on the White Man's War against the American Indian." Science and Society 36 (Winter 1972) : 417-442.

0311. Agnew, Miriam. "A Contrast of Parkman's The Oregon Trail to similar works in the same period of the early West." MA Thesis. Denver: University of Denver, 1937.

0312. Agogino, George. "A Study of the Stereotype of the American Indian." MA Thesis. Albuquerque: University of New Mexico, 1950.

0313. Almon, Bert. "Woman as Interpreter: Haniel Long's Malinche." <u>Southwest Review</u>, 59 (Summer 1974) : 221-239.

About Long's fictional account of Dona Marina (as the Spaniards called her), the Oluta Indian who served as interpreter to Cortes and became his mistess. According to Almon, the commentary that "relates the interpreter's story to the archetypes of religion and literature. . . offers valuable insights into a contemporary issue, the proper relationship between man and woman." Almon says, "Long suggests that the heroine of his tale represents a key archetype. . . woman as interpreter and guide. . .a 'third type of heroine.'"

0314. Ames, Max B. "An Investigation of the Literary Treatment of American Injustices to the Indian." MA Thesis. Denver: University of Denver, 1959.

0315. Anderson, Brenda Jean. "The North American Indian in Theatre and Drama from 1605 to 1970." Ph. D. dissertation, University of Illinois at Urbana-Champaign, 1978.

0316. Anderson, Marilyn Jeanne. "The Best of Two Worlds: The Pocahontas Legend as Treated in Early American Drama." <u>Indian Historian</u> 12 (Summer 1979) : 54-59, 64.

0317. Anderson, Marilyn Jeanne. "The Image of the American Indian in American Drama from 1766 to 1845." Ph.D. Diss. Minneapolis: University of Minnesota, 1974.

0318. Anderson, Marilyn Jeanne. "The Image of the American Indian in American Drama during the Jacksonian Era, 1829-1845." <u>Journal of American Culture</u> 1 (Winter 1978) : 800-810.

0319. Anderson, Marilyn Jeanne. "<u>Ponteach</u>: The First American Problem Play." <u>American Indian Quarterly</u> 3 (Autumn 1977) : 225-241.

0320. Arnold, Dorie Mae. "American Indians in Fiction." MA Thesis. Sherman, Texas: Austin College, 1938.

0321. Astor, G. "Good Guys Wear War Paint." <u>Look</u>, 34 (December 1, 1970) : 56-61.

On the making of <u>Little Big Man</u>. Interview with Dustin Hoffman, Richard Mulligan (who played Custer) and Arthur Penn.

0322. Atkeson, Mary Meek. "A Study of the Local Literature of the Upper Ohio Valley, with Especial Reference to

the Early Pioneer and Indian Tales, 1820-1840." Ph. D.
Diss.   Columbus: Ohio State University, 1919; <u>Ohio
State University, Bulletin Contributions English</u> No.
2, Columbus: Ohio State University, 1921.

0323. Axtell, James.   "The Scholastic Philosophy of the
Wilderness." <u>William and Mary Quarterly</u>, 29 (July
1972) : 335-366.

0324. Bahr, Howard M. and Chadwick, Bruce A. "Contemporary
Perspectives on Indian Americans: A Review Essay."
<u>Social   Science   Quarterly</u>,   53 (December 1972) :
606-618.

        A   review   of   five   books   about
    Indian-white relations.

0325. Ballotti, Geno A. "The Southwest Indian in Fiction."
MA Thesis.   Laramie: University of Wyoming, 1955; in
<u>Studies   in the Literature of the West</u>. Laramie:
University of Wyoming, 1956, pp. 130-156.

0326. Barnett, Louise K. <u>Ignoble Savage: American Literary
Racism, 1790-1890</u>. Contributions in American Studies
No. 18. Westport, CT: Greenwood Press, 1975.

        220   p.   Author examines frontier
    romances; describes three stereotypes: bad
    Indian, noble savage and good Indian; argues
    Hawthorne's   and Melville's novels are
    paradigms for racism.

0327. Barnett, Louise K. "The Indian in American Fiction,
1790-1860." Ph. D. Diss. Bryn Mawr, PA: Bryn Mawr
College, 1972.

0328. Barnett, Louise K. "Nineteenth Century Indian Hater
Fiction: A Paradigm for Racism." <u>South Atlantic
Quarterly</u>, 74 (Spring 1975) : 224-236.

        A   discussion of the western ethic,
    manifest destiny, Aryan supremacy, and
    violence as portrayed in nineteenth century
    fiction.

0329. Barre, Elizabeth Freeman. "A Study of the Indian in
William Gilmore Simms' Novels and Short Stories." MA
Thesis.   Columbia, SC: University of South Carolina,
1941.

0330. Bates, Lorna Doone. "The Noble Savage in the Works of
Thoreau." MA Thesis. Iowa City: University of Iowa,
1934.

0331. Bataille, Gretchen, and Silet, Charles. L. P. "The
Entertaining Anachronism: Indians in American Films."

In *The Kaleidoscopic Lens: How Hollywood Views Ethnic Groups*, edited by Miller, Randall M., pp. 36-53. Englewood, New Jersey: Jerome S. Ozer Pubishers, Inc., 1980.

0332. Bataille, Gretchen M. and Silet, Charles L. P., eds. *The Pretend Indians: Images of Native Americans in the Movies*. Ames, Iowa: Iowa State University Press, 1980.

> Collection of essays. Discusses myths, stereotypes about Indians from earliest movies to contemporary ones; traces development of image of Indian in both literature and media and gives reasons for various aspects of it.

0333. Becker, I. H. "Primitivism and Civilization in 'The Leatherstocking Tales.'" MA Thesis. Baton Rouge, LA: Louisiana State University, 1955.

0334. Beer, David F. "Anti-Indian Sentiment in Early Colonial Literature." *The Indian Historian*, 2 (Spring 1969) : 29-33, 48.

> Discusses attitudes of serveral early writers, including John Smith, Alexander Whitaker, William Bradford, Thomas Morton, Edward Johnson, William Hubbard, Mary Rowlandson, Increase Mather, Cotton Mather, William Fleming, Samuel Penhallow, and Robert Beverley. Also gives references.

0335. Behlen, Dorothy M. F. "The Captivity Story in American Literature, 1577-1826: An Examination of Written Reports in English, Authentic and Fictitious, of the Experiences of White Men Captured by the Indians North of Mexico." Ph. D. Diss. Chicago: University of Chicago, 1952.

0336. Beidler, Peter G. *Fig Tree John: An Indian in Fact and Fiction*. Tucson: University of Arizona Press, 1977.

0337. Beidler, Peter G. "The Popularity of Dan Cushman's *Stay Away, Joe* among American Indians." *Arizona Quarterly* 33 (Autumn 1977): 216-240.

0338. Bell, Carolyn L. "The Pre-School Child's Image of the American Indian." Bethesda, MD: EDRS: ED 051 914, May 1971.

> 48 p. Survey of books, nursery rhymes, coloring books, clothing, TV programs, and toys which tend to stereotype American Indians.

0339. Berkhofer, Robert F., Jr. _The White Man's Indian: Images of the American Indian from Columbus to the Present_. New York: Alfred A. Knopf, Inc., 1978.

>   He explores the white image and idea of the Indian through five centuries of contact in science, art, and government policy. The third part is entitled: "Imagery in Literature, Art, and Philosophy: the _Indian_ in White Imagination and Ideology."

0340. Berkman, Brenda. "The Vanishing Race: Conflicting Images of the American Indian in Children's Literature, 1880-1930." _North Dakota Quarterly_, 44 (Spring 1976) : 31-50.

>   Author examines two images frequent during period: Indian as savage and Indian as noble; focuses on treatment by five writers.

0341. Bernstein, Gene M. "Robert Altman's _Buffalo Bill and the Indians or Sitting Bull's History Lesson:_ A Self-Portrait in Celluloid." _Journal of Popular Culture_ 13 (Summer 1979): 17-25.

>   Film.

0342. Berthrong, Donald J. "Walter Stanley Campbell: Plainsman." _Arizona and the West_, 7 (February 1965) : 91-104.

>   Biographical and critical account of Campbell's writing life with particular attention to his treatment of Indians in his writing. Professor Berthrong was a member of the history faculty at the University of Oklahoma at the time this article was written.

0343. Bissell, Benjamin H. _American Indians in English Literature of the Eighteenth Century_. Yale Studies in English, No. 68. New Haven, CT: Yale University Press, 1925; reprint edition, Hamden,CT: Shoestring Press, Inc., 1968.

0344. Black, Nancy B. and Weidman, Bette S. _White on Red: Images of the Americn Indian_. Port Washington, NY: Kennikat Press, 1976.

>   The espoused purpose of this work is "to draw together literary treatment of the North American Indian, written by whites in the course of a three-hundred year period, roughly from the settlement of Virginia in 1607 to the Battle of Wounded Knee in 1890." Second section deals with selections of

drama, poetry and fiction from the nineteenth century.

0345. "Black Perceptions and Red Images: Indian and Black Literary Links." Phylon 44:1 (March 1983): 44-55.

0346. Blaine, Harold Arlo. "The Frontiersman in American Prose Fiction: 1800-1860." Ph. D. Diss. Cleveland, Ohio: Case Western Reserve University, 1936.

        138 p. "The Indian was the chief attribute of the American frontier." Regards Cooper and Simms as romantic, not realistic.

0347. Bleasby, George. "The Frontier in Cooper's 'The Leatherstocking Tales.'" Ph. D. Diss. Pittsburgh, PA: University of Pittsburgh, 1951.

0348. Blessing, Edith Stephen. "The North American Indian as Presented in Early Chronicles." MA Thesis. Albuquerque: University of New Mexico, 1941.

0349. Blicksilver, E. "Traditionalism vs. Modernity: Leslie Silko on American Indian Women." Southwest Review 64 (Spring 1979): 149-160.

0350. Boettler, Fred W. "Topics Commonly Ignored." Indian Historian, 3 (Summer 1970) : 22.

0351. Bongartz, Roy. "'Who Am I?' The Indian Sickness." The Nation, 210 (April 27, 1970) : 496-498.

0352. Bonney, India H. "Mary Austin's Interpretation of the American Indian." MA Thesis. Baton Rouge: Louisiana State University, 1936.

0353. "Book Ignites an Indian Uprising." Time, 115 (May 5, 1980) : 98.

        Discusses controversy over Sioux portrayal in Ruth B. Hill's novel, Hanta Yo.

0354. Boutelle, A. E. "Hemingway and Papa: Killing of the Father in the Nick Adams Fiction." Journal of Modern Literature 9:1 (1981-1982): 133-146.

0355. Bowman, Jack. "Western Movies, by an Indian Lover." Navajo Times (January 16, 1969) : n.p.n.

0356. Boyer, Mary G. "The Peoples--The Spaniards, the Indians, the Americans--and Nature in the Literature of Arizona." MA Thesis. Tucson: University of Arizona, 1930; Glendale: A. H. Clark, 1934.

        574 p.

0357. Brandon,   William. "American Indians and American
      History." American West, 2 (February 1965) : 14-25,
      91-93.

             A   critical   backward   look   at   how
      historians   have   portrayed   the   American
      Indian: "The traditional view of Indians in
      American   history   sees   them   as   natural
      features of the land, rather like mountains
      or   rivers   or   buffalo   or   troublesome,   if
      colorful, wild varmints, affecting American
      history only by occasionally impeding the
      civilizing progress of advancing settlers."

0358. Brauer,   Ralph   and   Brauer,   Donna. "Indians, Blacks,
      Mexicans, Old People, Long Hairs, and Other Assorted
      Deviants." The Horse, the Gun, and the Piece of
      Property: Changing Images of the TV Western. Bowling
      Green, Ohio: Bowling Green University Popular Press,
      1975.

0359. Brenzo,   Richard   Allen.   "American   Indians   vs.
      American   Writers."   Margins   14   (October/November
      1974):40-55, 88.

0360. Brenzo,   Richard Allen. "Civilization   against   the
      Savage: The   Destruction   of   Indians   in   American
      Novels,   1823-1854."   Ph. D.   Diss.   Milwaukee:
      University of Wisconsin, 1973.

             258 p.

0361. Brereton,   Lewis   Hyde. "American Indians of the
      Southeast   and   Southwest   in   the   Works   of   Charles
      Sealsfield, Karl May and Friedrick Armand Strubberg."
      MA Thesis. Austin: University of Texas, 1969.

0362. Brisco,   Robert L.   "The Stereotype of the Indian in
      the   New   Mexico Press." MA Thesis.   Albuquerque:
      University of New Mexico, 1954.

0363. Brown, Mark.   "Chief Joseph and the 'Lyin' Jack'
      Syndrome." Montana, 22 (October 1972) : 72-73.

0364. Brown, Mark.   "The Joseph Myth." Montana, 22 (January
      1972) : 2-17.

0365. Brown, Richard William. "Characteristics and Concepts
      of American Indians in Children's Fictional Literature
      Published   between   1963 and 1973." Ed. D. Diss.
      Philadelphia: Temple University, 1978.

0366. Bryant, Loy Young. "The Pocahontas Theme in American
      Literature." MA Thesis. Chapel Hill: University of
      North Carolina, 1935.

0367. Buntin, Arthur Roy. "The Indian in American Literature, 1680-1760." Ph. D. Diss. Seattle: University of Washington, 1961.

698 p. With the idea that, "the Indian's presence was more of a living issue in the lives of a greater precentage of the people in the years prior to 1760 than in any other period of American history," this work sets out to "describe the emotions and patterns of experience communicated in literature born of this great Indian Adventure." Additionally, its purpose "is to demonstrate what works were available at a given point in time and to suggest that captivity narratives, historical and travel narratives, sermons and essays, verse, and printed Indian treaties may have helped shape or confirm the thoughts of literate colonials about their Indian neighbors."

0368. Butler, M. D. "Narrative Structure and Historical Process in The Last of the Mohicans." American Literature 48 (May 1976): 117-139.

0369. Byers, John R., Jr. "The Indian Matter of Helen Hunt Jackson's Ramona: From Fact to Fiction." American Indian Quarterly 2:4 (Winter 1975-1976) : 331-346.

Compares Jackson's novel, Ramona, with her government report on the mistreatment of American Indians.

0370. Calder, Jenni. "Taming the Natives." There Must Be a Lone Ranger. London: Hamish Hamilton, 1974 : 38-57.

Examines films of the last 25 years. Author looks at literary sources from which many movie westerns came as well as at the films.

0371. Calhoun, Robert Francis. "Indian Characterization in Brown, Cooper and Simms." MA Thesis. Charlottesville: University of Virginia, 1959.

0372. Carey, Larry Lee. "A Study of the Indian Captivity Narrative as Popular Literary Genre." Ph. D. Diss. East Lansing: Michigan State University, 1978.

0373. Carlson, Ruth Kearney. "At the Edge of Two Worlds: The Indian Way and the Way of the White Man." Chapter 7 of Emerging Humanity: Multi-Ethnic Literature for Children and Adolescents. Dubuque: William C. Brown, 1972.

0374. Castro,   Michael.   Interpreting   the   Indian:
Twentieth-Century   Poets   &   the   Native   American.
Albuquerque: University of New Mexico Press, 1983.

0375. Cata, Juanita Opal. "The Portrait of American Indians
In Children's Fictional Literature." Ph. D. Diss.
Albuquerque: University of New Mexico, 1977.

0376. Cauthers, Janet Helen. "The North American Indian as
Portrayed   by   American   and   Canadian   Historians,
1830-1930."   Ph.   D.   Diss.   Seattle: University   of
Washington, 1974.

0377. Cawelti,   John.   "Cowboys,   Indians, Outlaws: The West
in Myth and Fantasy." American West, 1 (Spring 1964) :
28-35, 77-79.

              Explores   the idea that, "the Western, as
     we know it today in novels, movies, and
     television, is essentially the elaboration of
     the   image   of   the   West   created by the Wild
     West Show of Buffalo Bill and the dime novels
     of the later nineteenth century."

0378. Chappell, Charles Milton.   "The Defeat of the Indian
in Faulkner's Wilderness." MA Thesis. Atlanta, GA:
Emory University, 1965.

0379. Christensen,   J. A. "Honest Injun." Media & Methods, 8
(October 1971) : 38-43, 70-71.

              Critical   essay   on books about Indians;
     some fiction, poetry, collections of legends,
     tales.

0380. Churchill,   Ward.   "Literature and the Colonization of
the American Indian." Journal of Ethnic Studies 10:3
(Fall 1982): 37-56.

0381. Churchill, Ward; Hill, Norbert; and Hill, Mary Ann.
"Media   Stereotyping   and   Native   Response: An
Historical Overview."   Indian Historian 11 (December
1978): 45-56, 63.

0382. Clark,   Harold   Edward.   "Fenimore   Cooper's
Leatherstocking Tales: A Problem in Race." Ph. D.
Diss. Bloomington: Indiana University, 1955.

              "Discusses   Cooper's   presentation   of
     Indian-White relationships and his arguments
     against racial equality."

0383. Clark, La Verne Harrell. "The Indian Writings of Mari
Sandoz: A Lone One Left from the Old Times." American
Indian Quarterly 1:3 (Autumn 1974) : 183-192.

0384. Clausen, Dennis Monroe. "The Search for Identity in Cooper's _Leaterstocking Tales_: Nature as the Determinant of American Character." Ph. D. Diss. Riverside, CA: University of California at Riverside, 1971.

0385. Clayton, Thomas W. "The Indian Case Against the White Man in Pre-Civil War American Fiction." Ph. D. Diss. West Lafayette, Indiana: Purdue University, 1973.

0386. Coad, Oral S. "Jersey Gothic." _Proceedings of the New Jersey Historical Society_ (Now called _New Jersey History_) 84 (February 1966) : 89-112.

> Examines history of gothic story type in New Jersey and in so doing treats Indian legends.

0387. Collett, Beryl Bishop. "The Character of the California Indian as Portrayed in California Literature." MA Thesis. Stanford, CA: Stanford University, 1922.

> Stanford said they had archival copy only and that it was non-circulating.

0388. Collier, Peter. "Red Man's Burden." _Ramparts Magazine_, 8 (February 1970) : 26-38.

0389. Connolly, Sarah Ward. "Mary Austin's Philosophy of the Land." MA Thesis. Dallas: Southern Methodist University, 1951.

> "Influence of the Indian 'Earth Mother' on Mary Austin."

0390. Council on Interracial Books for Children. _Chronicles of American Indian Protest_. New York: Fawcett-Premier, 1971.

> 376 p. Reviewed by Jo Hudson in _Freedomways_, 12 (Winter 1972) : 76-77.

0391. Cox, Paul Ronald. "The Characterization of the American Indian in American Indian Plays 1800-1860 as a Reflection of the American Romantic Movement." Ph.D. Diss. New York: New York University, 1970.

0392. Cracroft, Richard Holton. "The American West of Washington Irving: The Quest for a National Tradition." Ph. D. Diss. Madison: University of Wisconsin, 1970.

0393. Crane, Fred Arthur. "The Noble Savage in America, 1815-1860: Concepts of the Indian with Special

Reference to the Writers of the Northwest." Ph. D. Diss. New Haven, CT: Yale, 1952.

0394. Craven, Wesley F. White, Red and Black: The Seventeenth Century Virginian. Charlottesville: University of Virginia Press, 1971.

114 p. Index. References. Reviewed by Gerald W. Mullin in Journal of American History, 59 (December 1972) : 678-679.

0395. Cronyn, George William. "The Frontier in American Literature Prior to the Civil War." MA Thesis. New York: Columbia University, 1917.

0396. "Crying Wind is Back, but Not as a Biography This Time." Christianity Today, 25 (January 23, 1981) : 44.

About controversy over book on Indian life published by Harvest House Publishers.

0397. Cunningham, Mary E., ed. James Fenimore Cooper: A Re-Appraisal New York History, 35. Cooperstown, NY: New York Historical Association, 1954.

Contains critical essays on Cooper, including: Arthur C. Parker's "Sources and Range of Cooper's Indian Lore," 447-456, and Paul A. W. Wallace's "Cooper's Indians," 423-446.

0398. Dabney, E. Jeanne. "Romantic and Realistic Conceptions of the Indian in American Literature." MA Thesis. Laramie: University of Wyoming, 1963.

80 p. Examines the writings of Philip Freneau, Washington Irving, James Fenimore Cooper, William Gilmore Simms, Mark Twain, Helen Hunt Jackson, and Hamlin Garland. Concludes: "The early idealization of the Indian in American romantic fiction was an outgrowth. . . of the exaltation of the primitive state of man. . . in contrast with the ills and assorted vices that civilization is prone to develop. . . (and that) running parallel to this ennobling concept. . . are devastating descriptions of the bloodthirsty, cruel savage. . . (which) can actually be considered a romantacizing of horror, and. . . is found in the same works that are criticized for being unnaturally romantic in the treatment of the Indian." Points out varying knowledge and experience of authors with Indians and cites these as factors in treatment.

0399. Dabney, Lewis M. The Indians of Yoknapatawpha: A Study in Literature and History. Baton Rouge: Louisiana State University, 1973.

136 p.

0400. Darnell, Donald. "Uncas as Hero: the 'Ubi Sunt' Formula in The Last of the Mohicans." American Literature 37:3 (1965) : 259-266.

0401. Daugherty, George Henry. "North American Indian Literature." Ph. D. Diss. Chicago: University of Chicago, 1925.

0402. David, J. The American Indian: The First Victim. New York: William Morrow, 1972.

192 p.

0403. Davidson, Levette J. "White Versions of Indian Myths and Legends." Western Folklore 7 (April 1948):115-128.

0404. Dempsey, Hugh A. "Fiction, Fact or Folklore?" Alberta Historical Review, 20 (1972) : 1-29.

0405. Diket, A. L. "The Noble Savage Convention as Epitomized in John Lawson's A New Voyage to Carolina." North Carolina Historical Review, 43 (April 1966) : 413-429.

"John Lawson's book. . . published in 1709, was remarkable for its careful and observant description of the Carolina frontier. It was also a milestone among an extensive number of descriptive and historical works concerning the southern portion of the British Empire in North America which assisted in an outstanding manner the development in literature of an ideal that engraved its image deep in Western thinking, the concept of the Noble Savage."

0406. DiPisa, Diane. "A Sioux Poem of Power." Paper presented at the Conference on Multi-Ethnic Literature, Chicago State University, May 10, 1974; Bethesda, MD: EDRS, ED 095 528, May 10, 1974.

"An assessment of Black Elk's poetry reveals that Indian attitudes toward words differ from ours. . . . "

0407. Dippie, Brian W. "Bards of the Little Big Horn." Western American Literature, 1 (March 1966) : 175-195.

Examines some "poetic celebrations of Custer, his Last Stand, and the legends that

surround both." Among the poets are John G.
Neihardt, Henry Wadsworth Longfellow,
Frederick Whittaker, John Greenleaf
Whittier, Francis Brooks. (See also Austin
and Alta Fife, "Ballads of the Little Big
Horn.")

0408. Dippie, Brian W. "'His Visage Wild; His Form
Exotick': Indian Themes and Cultural Guilt in John
Barth's The Sot-Weed Factor." American Quarterly 21
(Spring 1969) : 113-121.

0409. Dippie, Brian W. "Jack Crabb and the Sole Survivors
of Custer's Last Stand." Western American Literature
4:3 (1969) : 189-202.

0410. Dlugokinski, Eric. "Review of an Old Stereotype: The
Silent Indian." Journal of American Indian Education,
11 (May 1972) : 23-25.

0411. Doerr, Donald J., Sr. "On Literature." The Indian
Historian, 5 (Spring 1972) : 55.

Encourages the study of Native American
Literature by graduate students and as a part
of college curricula.

0412. Dondore, Dorothy Anne. "The Prairie and the Making of
Middle America; Four Centuries of Description." Ph.D.
Diss. New York: Columbia University, 1926; Torch
Press, 1926.

472 p. Literary descriptions; much on
Indians.

0413. Dorain, Edith McEwen. "Indian Warfare in Early New
England Literature." MA Thesis. New York: Columbia
University, 1927.

85 p.

0414. Dring, Lovilla Ruth. "Literary Backgrounds of the
Santa Fe Trail." MA Thesis. Albuquerque: University of
New Mexico, 1934.

0415. Duckett, Margaret. "Bret Harte and the Indians of
Nothern California." Huntington Library Quarterly 18:1
(1954) : 59-83.

0416. Duke, Mary Fender. "The Indian in American Literature
since 1920." MA Thesis. Dallas: Southern Methodist
University, 1942.

Discusses John Seger as source of
information for Stanley Vestal (Walter
Stanley Campbell), Hamlin Garland; discusses

Edwin Corle, Owen Wister, Oliver La Farge, Kenneth Roberts, Walter Edmunds.

0417. Dundes, Alan. "The Study of Folklore in Literature and Culture: Identification and Interpretation." Journal of American Folklore, 78 (1965) : 136-142.

0418. Easy, Peter. "The Treatment of American Indian Materials in Contemporary American Poetry." Journal of American Studies. 12 (April 1978): 81-98.

0419. Edwards, Karl Ormond. "A Theoretical and Methodological Exploration of Portrayals of Native Americans in Children's Fiction." Master's Thesis. Missoula: University of Montana, 1983.

0420. Elliott, Karen Sue. "The Portrayal of the American Indian Woman in a Select Group of American Novels." Ph. D. dissertation, University of Minnesota, 1978.

0421. Engel, Grace Margaret. "Pocahontas in American Literature." MA Thesis. New York: Columbia University, 1937.

0422. Evans, James Leroy. "The Indian Savage, the Mexican Bandit and the Chinese Heathen--Three Popular Stereotypes." Ph.D. Diss. Austin: University of Texas, 1967.

0423. Ewers, John C. "The American Indian in Current Books." Natural History, 70 (November 1961) : 4, 6-9.

        Reviews a number of non-fiction books on Indians.

0424. Fairchild, Hoxie Neale. The Noble Savage, A Study in Romantic Naturalism. New York: Columbia University Press, 1928.

        Author examines how French and British writers of romantic naturalism from 1730-1830 used the idea--or regarded the idea--of the noble savage.

0425. Falkenhagen, Maria. "Treatment of Native Americans in Recent Children's Literature." Integrated Education, 11 (July-October 1973) : 58-59.

        Summarizes a study which concentrated on determining the generalizations and concepts concerning Native Americans in trade books available to high school equivalency program students at the College of Education at Washington State University.

0426. Falkenhagen, Maria and Kelly, Inga K. "The Native American in Juvenile Fiction: Teacher Perception of Stereotypes." Journal of American Indian Education, 13 (January 1974) : 9-13.

What do teachers judge to be stereotypical of Native Americans in trade books for children? How do teachers' perceptions of stereotypes compare with findings of current research on the topic? What guidelines are today's teachers prepared to apply to the selection of fictionalized juvenile literature about Native Americans? To what extent is there a need for explicit criteria for book selection in this area?

0427. Farmer, Freda M. "The Changing Attitudes of American Authors toward the Indians." MA Thesis. Muncie, Indiana: Ball State University, 1953.

0428. Ferrin, George W. and Everson, William K. The Western: From Silents to Cinerama. New York: Orian Press, 1962

Contains a section on the treatment of the Indian in films.

0429. Ferris, Edward G. Just Another Redskin. Philadelphia: Dorrance, 1973.

0430. Fiedler, Leslie A. The Return of the Vanishing American. New York: Stein and Day, 1968.

Fiedler defines the West by the presence in it of the Indian, whether literally or abstracted into some non-Indian "other," and the western novel as focusing on the conflict between "Indian" (in whatever sense) and "white-European" (however represented). The "ultimate West," he suggests, may be psychic, where psychotics meet sanes.

0431. Field, Nadine Eaton. "Portraiture of the American Indian in the Novels of Cooper, Bird and Simms." MA Thesis. Stillwater: Oklahoma State University, 1957.

0432. Fife, Austin and Fife, Alta. "Ballads of the Little Big Horn." American West, 4 (February 1967) : 46-49, 86-89.

Songs about the Custer battle. (See also Brian Dippie, "Bards of the Little Big Horn.")

0433. Fisher, Laura. "All Chiefs, No Indians: What Children's Books Say about American Indians." Elementary English, 51 (February 1974) : 185-189.

Summarizes how Indians are stereotyped
and false impressions and misconceptions are
created. Discusses a few books that treat
Indians positively. Includes bibliography of
children's books about Indians.

0434. Folsom, James K. The American Western Novel. New
Haven: College and University Press, 1966.

Contains bibliography and index. Deals
with the treatment of the Indian as
character.

0435. Fox, Velda Mae. "The Development of the Pocahontas
Story in American Literature, 1607-1927." MA Thesis.
Iowa City: University of Iowa, 1927.

0436. Frederick, J. T. "Cooper's Eloquent Indians."
Publications of the Modern Language Association 71
(December 1956) : 1004-1017.

0437. French, P. "The Indian in the Western Movie." Art in
America, 60 (July 1972) : 32-39.

Discusses roles of Indian in movies
since 1950. This issue of magazine devoted
to the Indian.

0438. French Philip. "Indians and Blacks." in Westerns:
Aspects of a Movie Genre. London: Secker and Warberg,
Ltd., 1973 : 76-99.

Describes treatment of Indians in
western movies during 1950's and 1960's.

0439. Friar, Ralph E. The Only Good Indian: The Hollywood
Gospel. New York: Drama Book Specialists, Publisher,
1973.

Explores the role of the Indian in the
movies. Evaluates many films, but authors
also investigate misrepresentation of Indians
in other media.

0440. Fulton, Joan Lee. "A Study of the Upper Plains
Indians in an Adolescent Historical Fiction." MA
Thesis. Iowa City: University of Iowa, 1967.

Shows how the adolescent novel written
by the author, Walk the Red Road, gives an
accurate representation of the Indian of the
Upper Plains during the last years of the
Upper Plains culture. The author says, "The
handling of the Indian character and his
culture, not the literary quality of Walk the
Red Road, is the concern here."

0441. Gage, Duane. "William Faulkner's Indians." <u>American Indian Quarterly</u> 1:1 (Spring 1974) : 27-33.

0442. Garwin, Elaine Judith. "An Analysis of the Treatment of the American Indian in Juvenile Fiction." MA Thesis. Chicago: University of Chicago, 1961.

0443. Gast, David K. "The Dawning of the Age of Aquarius for Multi-Ethnic Children's Literature." <u>Elementary English</u>, 47 (May 1970) : 661-665.

        Discusses treatment of minorities in literature, including Indians. Classifies some approaches to treatment.

0444. Gast, David K. "Minority Americans in Children's Literature." <u>Elementary English</u>, 44 (January 1967) : 12-23.

        Describes an analysis of characterizations of minority group Americans as presented in contemporary children's literatuare. Problem, population and method are described; findings, conclusions and recommendations given.

0445. Gaston, Edwin Willmer. "The Early Novel of the Southwest: A Critical Study." Ph. D. Diss. Lubbock: Texas Tech University, 1959.

0446. Gentry, Dorothy Delores. "The Treatment of the American Indian in the American Novel, 1929-1953." MA Thesis. Washington, D.C.: Howard University, 1954.

        According to Elwood Jones in his dissertation (Ph. D. NYU, 1958), this thesis discusses novels in which Indians are heroes.

0447. Georgakas, Dan. "They Have Not Spoken: American Indians in Film." <u>Film Quarterly</u>, 25 (Spring 1972) : 26-32.

        Criticism of films for not portraying Indian culture and for not portraying it accurately. Discusses <u>A Man Called Horse</u>, <u>Soldier Blue</u>, <u>Little Big Man</u>, and <u>Tell Them Willie Boy is Here</u>.

0448. Gill, Eloise Wise. "The Changing Attitude toward the Indian in American Literataure." MA Thesis. Baton Rouge: Louisiana State University, 1935.

0449. Gillard, Kathleen Isabel. "Michigan as Recorded in Its Writings." Ph. D. Diss. Nashville: George Peabody College for Teachers, 1950; published as <u>Our Michigan Heritage</u>. New York: Pageant Press, 1955.

The Indian in Michigan history and
literature.

0450. Gimlin, Joan Sherako. "Henry Thoreau and the American
Indian." Ph. D. Diss. Washington, D.C.: George
Washington University, 1974.

0451. Gingerich, W. "Old Voices of Acoma: Simon Ortiz's
Mythic Indiginism." Southwest Review 64 (Winter 1979):
18-20.

0452. Gossett, Thomas Frank. "The Idea of Anglo-Saxon
Superiority in American Thought, 1865-1915." Ph. D.
Diss. Minneapolis: University of Minnesota, 1953.

        Considers ethnology and Anglo-Saxon
    concepts of relations between whites and
    Indians.

0453. Graham, William Alexander. The Custer Myth. New
York: Bonanza Books, n. d.

0454. Greenway, John. "Will the Indians Get Whitey?"
National Review, 21 (March 11, 1969) : 223-228.

        Critical of guilt-ridden intellectuals
    apologizing to the Indians: "history as
    practiced by these writers is. . . a pastime,
    like leaning against a wall and spitting.
    They write about the Indian because the Indian
    in the Amercan mind is as imaginary as
    Sandburg's Lincoln, a creation of fantasy,
    guilt and ignorance, on which everyone is
    his own authority." He takes to task ten
    "popular, non-scholarly" books on the Indian.
    Titles include The Long Death: The Last Days
    of the Plains Indians by Ralph K. Andrist,
    The Nez Perce Indians and the Opening of the
    Northwest by Alvin M. Josephy, Jr.,
    Disinherited: The Lost Birthright of the
    American Indian by Dale Van Every, and The
    Indian and the White Man by Wilcomb Washburn.

0455. Grose, Burl Donald. "'Here Come the Indians': An
Historical Study of the Representations of the Native
American upon the North American Stage, 1808-1969."
Ph. D. dissertation, University of Missouri-Columbia,
1979.

0456. "Growing War over Hanta Yo Pits Chief Lame Deer and
Wojo vs. Ruth Beebe Hill and David Wolper, D. Sheff
and J. Fincher." People, 13 (June 23, 1980) : 82+.

0457. Guptara, P. "Clutching a Feather in a Maelstrom:
Rudy Wiebe's Critique of the Contemporary West."

Journal of Commonwealth Literature 17:1 (1982): 146-152.

0458. Haberly, D. T. "Women and Indians: The Last of the Mohicans and the Captivity Tradition." American Quarterly 28 (Fall 1976): 431-443.

0459. Haines, Francis D. "Don't Stereotype Our Indians." Oregon Educational Journal, 27 (February 1953) : 11, 30.

0460. Hamilton, Wynette. "The Correlation between Societal Attitudes and Those of American Authors in the Depiction of American Indians, 1607-1860." American Indian Quarterly, 1 (Spring 1974) : 1-26.

0461. Hamm, V. M. "Greeks and Indians: A Study in Mythic Syncretism." Thought 50 (December 1975): 351-366.

0462. Hanson, Elizabeth Irene. "The Indian Metaphor in the American Renaissance." Ph. D. dissertation, University of Pennsylvania, 1977.

0463. "Hanta Yo: A Gross Insult is Offered to Indian People." Wassaja/The Indian Historian 13 (November 1980): 15-23.

0464. Hardman, Marion Payzant. "Terror in American Prose Fiction to 1835." Ph. D. Diss. Minneapolis: University of Minnesota, 1939.

        Considers the Indian as an element of terror in novels.

0465. Harrington, John. "Understanding Hollywood's Indian Rhetoric." Canadian Review of American Studies, 8 (Spring 1977) : 77-88.

        Critical essay on Hollywood's treatment of Indians.

0466. Harris, H. L. "Mark Twain's Response to the Native American." American Literature 46 (January 1975) : 495-505.

        Twain portrayed as "hostile" toward American Indian, insistent on Indian's inferiority as a young writer, somewhat sympathetic in later life but unexpressive of sympathy in his writings.

0467. Harris, John West. "The Glorification of American Types in American Literature from 1775 to 1825." Ph. D. Diss. Chapel Hill: University of North Carolina, 1928.

Indians throughout, especially as examples in certain historical novels.

0468. Harris, J. "Moulting of the Plumed Serpent: A Study of the Relationship Between the Novel and Three Contemporary Tales." Modern Language Quarterly 39 (June 1978): 154-168.

0469. Hartman, Hedy. "A Brief Review of the Native American in American Cinema." Indian Historian, 9 (Summer 1973) : 27-29.

Author discusses stereotypes and inaccuracies of Indians in movies; lists 11 complaints of AIM.

0470. Haslam, Gerald W. Forgotten Pages of American Literature. Boston: Houghton Mifflin Co., 1970.

398 p. About 77 pages on the American Indian.

0471. Hazard, Lucy Lockwood. "The Frontier in American Literature." Ph. D. Diss. Berkeley: University of California, 1925; New York: T. Y. Crowell, 1927.

A chronological discussion of the literary treatment of America's succeeding frontiers. Hazard examines three successive types of pioneer: the regional pioneer, whose conflict was with nature; the industrial pioneer, whose conflict was primarily with the labor of other men; and the spiritual pioneer, whose conflict was/is with himself. She analyzes a number of writings typical of each category in treatment of the frontier.

0472. Herbert, Jeanne Clark. "The Growth of Racism in the Treatment of the Southwestern Indian in Fiction since 1900." MA Thesis. Tucson: University of Arizona, 1961.

0473. Herbst, Laura. "That's One Good Indian: Unacceptable Images in Children's Novels." Top of the News (January 1975) : 192-198.

Discusses three objecticnable treatments of Indians and Indian culture in books.

0474. Hirschfelder, Arlene B. American Indian Stereotypes in the World of Children: A Reader and Bibliography. Metuchen, New Jersey: Scarecrow Press, Inc., 1982.

0475. Hoagland, Robert John. "A Comparison of the Indians of James Fenimore Cooper and Those Seen by Indian

Agents, Travelers, and Scientists." MA Thesis. New York: Columbia University, 1930.

0476. Hoilman, Grace Dona Gubler. "Voices and Images of the American Indian in Literature for Young People." Ph. D. Diss. Muncie, Indiana: Ball State University, 1981.

> Examines treatment of Indian in literature for young people over a span of time. Concludes that stereotypes are still being perpetuated, but that careful selection can result in excellent realistic and humane examples. Discusses usefulness of Indian folktales and poetry in classroom. 464 p.

0477. Hopcraft, Margaret Lindsay. "Attitudes toward the Indian as Found in American Literature, 1700-1800." MA Thesis. Albuquerque: University of New Mexico, 1943.

> Examines journals, narratives of captivity and diaries, histories, essays and letters, poetry, drama, and novels. Novelists include Charles Brockden Brown, Hugh Henry Breckenridge, Charlotte Ramsay Lennox, and Susannah Rawson. Conclusions about each type of literature are summarized at the end.

0478. Howell, Elmo. "The Chickasaw Queen: In Willia Faulkner's Story," Chronicles of Oklahoma 49:3 (Autumn 1971) : 334-339.

0479. Howell, Elmo. "President Jackson and William Faulkner's Choctaws." Chronicles of Oklahoma 45:3 (1967) : 252-258.

0480. Howell, Elmo. "William Faulkner and the Chickasaw Funeral." American Literature 36 (January 1965) : 523-525.

> Critical of Faulkner's Indians--accuses him of indifference to historical accuracy, but says his Indian stories are artistically valid.

0481. Howell, Elmo. "William Faulkner and the Mississippi Indians." Georgia Review 21:3 (1967) : 386-396.

0482. Howell, Elmo. "William Gilmore Simms and the American Indian." South Carolina Review 5:2 (1973) : 57-64.

0483. Howells, C. A. "History from a Different Angle: Narrative Strategies in The Temptation of Big Bear." Journal of Commonwealth Literature 17:1 (1982): 161-171.

0484. Huddleston, E. L. "Indians and Literature of the Federalist Era: The Case of James Elliot." New England Quarterly 44 (June 1971) : 221-237.

0485. Huff, Martha Rebecca. "The Indian Element in Twentieth Century Spanish-American Novels." MA Thesis. Austin: University of Texas, 1940.

0486. Hunter, C. "Historical Context in John Joseph Mathews' Sundown." MELUS 9 (Spring 1982): 61-72.

0487. Hunter, C. "Protagonist as a Mixed-Blood in John Joseph Mathews' Sundown." American Indian Quarterly 6 (Fall-Winter 1982): 319-337.

0488. Hutchinson, W. H. "The Remaking of the Amerind: a Dissenting Voice Raised against the Myth of the Noble Savage." Westways, 64 (October 1972) : 18-21, 94.

> Assails the ideas that there is such a person as a "Native American," that there ever was a uniform Indian society in America, that the Indian had a perfect democracy, or that the Indian lived in especially healthy harmony with nature, among others.

0489. "The Indian in Adolescent Novels." Indian Historian, 8 (Winter 1975) : 32-35.

> Nine novels from 1930 compared with 13 from 1960 to see what stereotypes, if any, existed in 1930 and if they persist in 1960.

0490. "An Indian Epic." Newsweek 93 (April 16, 1979): 86, 90.

> About novel, Hanta Yo.

0491. "Indians Protest TV Misrepresentation." Christian Century, 77 (February 10, 1960) : 157.

0492. Jacobs, Wilbur. Dispossessing the American Indian. New York: Charles Scribner's Sons, 1972.

> Attempts to correct "false historical impressions" about Indian-white relations. Focuses on the confrontations between eastern woodland Indians and Anglo-American pioneers of the 18th century. Essentially an historical study rather than a literary one.

0493. Jamison, Blanche Noma Miller. "The Western American Indian: Cross-Cultural Literary Attitudes, 1830-1975." Ed. D. dissertation, East Texas State University, 1978.

0494. Jenkins, William Warren. "Three Centuries in the
Development of the Pocahontas Story in American
Literature: 1608-1908."   Ph.   D.   dissertation,
University of Tennessee, 1977.

0495. Job, Marcus. "A Comparative Study of Culture Hero
Motifs in the Bible and in the Folklore of the Plains
Indians." MA Thesis. Aberdeen, South Dakota: Northern
State College, July 1970.

0496. Johannsen, Albert. The House of Beadle and Adams and
Its Dime and Nickle Novels: The Story of a Vanished
Literature. 2 vols. Norman: University of Oklahoma
Press, 1950.

    Part 3 lists various series of novels
published by House of Beadle and Adams with
brief synopses of most from 1860's to 1900's.

0497. Jones, George Elwood, Jr. "The American Indian in the
American Novel (1875-1950)." Ph. D. Diss. New York:
New York University, 1958.

0498. Jones, Henry Broadus. "The Death Song of the Noble
Savage: A Study in the Idealization of the American
Indian." Ph. D. Chicago: University of Chicago, 1924.

0499. Jones, Lucy Thweatt. "A Comparative Study of the
American Indian in Prose Fiction, from Edgar Huntley
to Ramona." MS Thesis. Charlottesville: University of
Virginia, 1925.

0500. Josephy, Alvin M., Jr. "Indians in History: The White
Man's Books Speak with Forked Tongue." The Atlantic,
225 (June 1970) : 67-72.

    Decries the inaccurate portrayal of
Indians in history and literature and the
omission of Indians from American history.
Discusses a number of works that are
inadequate and a number that both attempt to
be complete and are realistic. Concludes the
situation seems to be improving, as schools,
Indian groups, television, work to correct
deficiencies, and to keep the record straight
from here on, but that "there is plenty of
work to do, by Indians and non-Indians
laboring together, to set straight the
chapters already written."

0501. Kaufmann, Donald L. "The Indian as Media
Hand-Me-Down." Colorado Quarterly, 23 (1975) :
489-504.

    Author traces image of Native American
from early American writers to television.

This has been reprinted in <u>The Pretend Indians: Images of Native Americans in the Movies</u>, edited by Gretchen M. Bataille and Charles Silet (Ames, Iowa: Iowa State University Press, 1980).

0502. Keim, Charles J. <u>From String Stories to Satellites: Portrayal of the Alaska Native in Literature and Folklore</u>. n.p.: n.p., 1972.

Washington Library Network shows a reference number for this of 74-010584, which could be a Library of Congress number.

0503. Keiser, Albert. <u>The Indian in American Literature</u>. New York: Oxford University Press, 1933; New York: Octagon, 1970.

This seems to be the first really comprehensive look at the treatment of the American Indian in fiction. It analyzes fiction from 1600's to early 20th century. Chapters devoted to the Pocahontas legend, Puritan attitudes and Indian captivities, Philip Freneau's treatment of the Indian, Charles Brockden Brown's Indians, Lydia Maria Frances (Child) and the idea of Indian-white marriage, James Kirk Paulding and the humorous treatment of Indians, Washington Irving's optimistic point of view of Indians, Indian drama, James Fenimore Cooper and his critics, realism and Dr. Robert Montgomery Bird's <u>Nick of the Woods</u>, William Gilmore Simms' romantic naturalism, poets John Greenleaf Whittier and William Cullen Bryant, poet Alfred B. Street's view of the Iroquois as "Romans," Henry Longfellow's <u>Hiawatha</u> and Heckewelder's influence on Longfellow, Henry Thoreau's notebooks on Indians (There are 11 of them; sources include Heckewelder and Schoolcraft.), Joaquin Miller's romantic ideas, Helen Hunt Jackson's <u>Ramona</u>, Adolph Bandelier's <u>The Delight Makers</u>, John G. Neihardt (whose theories Keiser criticizes), Hamlin Garland, and comments on the influence of Rosseau, Chateaubriand and others.

0504. Keiser, Albert. "Thoreau's Manuscripts on the Indians." <u>Journal of English and Germanic Philology</u>, 27 (n.d.) : 183-199.

According to Keiser, "Thoreau had intended to write an elaborate work on the American Indians, and for more than ten years he busied himself collecting the material from all available sources. There are in the

Pierpont Morgan Library in New York city
eleven autograph manuscript notebooks of his,
containing about 2800 pages and approximately
540,000 words, mainly extracts relating to
the aborigines of America." Keiser describes
the contents of the manuscripts and comments
on them.

0505. Kelley, James Richard. "The Bloody Loam." Ph. D.
dissertation, State University of New York at Stony
Brook, 1976.

About treatment of Indians in writings
by Francis Parkman and Henry David Thoreau.

0506. Kelly, William Patrick III. "The Leatherstocking
Tales: Fiction and the American Historical
Experience." Ph. D. dissertation, Indiana University,
1977.

0507. Kendall, Martha. "Forget the Masked Man: Who Was
His Indian Companion?" Smithsonian 8 (September 1977):
113-120.

0508. Kennedy, Mrs. Ella Bryce (Morris). "The Indian in
Southwestern Fiction." MA Thesis. Albuquerque:
University of New Mexico, 1938; published University of
New Mexico Research I, No. 3 (1937) : 212-225.

0509. Koppell, Kathleen Sunshine. "Early American Fictioı
and the Call of the Wild: Nature and the Indian in
Novels before Cooper." Ph. D. Cambridge, MA: Harvard,
1968.

0510. Krefft, James Harvey. "Possible Source for Faulkner's
Indians: Oliver LaFarge's Laughing Boy." Tulane
Studies in English 23 (1978): 187-192.

0511. Krefft, James Harvey. "The Yoknapatawpha Indians:
Fact and Fiction." Ph. D. dissertation, Tulane
University, 1976.

0512. Kummings, Donald D. "'Nature's Children': The Image
of the Indian in Philip Freneau." Journal of American
Studies (Hyderabad-500007, India) 11:1 (January 1981):
25-38.

0513. Lacey, R. "Alternatives to Cinema Rouge." Media &
Methods, 7 (April 1971) : 45+.

0514. Lane, Lauriat, Jr. "Thoreau's Autumnal Indian."
Canadian Review of American Studies 6 (Fall 1975):
228-236.

0515. Lavender, David. "The Petrified West and the Writer."
American Scholar, 37 (Spring 1968) : 293-306.

Sees the west as "America's mythic
land," fertile, and rich with resources for
the imagination--if the stereotype of it can
be gotten around, the formula outdistanced.

0516. Lawson, Lewis A. "Old Fish Hawk: From Stereotype to
Archetype." American Indian Quarterly 3 (Winter
1977-1978): 321-333.

0517. Lawson, Marian. "Cooper's Indians Re-examined." MA
Thesis. Iowa City: University of Iowa, 1939.

0518. Leary, Lewis Gaston. Articles on American Literature,
1900-1950. Durham, North Carolina: Duke University
Press, 1954.

437 p. Section on Indians: pages
367-368

0519. Leary, Lewis Gaston. Articles on American Literature,
1950-1967. Durham, North Carolina: Duke University
Press, 1970.

0520. Leechman, Douglas. "The Indian in Literature." Queens
Quarterly, 50 (May 1943) : 155-163.

Types a number of literary Indians.
Author explores 8 stages in the growth of the
modern popular conception of North American
Indians.

0521. Leechman, Douglas. "The Popular Concept of the Red
Indian as Revealed in Literature." MA Thesis. Ottawa,
Ontario: University of Ottawa, 1940.

0522. Leechman, Douglas. "The Red Indian of Literature: A
Study in the Perpetuation of Error." Ph. D. Diss.
Ottawa, Ontario: University of Ottawa, 1941.

0523. Leeds, Josephene Frederica. "Longfellow's Use of
Indian Lore." MA Thesis. New York: Columbia
University, 1929.

0524. Lemons, William Everett. "John G. Neihardt's
Conception of the Plains Indian." MA Thesis. Boulder:
University of Colorado, 1950.

0525. Levernier, James A. "The Captivity Narrative as
Children's Literature." Markham Review 8 (Spring
1979):54-59.

0526. Levernier, James Arthur. "Indian Captivity
Narratives: Their Function and Form." Ph. D. Diss.
Philadelphia: University of Pennsylvania, 1975.

Analyzes the literary history of Indian

captivity narratives in the light of the
relationship between their cultural uses and
their forms and explores some of the
theoretical questions the narratives pose,
such as "the general relationship in America
between literary forms and cultural needs,
and the effect of popular literature on the
development of more sophisticated forms of
American expression."

0527. Levernier, James A., and Cohen, Hennig, eds. The
Indians and Their Captives. Contributions in American
Studies, No. 31. Westport, CT: Greenwood Press, 1977.

0528. Littlefield, Daniel F., Jr. "Washington Irving and
the American Indian." American Indian Quarterly 5:2
(May 1979) : 135-154.

0529. Littlefield, Daniel F., Jr. and Parins, J. W. "Short
Fiction Writers of the Indian Territory." American
Studies 23 (Spring 1982): 23-38.

0530. Littlefield, Daniel F., Jr. and Underhill, Lonnie.
"Renaming the American Indian: 1890-1913." American
Studies 12 (Fall 1971):33-45.

0531. Livingston, Richard O., Jr. "Carol Burnett Show
Degrades the American Indian." (letter) Indian
Historian, 6 (Spring 1973) : 23.

0532. Lockwood, Mary Margaret. "Pioneer Life as It Is
Reflected in American Literature." MA Thesis. Tucson:
University of Arizona, 1931.

        Some on Iroquois, Delaware, Mandan and
    Dakota.

0533. Lorch, Fred W. "Mark Twain's Early Views on Western
Indians." Twainian 4 (April 1945) : 1-3.

0534. Ludovici, Paola. "The Struggle for an Ending: Ritual
and Plot in Recent American Indian Literature." Ph. D.
Diss. Washington, D. C.: The American University,
1979.

0535. Lyttle, Thomas James. "An Examination of Poetic
Justice in Three Selected Types of Nineteenth Century
Melodrama: The Indian Play, the Temperance Play, and
the Civil War Play." Ph. D. Diss. Bowling Green,
Ohio: Bowling Green State University, 1974.

0536. McCaffery, L. "Absurdity and Oppositions in William
Eastlake's Southwestern Novels." Critique 19:2 (1977):
62-76.

0537. McCullough, Joseph B., and Dodge, Robert K. "The Puritan Myth and the Indian in the Early American Novel." _Pembroke Magazine_ No. 7 (1976): 237-244.

0538. McHargue, Georgess. "Countering Old Myths." _American Library_, 6 (March 1975) : 166-167.

> Critical review of several children's books, fiction and nonfiction, which counter stereotypes.

0539. McKenna, Frances. "Mary Hunter Austin, Interpreter of the American Indian." MA Thesis. Lawrence: University of Kansas, 1942.

0540. McLaurin, Nancy Della. "A Study of the Southern Frontier in Prose Fiction Prior to 1868." Ph. D. Diss. Columbia, South Carolina: University of South Carolina, 1958.

> The first part refers to efforts to conquer hostile Indians.

0541. McNickle, D'Arcy. "American Indians Who Never Were." _Indian Historian_, 3 (Summer 1970) : 4-7.

0542. McNutt, James C. "Mark Twain and the American Indian: Earthly Realism and Heavenly Idealism." _American Indian Quarterly_ 4 (August 1978): 223-242.

0543. McWilliams, Wilson Carey. "Natty Bumpo and the Godfather." _Colorado Quarterly_ 24 (Autumn 1975): 133-144.

0544. Mansfield-Kelley, Deane. "Oliver LaFarge and the Indian Woman in American Literature." Ph. D. Diss. Austin: University of Texas, 1979.

0545. Mardock, Robert W. "Irresolvable Enigma." _Montana_, 7 (1957) : 36-57.

0546. Marovitz, Sanford Earl. "Frontier Conflicts: Villians, Outlaws, and Indians in Selected 'Western' Fiction: 1799-1860." Ph. D. Diss. Durham, North Carolina: Duke University, 1968.

0547. Martin, T. "Surviving on the Frontier: The Doubled Consciousness of Natty Bumppo." _South Atlantic Quarterly_ 75 (Autumn 1976): 447-459.

0548. Marvin, Ann. "The Cowboy as Scientific Apache." _New York Folklore_ 1:1/2 (1975): 109-112.

0549. Meade, James Gordon. "The Westerns of the East: Narratives of Indian Captivity from Jeremiad to Gothic

Novel." Ph. D. Diss. Evanston, Illinois: Northwestern
University, 1971.

0550. Medicine, Bea. "Hanta-Yo: A New Phenomenon." Indian
Historian 12 (Summer 1979): 2-5.

0551. Meinhardt, Warren Lee. "The Mexican Indianist Novel."
Ph. D. Diss. Berkeley: University of California,
1965.

0552. Meyer, Roy W. "Hamlin Garland and the American
Indian." Western American Literature 2:2 (1967) :
109-125.

0553. Milder, R. "Last of the Mohicans and the New World
Fall." American Literature 52 (November 1980):
407-429.

0554. Miller, Mary Rita. "Attestations of American Indian
Pidgin English in Fiction and Nonfiction." American
Speech, 42 (1967) : 142-147.

        Explores some of the possible reasons
    why Indians speak pidgin English when they
    speak in works written by English-speaking
    writers.

0555. Moen, Ole O. "The Voice of Siouxland: Man and
Nature in Frederick Manfred's Writing." Ph. D.
dissertation, University of Minnesota, 1978.

0556. Monical, David G. "Changes in American Attitudes
toward the Indians as Evidenced by Captive
Literature." Plains Anthropologist, 14 (1969) :
130-136.

        An abstract of the article at the
    beginning of it says, "this study presents an
    analysis of the changes in the attitude of
    the American settler toward the Indian over a
    period of 120 years. Based on a comparison
    of the narratives of the white captives of
    the Indians three signficant periods are
    delineated: the colonial; transition; and,
    expansion."

0557. Monjo, F. N. "Monjo's Manifest Destiny: Authors Can
Claim Any Territory in Literature." School Library
Journal, 20 (May 1974) : 36-37.

        Monjo responds to criticism by Mary G.
    Byler (Library Journal February 15, 1974, p.
    546.) that his book, Indian Summer, presents
    a stereotyped and derogatory picture of the
    American Indian. See note under Byler in
    bibliographies section.

0558. Monkman, Leslie. <u>A Native Heritage: Images of the Indian in English-Canadian Literature</u>. Toronto: University of Toronto Press, 1981.

       See note below.

0559. Monkman, Leslie. "White on Red: Perspectives on the Indian in English-Canadian Literature." Ph. D. Diss. Canada: York University, 1975.

       Chronological examination of the treatment of the Indian in English-Canadian literature. Concludes: "We learn relatively little about the red man and his culture in the literature written by whites. Instead, the Indian and his culture serve in each historical period as vehicles for the definition of the white man's understanding of his physical environment and for his establishment of a sense of national, social or personal identity."

0560. Monroe, Barbara Ann. "An Investigation of Fictional Books for Children Which Deal with the American Indian in the United States." MA Thesis. Ithaca, New York: Cornell University, 1956.

0561. Montgomery, E. D. "A Study of the Indian in American Fiction (1820-1850)." MA Thesis. Iowa City, IA: University of Iowa, 1927.

0562. Moore, Jack Bailey. "Making Indians Early: The Worth of Azakia." <u>Studies in Short Fiction</u>, 13 (Winter 1976): 51-60.

       Briefly traces the making of white myths about Indians in an analysis of the short story, "Azakia."

0563. Moore, Jack Bailey. "Native Elements in American Magazine Short Fiction, 1741-1800." Ph. D. Diss. Chapel Hill, North Carolina: University of North Carolina, 1963.

0564. Moore, L. Hugh. "Francis Parkman on the Oregon Trail: A Study in Cultural Prejudice." <u>Western American Literature</u> 12 (Fall 1977): 185-197.

0565. Morgan, Paul. "The Treatment of the Indian in Southwestern Literature since 1915: A Study in Primitivism." Ph. D. Austin: University of Texas, 1954.

       According to the author, "the purpose of this study. . . is to determine the various reasons for which Indian primitivism was revived, during the war and postwar years, as a subject of popular interest among the writers on New Mexico and Arizona since 1915." Examines many types of literature.

0566. Morris, C. "Indians and Other Aliens: A Native American View of Science Fiction." Extrapolation 20 (Winter 1979): 301-307.

0567. Morris, M. "Charles Brockden Brown and the American Indian." American Literature 18 (November 1946) :244-247.

0568. Morris, Mable Marie. "The Democratic Influence in Charles Brockden Brown's Treatment of the Indian." MA Thesis. Iowa City: University of Iowa, 1926.

0569. Morsberger, Robert E. "Edgar Rice Burroughs' Apache Novels." Journal of Popular Culture 7:2 (1973) : 280-287.

0570. Mulvey, Kathleen A. "The Growth, Development, and Decline of the Popularity of American Indian Plays before the Civil War." Ph. D. dissertation, New York University, 1978.

0571. Murphy, J. J. "Cooper, Cather, and the Downward Path to Progress." Prairie Schooner 55 (Spring-Summer 1981): 168-184.

0572. Nahanee, Theresa. "Mind Benders." Tawow, 4 (1974) : 2-3.

The purpose of this article is "to catagorize the treatment of Indian people in the mass media and to show what Indian people themselves are doing to combat the after-effects of this assault."

0573. Napier, Georgia Pierce. "A Study of the North American Indian Character in Twenty Selected Children's Books." Ph. D. Diss. Fayetteville: Univeristy of Arkansas, 1970.

0574. Nelson, Horatia Dodson. "Indian Character and Customs as Portrayed in the Novels of James Fenimore Cooper." MA Thesis. Columbus: Ohio State University, 1932.

0575. Nelson, Mary. "Ode to the Future: Boarding Schools for Whites on Indian Reservations." Indian Historian, 3 (Fall 1970) : 31.

0576. Neumann, Edwin Julius. "Hamlin Garland and the Mountain West." Ph. D. Diss. Evanston, IL: Northwestern University, 1951.

"Considers Hamlin Garland's treatment of the Indian; his consideration of the social problems arising from the assimilation of the Indian."

0577. Newman, Jerry. "Indian Association Attacks Lies in Children's Literature." <u>Interracial Books for Children</u>, 2 (Summer 1969) : 2,8.

0578. Nichols, Roger L. "The Indian in the Dime Novel." <u>Journal of American Culture</u> 5 (Summer 1982): 49-55.

0579. Nichols, Roger L. "Printers Ink and Red Skins: Western Newspapers and Indians." <u>Kansas Quarterly</u> 3 (Fall 1971):82-87.

0580. Nigliazzo, Marc Anthony. "Faulkner's Indians." Ph. D. Diss. Albuquerque: University of New Mexico, 1973.

0581. O'Donnell, Thomas F. "More Apologies: The Indian in New York Fiction." <u>New York Folklore Quarterly</u>, 23 (1967) : 243-252.

0582. Oliva, Leo E. "The American Indian in Recent Historical Fiction: A Review Essay." <u>Prairie Scout</u> 1 (1973):95-120.

0583. O'Neill, M. C. "History as Dramatic Present: Arthur L. Kopit's <u>Indians</u>." <u>Theatre Journal</u> 34 (December 1982): 493-504.

0584. Orians, George H. <u>The Cult of the Vanishing American, 1834-1934</u>. Toledo, Ohio: University of Toledo, 1935.

Following the popular portrayal of the Indian in romance as "noble savage," it became popular to portray him as vanishing: "It was quickly discovered that the most romantic feature of the Indians was their decline."

0585. Orians, George H. "Pontiac in Literature." <u>Northwest Ohio Quarterly</u>, 35 (1963) 144-163; 36 (1964) : 31-53.

0586. Paine, Gregory Lansing. "The Indians of the Leatherstocking Tales." <u>Studies in Philology</u> 23 (1926) 16-39.

0587. Paine, Gregory Lansing. "James Fenimore Cooper as an Interpreter and Critic of America." Ph. D. Diss. Chicago: University of Chicago, 1924.

0588. "The Past: The Old Stories Showed Them a Way of Life." <u>Vista Volunteer</u>, 6 (January 1970) : 416-420.

0589. Pearce,   Roy   Harvey.   The   Savages   of   America.
Baltimore: Johns Hopkins University Press, 1953.

        Republished   in   1965   as   Savagism   vs.
        Civilization.   See below.

0590. Pearce, Roy Harvey. Savagism vs.   Civilization: A
Study of the Indian and the American Mind.   Baltimore:
Johns Hopkins University Press, 1965, 1967.

        This   work   and the one noted above which
        preceded   it   are   both based on Pearce's 1945
        Ph. D. Dissertation, "The Indian and the
        American Mind, 1775-1800: A Study in the
        History and Impact of Primitivistic Ideas."
        The   idea   of   the   title   is   explored   in
        political pamphlets, reports of missionaries,
        drama,   poetry,   novels   and   accounts   of
        anthropologists.

0591. Pearce,   Roy   Harvey.   "The   Significance of the
Captivity Narrative." American Literature, 19 (March
1947) : 1-20.

0592. Peavy,   Charles   D.   "The American Indian in the Drama
of the United States." The McNeese Review, 10 (Winter
1958) : 68-86.

        Traces   stage history of the Indians from
        1766 to 1905. Discusses 24 dramas.

0593. Pettit,   Paul   B.   "The   Important   American   Dramatic
Types to 1900, a Study of the Yankee, Negro, Indian
and Frontiersman." Ph. D. Diss.   Ithaca, New York:
Cornell University, 1949.

0594. Pitcher,   Edward W. R. "The Un-American Fiction of The
American   Moral   and Sentimental Magazine, with a
comment on the 'Captivity Narrative.'" Early American
Literature 14 (Winter 1979-1980): 312-315.

0595. Popp,   James A. "An Examination of Children's Books on
the American Indian." BIA Education Research Bulletin,
3 (January 1975) : 10-23.

        An analysis of 49 children's books.

0596. Porter, Mark. "Mysticism of the Land and the Western
Novel." South Dakota Review 11 (Spring 1973):79-91.

0597. Price, John A. "The Stereotyping of North American
Indians in Motion Pictures." Ethnohistory, 20 (Spring
1973) : 153-171.

0598. Price, John A. "Stereotyping in Motion Pictures." Native Studies: American and Canadian Indians, pp. 200-216. Toronto: McGraw-Hill Ryerson, Ltd., 1978.

0599. Prucha, Francis Paul, ed. Americanizing the American Indian: Writings by the "Friends of the Indian," 1880-1900. Cambaridge, MA: Harvard University Press, 1973.

0600. Rader, Alice Dresser. "The American Indian in the American Novel and Short Story." MA Thesis. Lawrence: University of Kansas, 1928.

0601. Ramsey, W. M. "Moot Points of Melville's Indian-Hating." American Literature 52 (May 1980): 224-235.

0602. Ram, Marie L. "An Analysis of the Lois Lenski Literature from a Sociological Point of View." 2 parts. Ed. D. Diss. Buffalo: State University of New York at Buffalo, 1958.

    Includes Indians in fiction, mainly Iroquois.

0603. Rans, Geoffrey. "Inaudible Man: The Indian in the Theory and Practice of White Fiction." Canadian Review of American Studies, 8 (Fall 1977) : 103-115.

    Author discusses works of J. F. Cooper, Washington Irving, Nathaniel West, William Faulkner, Thomas Berger, and Ken Kesey.

0604. Redekop, Ernest. "The Redmen: Some Representations of Indians in American Literature before the Civil War." Canadian Association for American Studies Bulletin, 3 (Winter 1968) : 1-44.

    Author discusses how Indians in 19th century American literature help to define white civilization, how 19th century writers almost universally placed Indian portrayals in a white context. Examines in particular treatments by Cooper, Brackenridge, Simms, Brown, and Melville; notes a variety of points of view among the writers.

0605. Reed, Perley I. Realistic Presentation of American Characters in Native American Plays Prior to 1870. Columbus: Ohio State University, 1918.

0606. Reichard, Gladys Amanda. "Literary Types and Dissemination of North American Myths." MA Thesis. New York: Columbia University, 1920.

    46 p. Indian tribes in general.

0607. Rice, S. "And Afterwards Take Him to a Movie." <u>Media</u>
      <u>& Methods</u>, 7 (April 1971) : 43-44+.

0608. Richburg, James R., and Hastings, Phyllis R. "Media
      and the American Indian: Ethnographical, Historical,
      and Contemporary Issues." <u>Social Education</u>, 36 (May
      1972) : 526-533.

0609. Roberts, Mrs. Brunidell (Sisson). "Character Types of
      the Southwest as Delineated in New Mexico Fiction." MA
      Thesis. Albuquerque: University of New Mexico, 1932.

0610. Robertson, Jennie R. Gould. "The Picture of the
      Indian in Fiction with South Dakota Setting." MA
      Thesis. Vermillion: University of South Dakota, 1951.

0611. Rose, Alan Henry. <u>Demonic Vision: Racial Fantasy and</u>
      <u>Southern Fiction</u>. Hamden, CT: Anchorbook, 1976.

              Author looks at humor of Old South,
           antebellum Southern fiction.

0612. Rosenburg, Bruce A. "How Custer's 'Last Stand' Got
      Its Name." <u>Georgia Review</u>, 26 (1972) : 279-296.

0613. Roucek, Joseph S. "The American Indian in Literature
      and Politics." <u>Politico</u> (Italy), 27 (1962) : 569-604.

0614. Rourke, Constance. <u>The Roots of American Culture</u>.
      New York: Harcourt, Brace, 1942.

              Indian Influence on theater pp. 60-74.

0615. Rucker, Mary E. "Natural, Tribal, and Civil Law in
      Cooper's <u>The Prairie</u>." <u>Western American Literature</u> 12
      (Fall 1977): 215-222.

0616. Russell, Jason Almus. "Hawthorne and the Romantic
      Indian." <u>Education</u> 48 (February 1928) : 381-386.

0617. Russell, Jason Almus. "The Indian in American
      Literature (1775-1875)." Ph. D. Diss. Ithaca, New
      York: Cornell University, 1932.

0618. Russell, Jason Almus. "Irving: Recorder of Indian
      Life." <u>Journal of American History</u> 25 (1931) : n.p.n.

0619. Russell, Jason Almus. "Longfellow: Interpreter of the
      Historical and the Romantic Indian." <u>Journal of</u>
      <u>American History</u> 22:4 (1928) : 327-347.

0620. Russell, Jason Almus. "Parkman and the Real Indian."
      <u>Journal of American History</u> 20 (April 1929) : 121-129.

0621. Russell, Jason Almus. "The Romantic Indian in
      Bryant's Poetry." <u>Education</u> 48 (June 1928) : 642-649.

0622. Russell, Jason Almus. "Southwestern Border Indians in
      the Writings of William Gilmore Simms." Education 51
      (November 1930) : 144-157.

0623. Russell, Jason Almus. "Thoreau: The Interpreter of
      the Real Indian." Queen's University Quarterly
      (October 1927) : 37-48.

0624. Ryan,   J.   S.   "Noble Savage: Attitudes to the
      Indigenous People in the American Novel." Armidale and
      District Historical Society [Australia] 14 (1971):
      12-32.

0625. Ryan, Patrick Edward. "The American Frontier
      Narratives Represented Primarily by a Selection of
      Indian Captive Narratives which Characterized the
      Indian as an Ignoble Savage." MA Thesis. Pocatello:
      Idaho State University, 1970.

0626. Sanders,   Ronald.   "Red Power at the Bookstore."
      Midstream, 18 (1972) : 49-67.

0627. Sando, Joe S. "White-Created Myths about the Native
      Americans." Indian Historian, 4 (Winter 1970) : 10-11.

0628. Saum, L. O. "The Fur Trader and the Noble Savage."
      American Quarterly 15 (Winter 1963) : 554-571.

0629. Sayre, Robert F. Thoreau and the American Indians.
      Princeton, New Jersey: Princeton University Press,
      1977.

0630. Sayre, Robert F. "Vision and Experience in Black Elk
      Speaks." College English, 32 (February 1971) :
      509-535.

0631. Scheick, William J. The Half-Blood: A Cultural Symbol
      in 19th-Century American Fiction. Lexington,
      Kentucky: University Press of Kentucky, 1979.

0632. Scheick, William J. "The Half-Breed in Snelling's
      Tales of the Northwest." Old Northwest 2 (June 1976):
      141-151.

0633. Schneider, Jack Ward. "Crime and Navajo Punishment:
      Tony Hillerman's Novels of Detection." Southwest
      Review 67 (Spring 1982): 151-160.

0634. Schneider, Jack Ward. "Patterns of Cultural Conflict
      in Southwestern Indian Fiction." Ph. D. dissertation,
      Texas Tech University, 1977.

0635. Schramm, W. L. "'Hiawatha' and Its Predecessors."
      Philological Quarterly 11 (October 1932) : 321-343.

0636. Schulman, Robert. "Parkman's Indians and American Violence." Massachusetts Review, 12 (Spring 1971) : 221-239.

0637. Schwartz, T. and Marshall, J. D. "Indian Epic: R. B. Hill's Novel, Hanta Yo." Newsweek, 93 (April 16, 1979) 86+.

0638. Scotch, N. A. "The Vanishing Villians of Television." Phylon Quarterly, 21 (Spring 1960) : 58-62.

0639. Scullin, Michael. "Reviewing the Mass Media." The Indian Historian, 2 (Spring 1969) : 49-50.

An analysis of articles on American Indians found through Reader's Guide to Periodical Literature which finds few of merit on Indians.

0640. Sears, Priscilla Flagg. "A Pillar of Fire to Follow: American Indian Dramas: 1808-1859." Ph. D. Diss. Medford, MA: Tufts University, 1975.

0641. Seyersted, Per. "The Indian in Knickerbocker's New Amsterdam." Indian Historian 7:3 (Summer 1974) : 14-28.

Irving's semi-fictional treatment of the Indians in his 'Knickerbocker's History of New York' is critiqued.

0642. Shames, Priscilla. "The Long Hope: A Study of American Indian Stereotypes in American Popular Fiction, 1890-1950." Ph. D. Diss. Los Angeles, CA: University of California at Los Angeles, 1969.

0643. Shaul, Lawana Jean. "Treatment of the West in Selected Magazine Fiction, 1870-1900: An Annotated Bibliography." MA Thesis. Laramie: University of Wyoming, 1954.

0644. Sheehan, B. W. "Paradise and the Noble Savage in Jeffersonian Thought." William and Mary Quarterly 53:26 (July 1969) : 327-359.

0645. Sheets, Sankey L. "The Rise of Anglo-Indian Literature: a Definition of the Term and the Place of the Letters and Journals of 1579-1626." Ph. D. Diss. Boston: Boston University Graduate School, 1938.

0646. Sheff, David, and Fincher, Jack. "A Growing War over Hanta Yo Pits Chief Lame Deer and Wojo vs. Ruth Beebe Hill and David Wolper." People Weekly 12 (June 23, 1980): 82+.

0647. Silet, Charles L. P. "The Image of the American Indian in Film." In The Worlds between Two Rivers: Perspectives on American Indians in Iowa, edited by Bataille, Gretchen M. and others, pp. 10-15. Ames: Iowa State University Press, 1978.

0648. Simonski, Ted. "Sioux versus Hollywood: The Image of Sioux Indians in American Films." Ph. D. dissertation, University of Southern California, 1979.

0649. Sitton, Fred. "The Indian Play in American Drama, 1750-1900." Ph. D. Diss. Evanston, Illinois: Northwestern University, 1962.

0650. Slotkin, Richard. "Dreams and Genocide: The American Myth of Regeneration Through Violence." Journal of Popular Culture 5:1 (1971): 38-59.

            A tracing of the mythology of
      regeneration through violence from Indian
      captivity narratives through literature about
      the Vietnam war.

0651. Slotkin, Richard. Regeneration through Violence: The Mythology of the American Frontier, 1600-1860. Middletown, CT: Wesleyan University Press, 1973.

            Evolution of the frontier myth and its
      influence on literature between 1620 and
      1850's.

0652. Smith, Garland Garvey. "The Indian in American Fiction before 1850." MA Thesis. Dallas: Southern Methodist University, 1923.

0653. Sommler, Henry Charles. "Washington Irving's A Tour on the Prairie." MA Thesis. Chapel Hill: University of North Carolina, 1965.

0654. Sonnichsen, C. L. "The Ambivalent Apache." Western American Literature 10 (August 1975): 99-114.

            Another source gave volume, number, and
      date as 10:2 (1976). Both sources indicate
      the article is about the attitudes of writers
      of Southwestern fiction (from the Civil War
      era to the present) towards the Apache who
      appears in their work more than any other
      Indian.

0655. Stallman, R. W. "Stephen Crane and Cooper's Uncas." American Literature 39 (November 1967) : 392-396.

0656. Stappenbeck, Herbert Louis, Jr. "Mark Twain and the American Indians." MA Thesis. Austin: University of Texas, 1958.

0657. Stark, Bernice Sutherland. "The Presence and Significance of the Indian in Modernism." Ph. D. Diss. Pittsburgh: University of Pittsburgh, 1970.

0658. Stensland, Anna Lee. "American Indian Culture: Promises, Problems, and Possibilities." English Journal, 60 (December 1971) : 1195-1200.

0659. Stensland, Anna Lee. "American Indian Culture and the Reading Program." Journal of Reading 14:1 (October 1971): 22-26.

> Includes bibliography.

0660. Stensland, Anna Lee. "The Indian Presence in American Literature." English Journal, 66 (March 1977) : 37-41.

0661. Stensland, Anna Lee. "Indian Writers and Indian Lives." Integrated Education, 12 (November-December 1974) : 3-7.

> A discussion of popular Indian stereotypes and counter-stereotypes in literature, based on the thesis that the introduction of the literature of the American Indian, traditional and modern, will help to increase an Indian child's pride in his culture and add to the understanding of the non-Indian child.

0662. Stensland, Anna Lee. Literature by and about the American Indian.

> See the bibliographies section.

0663. Stockton, Edwin Link, Jr. "The Influence of the Moravians upon The Leatherstocking Tales." Ph. D. Diss. Gainesville: University of Florida, 1960.

0664. Stoodt, B. D. and Ignizio, S. "American Indians in Children's Literature." Language Arts, 53 (January 1976) : 12-21.

0665. Stouck, D. "Willa Cather and the Indian Heritage." 20th Century Literature 22 (December 1976): 433-443.

0666. Sullivan, Cecille Gerard. "The Indian as Treated by Cooper and Simms." MA Thesis. New Haven: Yale University, 1925.

0667. Sullivan, Sherry Ann. "The Indian in American Fiction 1820-1850." Ph. D. dissertation, University of Toronto, 1979.

0668. Szasz, Margaret C., and Fernac M. "The American Indian and the Classical Past." Midwest Quarterly 17 (1975):58-70.

0669. Tapia, John Reyna. The Indian in the Spanish American Novel. Lanham, MD: University Press of America, 1981.

0670. Taylor, Allan R. "The Literary Offenses of Ruth Beebe Hill." American Indian Culture and Research Journal 4 (No. 3, 1980): 75-85.

0671. Ten Kate, Herman F. C. "The Indian in Literature." Smithsonian Report (1921) : 507-528; Indian Historian, 3 (Summer 1970) : 23-32.

        Author reviews principal literary works in which Indians figure as heroes by 37 writers between 1799 and 1916 from an ethnologist's and geographer's point of view.

0672. Thieme, J. "Scheherazade as Historian: Rudy Wiebe's 'Where is the Voice Coming From?'" Journal of Commonwealth Literature 17:1 (1982): 172-181.

0673. Thigpen, Buelah Virginia. "The Indians of the Leather-Stocking Tales: A Study of the Noble and Ignoble Savage." Ed. D. Diss. Commerce: East Texas State University, 1981.

        Traces the contrasting influences of Romantic ideas of the noble savage and of savagism in the Indians of Cooper's Leather-Stocking Tales to determine whether his Indians were true noble savages. Conludes that Cooper shows influences of both.

0674. Thomson, Peggy. "Ruth Hill Became Indian to Write Epic of the Sioux." Smithsonian 9 (December 1978): 111-128.

0675. Tiller, Solomon H. "'Indianismo' in the Spanish American Novel." Ph. D. Diss. Ann Arbor: University of Michigan, 1968.

0676. Timmerman, J. H. "Harmony in Dynamic Pattern: Frederick Manfred's Novelistic Art." Southwest Review 68 (Spring 1983): 153-161.

0677. Todd, Ruthwen. "The Imaginary Indians in Europe." Art in America, 60 (July-August 1972) : 42-47.

0678. Toelken, Barre. "The Native Aerican: A Review Article." Western Folklore, 29 (1970) : 268-278.

0679. Tompkins, J. P. "No Apologies for the Iroquois: A New
      Way to Read the Leatherstocking Novels." Criticism 23
      (Winter 1981): 24-41.

0680. Troy, Alice Anne. "The   Indian   in Adolescent
      Literature 1930-40 vs. 1960-70." Ph. D. Diss. Iowa
      City: University of Iowa, 1972.

0681. Troy, Anne. "The Stereotype of the American Indian in
      Adolescent Literature." Paper Presented to Annual
      Meeting of NCTE in 1973; Bethesda, MD: EDRS, ED 087
      042, 1973.

          She discusses what a stereotype is and
          how stereotypes of American Indian may have
          evolved.   One of her hypotheses is that
          novels of the past as well as history books
          made use of erroneous stereotypes.   Shows
          range of treatment.

0682. Troy, Anne. "The Indian in Adolescent Novels." Indian
      Historian, 8 (Winter 1975) : 32-35.

          Nine 1930 novels compared to fourteen
          1960 novels.   Article summarizes her Ph. D.
          dissertation,   "The   Indian   in Adolescent
          Literature,   1930-40   vs.   1960-70," cited
          above.

0683. Underhill, Lonnie E. "Hamlin Garland and the Indian."
      American Indian Quarterly 1:2 (Summer 1974) : 103-113.

0684. Underhill, Lonnie E. and Littlefield, Daniel F., Jr.
      "Hamlin Garland and the Navajos." Journal of Arizona
      History 13:4 (1972) : 275-285.

0685. Van Der Beets, Richard. "The Indian Captivity
      Narrative: An American Genre." Ph. D. Diss. Stockton,
      CA: University of the Pacific, 1973.

0686. Van Der Beets, Richard. "The Indian Captivity
      Narrative as Ritual." American Literature 43 (January
      1971): 548-562.

0687. Van Der Beets, Richard. "A Surfeit of Style: The
      Indian Captivity Narrative as Penny Dreadful."
      Research Studies 39:4 (1971): 297-306.

0688. Van Keuren, M. Luise. "American Indian Responses and
      Reactions to the Colonists as Recorded in Seventeenth
      and Eighteenth-Century American Literature." Newark,
      Delaware: University of Delaware, 1981.

0689. Van Norman, Carrie Elta. "An Investigation of the
      Concept of War in Historical Fiction Written for

Children." Ed.   D.   Diss.   Stanford,   CA: Stanford
University, 1941.

>Two chapters on Indian warfare.

0690. Vigil, Ralph H. "New Ethnic Literature: A Review
Essay." New Mexico Historical Quarterly, 49 (1974) :
153-170.

0691. Vogel, Virgil J. "The Indian in American History."
Bethesda, MD: EDRS, ED 033 783, 1968.

>Treatment   of   Indian   discussed with
reference to four methods of perpetuating
false   impressions: obliteration, defamation,
disembodiment, and disparagement.

0692. Wallace, P. A. W. "John Heckewelder's Indians and the
Fenimore Cooper Tradition." American Philosophical
Society Proceedings 96:4 (1952) : 496-504.

0693. Wardenaar,   Leslie   A.   "Humor   in   the Colonial
Promotional Tract: Topics and Techniques." Early
American Literature 9:3 (1975): 286-300.

0694. Wasserman, Maurice Marc. "The American Indian as Seen
by the Seventeenth Century Chroniclers." Ph. D. Diss.
Philadelphia: University of Pennsylvania, 1954.

0695. Waters, Frank. "Crossroads: Indians and Whites."
South Dakota Review 11 (Autumn 1973):28-38.

0696. Watkins, Floyd C. "James Kirk Paulding: Humorist and
Critic of American Life." Ph. D. Diss. Nashville, TN:
Vanderbilt University, 1952.

>Paulding (1778-1860) was one of the
earliest American authors to use Indians in
fiction.   This   dissertation   suggests he
anticipated others in use of Indian folklore.

0697. Weinkauf, M. S. "The Indian in Science Fiction."
Extrapolation 20 (Winter 1979): 308-320.

0698. Weixlmann, Joseph N., Jr. "Counter-Types and
Anti-Myths: Black and Indian Characters in the Fiction
of John Barth." Ph. D. Diss. Manhattan, Kansas:
Kansas State University, 1973.

0699. Wells, Helen G. "Navaho of the Painted Desert in
American Fiction." MA Thesis. Los Angeles: University
of Southern California, 1942.

0700. White, Clara Mae. "A Study of James Fenimore Cooper's
Social Teachings on American Democratic Culture." MS

Thesis. Kingsville, Texas: Texas A & I University,
1946.

> Cooper's ideas and reactions as he saw
> Indians.

0701. Woodall, Marian K. "The Economic and Social Changes
in the Southwest as Seen in the Novels of Harvey
Fergusson." MA Thesis. Tucson: University of Arizona,
1964.

> Discusses this New Mexican author's
> Indian characterizations.

0702. Zolla, Elemire. The Writer and the Shaman: A
Morphology of the American Indian. trans. R.
Rosenthal. New York: Harcourt, Brace Jovanovich, 1969,
1973.

> Traces development of Indian images over
> course of American literature and literature
> in general.

Native American Literature

The purpose of this section is to list works by and about Indian authors and their literary products. It includes Native American works edited, translated, or retold by non-Indians. This list includes novels, story collections, single stories, myths, legends, tales, some poetry and some drama, as well as critical works about the literature, both oral and written, of Native Americans.

Where it has been determined that a work is aimed at a particular age level or type of reader this distinction has been noted. If the work is about or is aimed at a particular tribe, cultural group, or geographical region, this, too, has been noted, usually, unless the title provides this information.

This section might have been much larger, but other books are available which list Native American works much more comprehensively and/or specifically than this one can. To avoid needless duplication of information commonly available, I have tried to include in this collection only titles that are not, in most cases, to be found in what I believe to be the most thorough bibliographies--at least not to be found exactly as I have listed them. In some cases I have added a brief description; in other cases all I have added is a bit of bibliographic information such as the name of an additional publisher or a title variation. Of course, I have endeavored to list all works published since the publication of the major bibliograhies I am about to mention. There is some overlap between this work and these others, but consider this section as a supplement to them, to be used in conjunction with them, and not as an alternative.

Perhaps the most comprehensive gatherings of Indian literary materials are Jack W. Marken's The American Indian: Language and Literature (180) and Daniel F. Littlefield and James W. Parins's A Bibliography of Native American Writers, 1772-1924 (172). Little written, narrated or dictated by American Indians up to 1978 has been left out of Marken's collection. Littlefield and Parins list translations but not dictations among their 4,000-plus entries. Neither work is annotated.

Angeline Jacobsen's <u>Contemporary Native American Literature</u> (154) concentrates on works written between 1960 and 1976 and is quite thorough in its listing of poems. The poems are not annotated, but all other entries in Jacobsen's collection are.

Judith Ullom's <u>Folklore of the North American Indians: An Annotated Bibliography</u> (282) provides an extensively annotated listing of 152 works collecting or retelling myths, tales and legends.

Perhaps the most useful bibliography for teachers, but an invaluable aid to any student, is Anna Lee Stensland's <u>Literature by and about the American Indian</u> (265). The first 63 pages of this book are devoted to materials, methods and problems related to teaching the literature of the American Indian. Included in the introduction are discussions of themes and stereotypes. Guides to curriculum planning are listed along with items for a basic library of Indian Literature. Sources of additional materials are cited. The bibliography section touches virtually all areas of Indian literature. Because of the broad scope and thorough annotation each entry is given, the bibliography must be considered very selective.

A book which should prove a valuable resource to educators and parents, is Hap Gilliland's <u>Indian Children's Books</u> (119). An annotated list of children's books of all types is presented arranged alphabetically by title on color-coded pages. Books listed were evaluated for suitability for children, and each was assigned a rating.

Several works by Arlene B. Hirschfelder should be pointed out as major lists of Indian literature, including: <u>American Indian Authors: A Bibliography of Contemporary and Historical Literature Written or Narrated by Native Americans</u> (138), <u>American Indian and Eskimo Authors: A Comprehensive Bibliography</u> (140), and <u>American Indian Stereotypes in the World of Children: A Reader and Bibliography</u> (141).

Some other bibliographies of note are an earlier one by Jack Marken entitled <u>The Indians and Eskimos of North America: A Bibliography of Books in Print through 1972</u> (181) and the four volumes (1970-1973) of the <u>Index to Literature on The American Indian</u> (133) edited by Jeanette Henry, each volume of which indexes a year's worth of writings on or by Indians.

Newspapers and periodicals edited and published by Native Americans are indexed in two sources: <u>American Indian and Alaska Native Newspapers and Periodicals, 1826-1924</u> by Daniel F. Littlefield and James W. Parins (173) and <u>Native American Periodicals and Newspapers, 1828-1982</u> edited by James P. Dankey and compiled by Maureen E. Hady (71).

Each of the books just cited applies a unique strength to the task of compiling bibliographical materials on Indian Literature. Together they provide a solid foundation which might serve as a point of departure for the exploration and classification a large and complex body of literature--a literature which it seems we have only re-

cently begun to realize deserves a full-sized niche in
American arts and letters.
   Additionally, researchers should check out lists on
Native American languages and native texts prepared by
linguists and anthropologists among others. Perhaps the
vast majority of Indian oral literature that has been
recorded is the byproduct of scientists mapping culture.
   American Indian Fiction by Charles R. Larson (1154) is
among the few critical books--perhaps it is the only
one--dealing exclusively with fiction by American Indian
writers. Larson provides an historical overview of the
development of American Indian fiction and detailed
criticism of the major Indian writers. Footnotes,
bibliography and index make the work an excellent starting
place for the student of Indian fiction.

0703. Abbott, Katherine M. Old Paths and Legends of the New
      England Border: Connecticut, Deerfield, Berkshire.
      Reprint of 1907 edition, Detroit: Gale Research Co.,
      1970.

0704. Abrahall, John Hoskyns. Western Woods and Waters:
      Poems and Illustrative Notes. London: Longman,
      Roberts and Green, 1864.

0705. Absaloka: Crow Children's Writing. (Indian Culture
      Series) Billings, MT: Montana Council for Indian
      Education, 1971.

0706. Adamson, Thelma. Folktales of the Coast Salish.
      Memoirs of the American Folklore Society 27 (1934).
      New York: Kraus Reprints, n.d.

0707. "African and Indian Myths: Literature Curriculum,
      Levels C-D (Grades 3 & 4): Teacher's Guide." Oregon
      Elementary English Project. Bethesda, MD: EDRS, ED 075
      845, 1971.

0708. Albert, Roy. Coyote Tales, English Version.
      Bethesda, MD: EDRS, ED 046 611, June 1970.

         Hopi storytellers told, in Hopi, 20
      stories for this supplementary reading
      series. Each was translated into English,
      graded 1.1 to 3.8 and illustrated. Stories
      normally serve to entertain and instruct
      children during winter nights. RC 005 039
      has same stories in Hopi.

0709. Alexander, Hartley Burr. God's Drum and Other Cycles
      from Indian Lore. New York: E. P. Dutton and Co.,
      1927

0710. Alexander, Hartley B. The World's Rim: Great
      Mysteries of the North American Indian. Lincoln:
      University of Nebraska Press, 1953, 1967.

0711. Alexander, Hartley Burr. "The Sense of Antiquity in Indian Mythology." Southwest Museum. The Masterkey, 7 (1933) : 132.

0712. Allen, Paula Gunn. "The Mythopoeic Vision in Native American Literature: The Problem of Myth." American Indian Culture and Research Journal 1, No. 1 (1974) : 3-13.

    Defines myth and discusses its function in Native American literature. Contains a bibliography.

0713. Allen, Paula G. "The Psychological Landscape of Ceremony." American Indian Quarterly 5:1 (February 1979) : 7-12.

0714. Allen, Paula G. "The Sacred Hoop: A Contemporary Indian Perspective on American Indian Literature." Cross Currents 26 (Summer 1976): 144-163.

0715. Allen, Paula G. "A Stranger in My Own Life: Alienation in Native American Prose and Poetry. (1)" Newsletter of the Association for Study of American Indian Literatures 3, No. 1 (Winter 1979) : 1-10.

    First of two parts. News letter is published by the Department of English, Columbia University, New York, NY.

0716. Allen, Paula G. "A Stranger in My Own Life: Alienation in Native American Prose and Poetry. (2)" Newsletter of the Association for Study of American Indian Literatures 3, No. 2 (Spring 1979) : 16-23.

0717. Allen, Paula G. "Symbol and Structure in Native American Literature: Some Basic Considerations." College Composition and Communication 24 (1973):267-270.

0718. Allen, Paula G., ed. Studies in American Indian Literature: Critical Essays and Course Designs. MLA Commission on the Literatures and Languages of America Series. New York: Modern Language Association of America, 1982.

0719. Allen, Paula, et al. Four Indian Poets. Vermillion, S. Dakota: Dakota Press, 1974.

0720. Allen, Phillipa. Whispering Wind: Folktales of the Navaho Indians Retold. Chicago: Thomas A. Rockwell, Co., 1930.

0721. Allen, Terry D., ed. Arrows Four: Prose and Poetry by Young American Indians. New York: Washington Square Press, 1974.

0722. Allen, Terry D., ed. The Whispering Wind: Poetry by Young American Indians. Garden City, NY: Doubleday and Co., Inc., 1972.

0723. American Indian II, South Dakota Review. Vermillion: Dakota Press, 1971.

    A second collection of contemporary Indian writing--10 authors.

0724. "American Indian Literature and American Literature: An Overview." Association of Departments of English (New York) Bulletin No. 75 (Summer 1983): 35-38.

0725. Anderson, Bernice G. Indian Sleep-Man Tales. New York: Bramhall House, 1940.

    For children.

0726. Andrade, Manuel. Quileute Texts. Columbia University Contributions to Anthropology, vol. 12. (1931).

0727. Andrist, John E. "Coyote and the Colville." Bethesda, MD: EDRS, ED 059 798, June 1, 1971.

    Contains 10 legends, 24 item bibliography.

0728. Aoki, Haruo. Nez Perce Texts. University of California Publications in Linguistics, vol. 90 (1979).

0729. Applegate, Frank B. Indian Stories from the Pueblos. Philadelphia: J. B. Lippincott Co., 1929; Glorieta, New Mexico: Rio Grande Press, 1971.

0730. Applegate, Frank B. Native Tales of New Mexico. Philadelphia: J. B. Lippincott Co., 1932.

0731. Armstrong, Virginia. I Have Spoken. Chicago: Sage Books, Swallow Press, Inc., 1971.

    Indian oratories 17th century to 20th century. Chronological.

0732. Astrov, Margot, ed. American Indian Prose and Poetry, an Anthology. New York: G. P. Putman's Sons, 1962.

    Songs, prayers, and stories of U. S. Mexico, Central America and Peru. Includes some Eskimo songs and dances.

0733. Astrov, Margaret. The Winged Serpent: An Anthology of American Indian Prose and Poetry. New York: Capricorn Books, 1962; New York: John Day Co., 1972.

Originally published as *The Winged Serpent*. New York: G. P. Putnam's Sons, 1946. Also listed under the title *American Indian Prose and Poetry*. Translations of North, Central and South American Indian songs, speeches, prayers, myths and narratives organized according to geographical regions. North and South America includes Mexico and Central America; in all, 10 culture areas. Index. Bibliography.

0734. Atkeson, Mary Meek. "A Study of the Local Literature of the Upper Ohio Valley, with Especial Reference to the Early Pioneer and Indian Tales, 1820-1840." Ph. D. Diss. Columbus, Ohio: Ohio State University, 1919.

0735. Austin, Mary. *American Rhythm: Studies and Reexpressions of American Indian Songs*. Reprint of 1930 edition. New York: Cooper Square Publishers, Inc., 1972.

0736. Austin, Mary. *One-Smoke Stories*. Boston: Houghton Mifflin Co., 1934

0737. Ayre, Robert. *Sketco the Raven*. Toronto: Macmillan Co. of Canada, n.d.

Tales of West Coast Indians for grades 5-8.

0738. Bagley, Clarence Booth. *Indian Myths of the Northwest*. n.p.: Lowman and Hanford Co., 1930; Seattle: Shorey Publications, 1970.

0739. Bahr, Donald M. *Pima and Papago Ritual Oratory*. San Francisco: Indian Historian Press, 1975.

0740. Bailey, Carolyn S. *Stories from an Indian Cave: The Cherokee Cave Builders*. Chicago: Albert Whitman and Co., 1935.

Twenty-five stories, adopted from Cherokee legends, retold for children.

0741. Baker, Betty. *At the Center of the World*. New York: Macmillan, 1973.

0742. Ballard, Arthur C. "Mythology of South Puget Sound." *Publications in Anthropology*, Vol. 1, No. 2. Seattle: University of Washington Press, 1929.

0743. Ballard, Arthur C. "Mythology of Southern Puget Sound." *Publications in Anthropology*, Vol. 3, No. 2. Seattle: University of Washington Press, 1929.

0744. Ballard, Arthur C. <u>Some Tales of the Puget Sound Salish</u>. Seattle: University of Washington Press, 1927.

0745. Ballard, Charles C. " The Deep Structure Content of Native American Literature." Paper presented at the annual meeting of the Rocky Mountain Modern Language Association, Santa Fe, New Mexico, October 21-23, 1976; Bethesda, MD: EDRS, ED 132 577, 1976.

> Discusses older tradition of Native American literature in terms of the systems of values which we bring to it, as well as those embedded in it. The analysis leads to a statement of some of the strengths of recent Native American literature, which carries from the past some of the value judgments that have always kept the group or the tribe intact.

0746. Bannon, Helen M. "Spider Woman's Web: Mothers and Daughters in Southwestern Native American Literature." In <u>The Lost Tradition: Mothers and Daughters in Literature</u>, edited by Broner, E.M and Davidson, Cathy N., pp. 286-299. New York: Frederick Ungar Publishing Co., 1980.

0747. Barnard, Herwana Becleer. "The Commanche and His Literature, with an Anthology of His Myths, Legends, Folktakes, Oratory, Poetry and Songs." MA Thesis. Norman: University of Oklahoma, 1941.

0748. Barnes, Nellie. <u>American Indian Love Lyrics</u>. New York: The Macmillan Co., 1925.

0749. Barnes, Nellie. <u>American Indian Song Lyrics</u>. New York: Macmillan Co., 1925.

0750. Barnes, Nellie. <u>American Indian Verse</u>. Lawrence: University of Kansas Press, 1921.

0751. Barnouw, Victor. <u>Wisconsin Chippewa Myths and Tales and Their Relation to Chippewa Life</u>. Madison: University of Wisconsin Press, 1977.

0752. Barrett, Samuel A. "Myths of the South Sierra Miwok." <u>Publications in American Archaeology and Ethnology</u>, Vol. 14, No. 16. Berkeley: University of California Press, 1919.

0753. Barrett, Samuel A. "Sioux legend 'Eagle Woman's Return,'" <u>Yearbook</u> Milwaukee Public Museum (1922) : 162.

0754. Barrett, Samuel A., ed. "Pomo Myths." <u>Bulletin of the Milwaukee Public Museum</u> 15 (1933); reprinted as

Pomo Myths. New York: Johnson Reprint Co., 1971.

108 myths.

0755. Barry, Nora Baker. "The Bear's Son Folk Tale in When the Legends Die and House Made of Dawn." Western American Literature 12 (Winter 1978): 275-287.

0756. Bartlett, Charles H. Tales of Kanakee Land. Reprint of 1907 edition, Barrien Springs, MI: Hardscrabble Books, 1977.

0757. Bass, Althea. Grandfather Grey Owl Told Me. Indian Culture Series. Billings: Montana Council for Indian Education, 1973.

0758. Bass, Althea. Nightwalker and the Buffalo. Indian Culture Series. Billings: Montana Council for Indian Education, 1972.

0759. Bataille, Gretchen M. "An Approach to the Study of American Indian Literature at the College Level." Ph. D. Diss. Des Moines, Iowa: Drake University, 1977.

See page 6128 in Volume 38/10-A of Dissertation Abstracts International.

0760. Bayliss, C. K. A Treasury of Eskimo Tales. New York: n.p., 1923.

0761. Baylor, Bird. And It Is Still That Way. New York: Scribner, 1976

0762. Beauchamp, William M. Iroquois Folk Lore. Reprint of 1922 edition. New York: AMS Press, Inc., 1974.

0763. Beck, Horace P. Gluskap the Liar and other Indian Tales. Freeport, Maine: Bond Wheelright Co., 1966.

Maine Indians, Penobscot.

0764. Beck, Mary. "Oral Literature of Native Alaska." Indian Historian, 4 : 2 (1971) : 17-19.

Tlingit and Haida literatures; totemic figures; stories of Killer Whale, Frog, Grizzly and Raven; culture heroes.

0765. Beck, Peggy V. and Walters, Anna. The Sacred Ways of Knowledge, Sources of Life. Tsaile, AZ: Navajo Community College Press, 1977.

0766. Beckwith, Martha W. Myths and Hunting Stories of the Mandan and Hidatsa Sioux. (Vassar College Folklore Foundation: Publication No. 10). Reprint of 1930 edition. New York: AMS Press, Inc., 1977.

0767. Beckwith, Martha W., ed. Mandan-Hidatsa Myths and Ceremonies. American Folklore Society Memoir Series, 1937; reprint edition, Millwood, NY: Kraus Reprint, 1969.

0768. Beidler, Peter G. "Animals and Human Development in the Contemporary Indian Novel." Western American Literature 14 (Summer 1979): 133-148.

0769. Beidler, Peter G. "Animals and Theme in Ceremony." American Indian Quarterly 5:1 (February 1979) : 13-18)

0770. Beidler, Peter G., ed. "Special Symposium Issue on James Welch's Winter in the Blood." American Indian Quarterly 4 (May 1978): entire issue.

0771. Belanger, Stephanie. "Running Bear." Weewish Tree, 1 (November 1971) : 30-34.

0772. Bell, Robert C. "Circular Design in Ceremony." American Indian Quarterly 5:1 (February 1979) : 47-62.

0773. Belting, Natalia M. The Earth is on a Fish's Back: Tales of Beginnings. New York: Holt, Rinehart and Winston, 1965.

       Grades 4-6.

0774. Belting, Natalia M. The Long-Tailed Bear and Other Indian Legends. Eau Claire, Wisconsin: E. M. Hale and Co., 1961; Indianapolis: Bobs-Merrill Corp., 1961.

       Grades 4-6.

0775. Benchley, Nathaniel. Only Earth and Sky Last Forever. New York: Harper and Row, 1972.

0776. Benedict, Ruth. Concept of the Guardian Spirit in North America. Reprint of 1923 edition, Millwood, NY: Kraus Reprint, n.d.

0777. Benedict, Ruth. Tales of the Cochiti Indians. Albuquerque: University of New Mexico Press, 1982.

0778. Benedict, Ruth. Zuni Mythology. 2 vols. (Columbia University Contributions to Anthropology Ser.: No. 21). Reprint of 1935 edition. New York: AMS Press, Inc., 1975.

0779. Bennett, Kay, and Bennett, Russ. A Navajo Saga. San Antonio, Texas: Naylor Co., 1969.

       Historical novel. Grade 8-up.

0780. Benton, Patricia. The Young Corn Rises. New York: Vantage Press, 1953.

Myths, legends.

0781. Berner, Robert L. "N. Scott Momaday: Beyond Rainy Mountain." American Indian Culture and Research Journal 3 (No. 1, 1979): 57-67.

0782. Bevis, William. "American Indian Verse Translations." College English 35:6 (March 1974) : 693-703.

One of the attractions of a strange culture is its strangeness. Free translations which familiarize the language and plant meanings which weren't in the originals give an incorrect impression of Indian poetry and the Indian culture it is from and may be culturally dangerous to a society hungry for Indian literature. Urges readers to adopt standard: "how well do they allow us to enter the imaginative world of the Indian's art?" The best translations may be the earliest ones by anthropologists and ethnologists. Bevis points out the weaknesses of a couple of free translations. (For an opposing point of view, read Peter Dillingham's article "The Literature of the American Indian.")

0783. Bierhorst, John, ed. Fire Plume: Legends of the American Indians Collected by Henry R. Schoolcraft. New York: Dial, 1969.

One source estimated reading level at about grades 4-6. Mostly tales of magic and sorcery. Algonquin; seven Chippewa legends and fables. Originals cut, modified, simplified.

0784. Bierhorst, John. Four Masterworks of American Indian Literature. New York: Farrar, Straus and Giroux, Inc., 1974.

Reviews:
Publisher's Weekly, 205 (January 24, 1974) : 56.
Library Journal, 99 (August 1974) : 1951.
Choice, 11 (October 1974) : 1132.
Book World (December 29, 1974) : 4
Booklist, 71 (September 15, 1974) : 65.
Atlantic Monthly, 234 (September 1974) : 103.

0785. Bierhorst, John, ed. The Red Swan: Myths and Tales of the American Indians. New York: Farrar, Straus, and Giroux, 1976; New York: Octagon Books, 1981.

0786. Bierhorst, John, ed. <u>The Ring in the Prairie: A</u>
<u>Shawnee Legend</u>. New York: Dial Press, 1970.

One source rated readibility at primary
level. Reviewed by Ernestine Fox in <u>The</u>
<u>Indian Historian</u>, 5 (Spring 1972) : 45-46.

0787. Bierhorst, John, ed. <u>Songs of the Chippewa</u>. New
York: Farrar, Straus and Giroux, 1974.

Grade 4--up.

0788. Bierhorst, John, ed. <u>The Sacred Path: Spells,</u>
<u>Prayers and Power Songs of the American Indians</u>. New
York: William Morrow and Co., Inc., 1982.

Grade 4 up.

0789. Bierhorst, John, ed. <u>In the Trail of the Wind:</u>
<u>American Indian Poems and Ritual Orations</u>. New York:
Farrar, Straus and Giroux, 1971.

0790. Bird, Traveller. <u>The Path to Snowbird Mountain:</u>
<u>Cherokee Legends</u>. New York: Farrar, Straus and
Giroux, 1972.

Author is Cherokee, Shawnee and
Commanche. He is a freelance photographer;
however, there are no photos in book. The
stories are those he remembers his
grandfather and others telling.

0791. Birland, Cottie. <u>North American Indian Mythology</u>.
New York: Tudor Publishing Co., 1965.

0792. Blackburn, Thomas C., ed. <u>December's Child: A Book of</u>
<u>Chumash Oral Narratives</u>. Berkeley: University of
California Press, 1975, 1980.

Includes bibliography.

0793. Blackerby, A. W. <u>Tale of an Alaskan Whale</u>. Portland,
Oregon: Binford and Mort Publishers, n.d.

Indian legend of the Alaska Cedar
Killer. Whate and Thlinget.

0794. Bloodworth, William. "Neihardt, Momaday, and the Art
of Indian Autobiography." <u>Where the West Begins</u>.
Arthur R. Huseboe and William Geyer, eds. Sioux
Falls, South Dakota: Center for Western Studies Press,
1978, pp. 152-160.

0795. Bloodworth, William. "Varieties of American Indian
Autobiography." <u>MELUS</u> 5 (Fall 1978):67-81.

0796. Bloomfield, Leonard. "Cree Tales." American Ethnological Society Publications, 16 (1934).

0797. Bloomfield, Leonard. Plains Cree Texts. (American Ethnological Society Publications Ser.: No. 16). Reprint of 1934 edition. New York: AMS Press, Inc., 1973.

0798. Bloomfield, Leonard. Sacred Stories of the Sweet Grass Cree. Reprint of 1930 edition. New York: AMS Press, Inc., 1974.

0799. Boas, Franz. "Abstract Character of Keres Tales." Proceedings International Congress of Americanists, 20 (1922) : 223.

0800. Boas, Franz. Bella Bella Tales. Reprint of 1932 edition. New York: Kraus Reprint Co., 1970.

0801. Boas, Franz. Chinook Texts. Bureau of American Ethnology Bulletin, No. 20 (1894).

0802. Boas, Franz. Kathlamet Texts. Bureau of American Ethnology Bulletin, No. 26 (1901).

0803. Boas, Franz. Keresan Texts. (American Ethnological Society Publications: No. 8). Reprint of 1928 edition. New York: AMS Press, Inc., 1973.

0804. Boas, Franz. Kwakiutl Tales. (Columbia University Contributions to Anthropology: No. 2). Reprint of 1910 edition. New York: AMS Press, 1970.

0805. Boas, Franz. Kwakiutl Tales: New Series. 2 vols. (Columbia University Contributions to Anthropology: No. 26). Reprint of 1943 edition. New York: AMS Press, Inc., 1979.

0806. Boas, Franz. The Mythology of the Bella Coola Indians. (Jesup North Pacific Expedition Publications: Vol. 1, Part 2). Reprint of 1898 edition. New York: AMS Press, Inc., 1973.

0807. Boas, Franz. Race, Language and Culture. New York: Macmillan, 1940.

        Contains eight essays on Native American Literature written between 1891 and 1925.

0808. Boas, Franz, ed. Bella Bella Texts. Columbia University Contributions to Anthropology, Vol. 5. New York: Columbia University Press, 1928; New York: AMS Press, 1969.

Bella Bella tales as narrated by Willy
Gladstone, Bella Bella Indian, in both Bella
Bella and English.

0809. Boas, Franz, ed. Folk Tales of Salishan and Sahaptim Tribes. Tait, J. A. et al, translators. Lancaster, PA: American Folklore Society, 1917; reprint edition, New York: Kraus Reprint, 1971.

0810. Boas, Franz, and Chamberlain, (no first name). "Kutenai Tales and Texts." Bulletin Bureau of American Ethnology, No. 59 (1918); reprint East St. Claire Shores, MI: Scholarly Press, n.d.

0811. Boatright, Mody C., ed. The Sky Is My Tipi. Texas Folklore Society Publications, 22 (1949); reprint edition, Dallas: Southern Methodist University Press, 1966.

Legends from Kiowa-Apache and Apache by
J. G. McAlister, J. Frank Dobie, and others.

0812. Bodiroga, Ronald, compiler. "Apache." Vol. I. Bethesda, MD: EDRS, ED 091 124, n.d.

0813. Bodiroga, Ronald, Compiler. "Apache." Vol. II. Bethesda, MD: EDRS, ED 091 125, n.d.

0814. Bonnin, Gertrude. American Indian Stories. Reprint of 1921 edition. Glorieta, New Mexico: Rio Grande Press, Inc., 1983.

0815. Borland, H. G. Rocky Mountain Tipi Tales. n.p.: n.p., 1924.

0816. Bouchard, Randy, and Kennedy, Dorothy, eds. Lillooet Stories. Sound Heritage 6, No. 1 (1977).

0817. Bower, Donald E. "The Native American: A Changing Perspective." American West, 10 (1973) : 48, 63.

0818. Boyd, Maurice and Pauahty, Linn. Kiowa Voices: Myths, Legends, and Folktales, Vol. II. Worcester, Donald and Pattie, Jane, eds. (Kiowa Voices Series). Fort Worth, TX: Texas Christian University Press, 1983.

0819. Boyer, L. Bryce. Childhood and Folklore: A Psychoanalytic Study of Apache Personality. n.p.: Library of Psychological Anthropology, 1979.

0820. Brandon, William. "American Indian Literature." Indian Historian, 4 (Summer 1971) : 53-55.

Argues the greatness of Indian
literature; cites several collections of
Indian literature as examples.

0821. Brandon, William. <u>The Magic World, American Indian
Songs and Poems</u>. New York: William Morrow and Co.,
Inc., 1971.

A new collection taken from old
collections.

0822. Bright, William. "Literature: Written and Oral." The
1981 Georgetown University Round Table on Languages
and Linguistics, Georgetown, Washington, D.C., pp.
271-283.

0823. Brinton, Daniel G. <u>Aboriginal American Authors</u>.
Philadelphia: n.p., 1883.

0824. Brinton, Daniel G., ed. <u>Library of American
Aboriginal Literature</u>. Philadelphia: 1882-1890. 8
vols. Reprint edition, New York: AMS Press, 1970.

This set of books includes translations
from Delaware, Iroquois, Creek, Nahuatl and
Maya. Several volumes in the series are
cited separately below.

0825. Brinton, Daniel G., ed. <u>Ancient Nahuatl Poetry</u>.
Library of Aboriginal American Literature Series, 7
(1890); reprint edition, New York: AMS Press, 1971.

0826. Brinton, Daniel G., ed. <u>The Annals of the Cakchiquel</u>
Library of Aboriginal American Literature Series, 6
(1885); reprint edition, New York: AMS Press, 1970.

0827. Brinton, Daniel G., ed. <u>The Comedy Ballet of
Guequence</u>. Library of Aboriginal American Literature
Series, 3 (1883); reprint edition, New York: AMS
Press, 1970.

0828. Brinton, Daniel G., ed. <u>The Lenape and Their Legends</u>.
Library of Aboriginal American Literature Series, 5
(1884); reprint edition, New York: AMS Press, 1970.

0829. Brinton, Daniel G., ed. <u>The Maya Chronicles</u>. Library
of Aboriginal American Literature Series, 1 (1882);
reprint edition, New York: AMS Press, 1970.

0830. Brinton, Daniel G., ed. <u>The Myths of the New World:
A Treatise on the Symbolism and Mythology of the Red
Race in America</u>. Americana Series, No. 37 (1876);
reprint Westport, CT: Greenwood Press, Inc., 1962;
New York: Haskell House Publishers, Inc., 1969; East
St. Clair Shores, MI: Scholarly Press, 1972; Detroit,
MI: Gale Research Co., 1974; in paperback as <u>Myths of</u>

the New World Indians.   Blauvelt, NY: Steinerbooks,
1976.

Listings of this work vary and are a bit
confusing.   Apparently it first appeared
under this title in 1868. Another version
then was published in 1876, and possibly
another in 1896. Since then a number of
reprint editions have been published.
Longwood Press reprinted the 1868 version in
1979.

0831. Brinton, Daniel G., ed. Rig Veda Americanus. Library
of Aboriginal American Literature Series, 8 (1890);
reprint edition, New York: AMS Press, 1971.

0832. Bromley, A. "Renegade Wants the Word: Contemporary
Native American Poetry." Literary Review 23 (Spring
1980): 413-421.

0833. Brotherston, Gordon. Image of the New World: The
American Continent Portrayed in Native Texts. New
York: Thames and Hudson, 1982.

Deals with native texts in native
script. Discusses how native script may be
read. Includes translations of pictographs,
ideograms, and others. Some 118 documentary
texts from the literature of the natives of
the Western Hemsiphere. Four maps, six
tables. Bibliography.

0834. Brown, Dee. Teepee Tales of the American Indian. New
York: Holt, Rinehart and Winston, 1979.

0835. Brown, Dorothy M. "Indian Tree Myths and Legends."
Wisconsin Archaeologist, Vol. 19, No. 2 (1938): 30-36.

0836. Brown, Joseph Epes. The Sacred Pipe: Black Elk's
Account of the Seven Rites of the Oglala Sioux.
Norman: University of Oklahoma Press, 1953; paper
Baltimore: Penguin Books, 1971.

0837. Brown, Joseph Epes. Spiritual Legacy of the American
Indian. Wallingford, PA: Pendle Hill Publications,
1964.

0838. Brown, Lisette. Tales of Sea Foam. Healdsburg, CA:
Naturegraph Publishers, 1971.

Grades 6 up.

0839. Brown, Vinson. Voices of Earth and Sky. Healdsburg,
CA: Naturegraph Publishers, 1976.

0840. Bruhac, Joseph, intro. by. Songs from This Earth on
Turtle's Back: An Anthology of Poetry by American

Indian Writers.   Greenfield Center, NY: Greenfield
Review Press, 1982.

0841. Brundage, Burr C. *The Phoenix of the Western World:*
Quetzalcoatl and the Sky Religion. Civilization of
the American Indian Series, 160. Norman: University
of Oklahoma Press, 1981.

0842. Brunson, Olive. "Some Indian Legends." *Pioneer*
History of North Lincoln County Oregon, v. 1. North
Lincoln Pioneer and Historical Association.
McMinnville, Oregon: Telephone Register Publishing
Co., 1951.

0843. Bruseth, Nels. *Indian Stories and Legends*.
Fairfield, WA: Ye Galleon Press, 1977.

0844. Budd, Lillian. *Full Moons: Indian Legends of the*
Seasons. New York: Rand, McNally and Co., 1969, 1971.

        One source recommends use grades K-8,
    another grades 4-6.

0845. Buller, Galen. "Commanche Oral Narratives." Ph. D.
Dissertation. Lincoln: University of Nebraska, 1977.

0846. Buller, Galen. "New Interpretations of Native
American Literature: A Survival Technique." *Indian*
Culture and Research Journal 4:1-2 (1980) : 165-177.

        Uses examples from works of several
    Native American Writers including Momaday,
    Silko, and Deloria to discuss five unique
    elements in American Indian literature:
    reverence for words, dependence on a sense of
    place, sense of ritual, affirmation of the
    need for community, and a significantly
    different world view.

0847. Bunnell, Clarence. *The Legends of the Klickitats*.
n.p.: n.p., 1935.

0848. Bunzel, Ruth. *Zuni Ritual Poetry*. 47th Annual Report
of the Bureau of Ethnology. Washington, D.C., 1932,
pp. 613-835.

0849. Bunzel, Ruth. *Zuni Texts*. Publications of the
American Ethnological Society, Vol. 15. New York:
Stechert, 1933.

0850. Bureau of American Ethnology, Smithsonian
Institution. *The Annual Bureau of American Ethnology*
Reports, 1-48. (Washington, D.C., 1881-1933); *Bureau*
of American Ethnology Bulletins. (Washington, D.C.,
1887 to date); and earlier *Introduction*, *Miscellaneous*
Publications and *Contributions*.

These   include   collections   of   American
Indian   tales,   songs,   myths,   legends,   and
poems.

0851. Burland,   Cottie   A.   <u>North American Indian Mythology</u>.
Feltham,   Middlesex,   England: The   Hamlyn   Publishing
Group,   Ltd.,   1968.

Describes   pre-historic   beliefs   of
natives from Arctic Eskimos to Navaho.

0852. Burlin,   Natalie   (Curtis).   See Curtis, Natalie Burlin
in this section.

0853. Burton,   Jimalee.   <u>Indian   Heritage,   Indian   Pride:
Stories   That   Touched   My   Life</u>.   Norman: University of
Oklahoma Press, 1981.

0854. Callaway,   Sydney   M.   and   Witherspoon,   Gary.
<u>Grandfather   Stories   of   the   Navahos</u>.   Rough   Rock,   AZ:
Navajo Curriculum Center Press, 1968.

Examples   of   stories   grandfathers   told   to
children.

0855. Campbell,   Diana.   <u>Teaching   Guide   for   Indian
Literature,   Vol.   I</u>.   Rough   Rock,   AZ: Navajo
Curriculum Center Press, 1983.

Grades 4-8.

0856. Campbell,   Joseph.   <u>The   Masks   of   God: Primitive
Mythology</u>.   New York: Viking, 1959.

A psychological approach to mythology.

0857. Canfield,   William   W.   <u>The   Legends of the Iroquois</u>.
Empire   State   Historical   Publications   Series, No. 93
(1902);   reprint   Port   Washington, NY: Kennikat Press,
1971.

0858. Canonage,   Elliott.   <u>Commanche Texts</u>.   Publications in
Linguistics   and   Related   Fields Series, No. 1.   Dallas,
Texas: Summer   Institute   of   Linguistics, 1958.

Available   in   paperback   and   on
microfiche.

0859. Capps,   Walter   H.   <u>Seeing   with   the   Native   Eye:
Contributions   to   the   Study   of   Native   American
Religion</u>.   New   York: Harper and Row Publishers, Inc.,
1976.

0860. Carpenter,   (no first name).   <u>Anerca</u> n.p.: n.d.

Eskimo poetry.

0861. Carroll, Raymonde. *Nukuoro Stories*. Nukuoro Texts Series, 1 (1980); Ann Arbor, MI: University Microfilms International, 1980.

0862. Cash, Joseph H. and Hoover, Herbert T., eds. *To Be an Indian: An Oral History*. New York: Holt, Rinehart and Winston, 1971.

    Indians interviewed in 1960's from many tribes on "things that guide the people."

0863. Caswell, Helen. *Shadows from the Singing House*. n.p. : n.d.

    Ancient Eskimo folk tales.

0864. Chafetz, Henry. *Thunderbirds and Other Stories*. New York: Pantheon, 1964.

    Three stories from mythology of American Indian.

0865. Chamberlain, Alexander F. "Mythology of Indian Stocks North of Mexico." *Journal of American Folklore* Vol. 18, No. 69 (April-June 1905): 111-122.

0866. Channing, Walter. "Essay on American Language and Literature (1815)." *American Indian Culture and Research*, Vol. 1, No. 4 (1976) : 3-6.

    The thrust of this essay is that American Indian oral literature is probably the nearest thing to a national literature in America.

0867. Chapin, Gretchen. "A Navajo Myth." *New Mexico Anthropologist* Vol. 5, No. 4 (1940): 63-67.

0868. Chapman, Abraham, ed. *Literature of the American Indian: Views and Interpretations. A Gathering of Indian Memories, Symbolic Contexts, and Literary Criticism*. Introduction by Abraham Chapman. New York: New American Library, 1975.

    This collection of 26 essays brings together "two currents of thinking and expression: first, traditional and contemporary Indian views and interpretations of the Indian cultures, literature, and symbolism from older and recent writings . . . Secondly is included a historical sequence of older and contemporary non-Indian interpretations of Indian literature and the cultures out of which it grew by American writers and anthropologists outside the Indian cultures . . . ."

0869. <u>Cheyenne   Short   Stories: A   Collection   of   Ten</u>
      <u>Traditional   Stories   of   the   Cheyenne.</u> (Cheyenne and
      English).   Billings: Montana   Council   for   Indian
      Education, 1977.

                Grade 2 up.

0870. Chief Eagle, Dallas. <u>Winter Count</u>. Colorado Springs,
      CO: Denton-Berkeland   Printing   Co.,   1967;   reprint
      edition, Denver: Golden Bell Press, 1968; reprint
      edition, Boulder, CO: Johnson Publishing Co., 1968.

                Novel set against the Indian relocation
            attempts   of   the   1870's and 1880's that
            resulted in Wounded Knee.

0871. Chief   Eaglewing. <u>Peek-wa Stories; Ancient Indian</u>
      <u>Legends   of   California.</u>   San   Francisco: George
      Lithograph Co., 1938.

                Karuk. Grade level 4-6.

0872. Clark,   Cora, ed. <u>Pomo Indian Myths and Some of Their</u>
      <u>Sacred Meanings</u>. Farmingdale, NY: Brown Book Co.,
      n.d.

0873. Clark, Ella. <u>Guardian Spirit Quest</u> Indian Culture
      Series.   Billings: Montana   Council   for   Indian
      Education, 1974.

                Grades 5-12.

0874. Clark, Ella Elizabeth. <u>Indian Legends of Canada</u>.
      Toronto: McClelland and Stewart, 1960.

                About 90 examples, arranged by theme, of
            myths,   personal narratives, and historical
            lore, from 30 tribes.

0875. Clark,   Ella   Elizabeth. <u>Indian Legends from the</u>
      <u>Northern Rockies</u>. Civilization of the American Indian
      Series, no. 6. Norman: University of Oklahoma Press,
      1966, 1977.

                Over 100 tribal traditions and legends
            obtained   directly from Indians as well as
            from printed and manuscript sources arranged
            by language families. Tribes represented: Nez
            Perce, Coeur d'Alene, Flathead, Kalispell,
            Kutenai, Shoshone, Bannock, Arapahoe, Gros
            Ventre, Blackfeet, Assiniboine, Crow, Sioux.

0876. Clark, Ella Elizabeth. <u>Indian Legends of the Pacific</u>
      <u>Northwest</u>. Berkeley: University of California Press,
      1953.

About 100 tales collected from Indians, govt. documents, old periodicals, old histories, and reports of anthropologists and folklorists. No index. Legends arranged by theme; originating tribe identified in table of contents.

0877. Clark, Ella Elizabeth. "Indian Story-telling of Old in the Pacific Northwest." Oregon Historical Society Quarterly Vol. 54, No. 2 (June 1953): 91-101.

0878. Clark, Ella, ed. In the Beginning. Billings, MT: Montana Council for Indian Education, 1977.

Grade 5 up.

0879. Clark, LaVerne Harrell. "Introduction to the Hopi Indians and Their Mythology." Arizona English Bulletin 13 (Spring 1971) : 1-14.

0880. Clements, William M. "Faking the Pumpkin: On Jerome Rothenberg's Literary Offenses." Western American Literature 16:3 (November 1981): 193-204.

0881. Clutesi, George. Son of Raven, Son of Deer. Sidney, B.C., Canada: Gray's Publishing, Ltd., 1970; Seattle: Superior Publishing Co., 1967.

Twelve stories for grades 5-8. Tales by elders of Nootka tribe retold for children.

0882. Coffer, William E. Spirits of the Sacred Mountains: Creation Stories of the American Indian. New York: Van Nos Reinhold Co., 1978.

0883. Coffer, William E. Where Is the Eagle? New York: Van Nos Reinhold Co., 1981.

0884. Coffin, Tristram P., ed. Indian Tales of North America: An Anthology for the Adult Reader. American Folklore Society Bibliographical and Special Series, No. 13. Austin: University of Texas Press, 1961.

45 tales.

0885. Coleman, Sister Bernard. Ojibwa Myths and Legends. Wayzata, MN: Ross and Haines, 1962.

A cultural study using traditional stories which reflect Ojibwa beliefs.

0886. Compton, Margaret and Bjorklund, Lorence F. American Indian Fairy Tales. New York: Dodd, Mead and Co., 1970.

Primary-grade 7.

0887. "Continuity and Change in American Indian Oral Literature." Association of Departments of English (New York) Bulletin No. 75 (Summer 1983): 43-46.

0888. Converse, Harriet. Myths and Legends of the New York State Iroquois. Reprint of 1908 edition. Detroit: Gale Research Co., 1975.

0889. Cook, Liz. "American Indian Literatures in Servitude." Indian Historian, 10 (Winter 1977) : 3-6.

        Citing numerous examples, this article argues that Native American literature cannot be taught from a "western" perspective. Decries academics who treat native oral literature as a stage in the progression toward literacy. Urges consideration of Indian literature in context and skepticism of translations.

0890. Cooke, Grace. Sun Men of the Americas. Marina Del Ray, CA: De Vorss and Co., n.d.

0891. Cornplanter, Jesse J. Legends of the Longhouse. Empire State Historical Publications Series, No. 24. Washington, NY: Ira J. Friedman, Inc., 1938; reprint edition, Port Washington, NY: Kennikat Press Corp., 1963.

        Myths and legends of the Seneca.

0892. Costello, Joseph A. Siwash: Their Life, Legends, and Tales. Seattle: Shorey Publications, 1895.

0893. Costo, Rupert. "How the Mockingbird Got Its Song." Weewish Tree, 1 (Spring 1972) : 13-20.

        Cahiulla.

0894. Costo, Rupert, ed. Indian Voices: The First Convocation of American Indian Scholars. San Francisco: Indian Historian Press, 1970.

        Articles by various Indian scholars.

0895. Costo, Rupert. "Review of Seven Arrows by Hyemeyohsts Storm." Indian Historian 5:2 (Summer 1972) : 41-42.

        Claims Seven Arrows "falsifies and desecrates the traditions and religion of the Northern Cheyenne, which it purports to describe." Describes reaction of Cheyenne people at Lame Deer (on Cheyenne Reservation in Montana) as "disbelief and anger." Offers some examples of author's distortions and innacuracies.

0896. Costo, Rupert. "Song of the Quail." <u>Weewish Tree</u>, 1 (November 1971) : 11-13.

0897. Dale, Edward E. <u>Tales of the Tepee</u>. Boston: D. C. Heath and Co., 1920.

0898. David, Jay, ed. <u>The American Indian</u>. New York: William Morrow & Co., 1972.

        Prose and poetry of American Indians.

0899. Day, A. Grove. <u>The Sky Clears: Poetry of the American Indians</u>. New York: Macmillan Co., 1951; reprint edition, Lincoln: University of Nebraska Press, 1951, 1964, 1968, 1970; reprint of 1951 edition, Westport, CT: Greenwood Press, 1983.

        Over 200 poems and lyrics from some 40 tribes. "Primarily a book to be read for pleasure. . . first consideration has been to select those translations which were literary rather than literal." Poems classified by geographical culture areas. First 35 pages are a discussion of types of Indian poetry, composition, sources, alien intrusion, translation, study of Indian poetry. Includes 211 item bibliography on North American Indian poetry.

0900. De Angulo, Jaime. <u>Indian Tales</u>. New York: A. A. Wyn, Inc., 1953; New York: Hill and Wang Inc., 1962.

        Author lived among Pitt River Indians of California for 40 years, transcribed some animal legends into tales. Some are literal translations, some totally De Angulo's fiction, some based partly on legends.

0901. DeFlyer, Joseph Eugene. "Partition Theory: Patterns and Partitions of Consciousness in Selected Works of American and American Indian Authors." Ph. D. Dissertation. Lincoln: University of Nebraska, 1974.

0902. De Huff, Elizabeth W. "'The Bear and the Deer' Taos Myth." <u>El Palacio</u>, 31:1 (1931): 3.

0903. De Huff, Elizabeth W. "'The Greedy Fox' Taos Myth." <u>El Palacio</u>, 31:2 (1931): 20.

0904. De Huff, Elizabeth, W.. "'Infidelity' Taos Myth." <u>El Palacio</u>, 31 : 13 (1931) : 200.

0905. De Huff, Elizabeth W. "Myths from San Juan, Acoma, Cochiti and Picuris." <u>El Palacio</u>, 11 : 11 (1921) : 140.

0906. De Huff, Elizabeth W. "Myths from San Juan, Taos,
Seama and Picuris." El Palacio, 11 : 7 (1921) : 86.

0907. De Huff, Elizabeth W. "The Navajo Flood Legend." New
Mexico Magazine, 11 (March 1933) : 18-19, 50-51.

0908. De Huff, Elizabeth, W.. "Taos Myths." El Palacio, 16
: 4 (1924) : 51.

0909. De Huff, Elizabeth, W.. "'The Venomous Snake Girl'
San Ildefonso Myth." El Palacio, 31 : 5 (1931) : 73.

0910. De Huff, Elizabeth, W. "'The Witch' Hopi Myth." El
Palacio, 31 : 3 (1931) : 37.

0911. De Huff, Elizabeth, W.. "Witch Myths from Tsia and
San Juan." El Palacio, 11 : 8 (1921) : 98.

0912. De Huff, Elizabeth, W.. "'Yellow House People' Taos
Myth." El Palacio, 30 : 23-24 (1931) : 269.

0913. De Huff, Elizabeth W., and Guinn, Homer. From Desert
and Pueblo; Five Authentic Navajo and Tewa Indian
Songs. Boston: n.p., 1924.

0914. Deloria, Ella. Dakota Texts. American Ethnological
Society Publications, 14. New York: G. E. Stechert
and Co., 1932; reprint edition, New York: AMS Press,
1974.

        Probably the most recent edition of this
    is an edited version put out by Dakota Press
    (See below). Teton Sioux tales from Standing
    Rock, Pine Ridge, and Rosebud Reservations
    transcribed   in   Sioux   direct   from
    storytellers. Each tale is accompanied by
    author's translation with notes on grammar
    and customs.

0915. Deloria, Ella. Dakota Texts. Picotle, Agnes and
Pavich, Paul, eds. Vermillion, S. Dakota: Dakota
Press, 1978.

0916. Denny, Walter A. Stories from the Old Ones. Gray,
Harold E. and Scott, Patria, eds. Havre, MT: Bearpaw
Books, 1979.

0917. De Pillis, Mario S. "Folklore and the American West."
Arizona and the West, 5 (1963) : 291-314.

0918. De Pisa, Diane. "A Sioux Poem of Power." Paper
Presented   at   the   Conference   on   Multi-ethnic
LIterature, Chicago State University, May 10, 1974.
Bethesda, MD: EDRS, ED 095 528, 1974.

        "An assessment of Black Elk's poetry

reveals that Indians' attitudes toward words
differ from ours."

0919. Dillingham, Peter. "The literature of the American
Indian." English Journal 62:1 (January 1973) : 37-41.

A brief critical survey designed for
high school teachers. Says, although
"standard anthologies of traditional American
Indian literature, Margaret Astrov's American
Indian Prose and Poetry (Capricorn) and G. W.
Cronyn's American Indian Poetry (Ballantine
Walden Editions), remain excellent sources
from which to draw supplementary material,
the translations are somewhat dated for use
in high school classes. William Brandon's
recently published anthology, The Magic
World: American Indian Songs and Poems
(Morrow), however, is a perfect text for
introducing high school students to the
lyricism and myth of traditional Indian
poetry. Brandon has a fine ear for the
translation as poem rather than ethnological
data, and a deep understanding of Indian
poetry as song. . . ." [For an opposing point
of view, contrast this article with that of
William Bevis (See above), "American Indian
Verse Translations."] Briefly describes a
number of other books of different
types--biography, poetry, fiction.

0920. Dillon, Leo and Diane. The Ring in the Prairie. New
York: The Dial Press, 1970.

A Shawnee legend.

0921. Dixon, (no first name). "Maidu Myths." American
Museum of Natural History Bulletin 17, Part 2 (1902):
33.

0922. Dobie, J. Frank, ed. Apache Gold and Yaqui Silver.
Boston: Little, Brown and Co., 1939.

0923. Dolch, Edward W. and Dolch, M. P. Lodge Stories.
Basic Vocabulary Series. Westport, CT: Garrard
Publishing Co., 1957.

Grades 1-6.

0924. Dolch, Edward W. and Dolch M. P. Navaho Stories.
Basic Vocabulary Series. Westport, CT: Garrard
Publishing Co., 1957.

Grades 1-6. Tales of how and what
different birds and animals mean.

0925. Dolch, Edward W. and Dolch, M. P. Pueblo Stories. Basic Vocabulary Series. Westport, CT: Garrard Publishing Co., 1956.

Grades 1-6.

0926. Dolch, Edward W. and Dolph M. P. Teepee Stories. Basic Vocabulary Series. Westport, CT: Garrard Publishing Co., 1956.

Grades 1-6.

0927. Dolch, Edward W. and Dolch, M. P. Wigwam Stories. Basic Vocabulary Series. Westport, CT: Garrard Publishing Co., 1956.

Grades 1-6.

0928. Dorris, Michael. "Native American Literature in an Ethnohistorical Context." College English 41 (October 1979):147-162.

0929. Dorsey, George A. The Mythology of the Wichita. Reprint of 1904 edition. New York: AMS Press, Inc., n.d.

0930. Dorsey, George A. The Pawnee: Mythology. Reprint of 1906 edition. New York: AMS Press, Inc., n.d.

0931. Dorsey, George A. Traditions of the Caddo. Reprint of 1905 edition. New York: AMS Press, Inc., 1974.

0932. Dorsey, George A. Traditions of the Osage. Reprint of 1904 edition. New York: AMS Press, Inc., n.d.

0933. Dorsey, George (with Murie, James R., Pawnee). Traditions of the Skidi Pawnee. Memoirs of the American Folklore Society, 8. Boston: Houghton Mifflin Co., 1904; reprint edition, New York: Kraus Reprint, 1970.

Pawnee tales about tribal origins, rituals, medicine men and encounters with animals.

0934. Dorson, Richard. "Comic Indian Anecdotes." Southern Folklore Quarterly 10 (1945):113-128.

0935. Dorson, Richard. "New England Popular Tales and Legends." Ph. D. Diss. Cambridge: Harvard University, 1943; under the title Jonathan Draws the Long Bow. Cambridge: Harvard University Press, 1946.

Contains brief section on Indian legends.

0936. Dubois, (no first name). "Diegueno Myths and the Mohave." *Proceedings*, International Congress of Americanists, 2:15 (1906): 129.

0937. Dubois, (no first name), and Dematracopoulou, (no first name). "Wintu Myths." University of California *Publications in American Archaeology and Ethnology* 28:5 (1931).

0938. Dundes, Alan. *The Morphology of North American Indian Folktales*. Folklore Fellows Communications, vol. 81, No. 195 (1964).

0939. Dutton, Bertha P. and Olin, Caroline. *Myths and Legends of the Indian Southwest*. Santa Barbara, CA: Bellerophon Books, 1978.

0940. Duxbury, William C. "A Legend of the Navajos." *Cosmopolitan* 22 (November 1896) : 73+.

0941. Earl, Guy C. *Indian Songs and Legends*. Glendale, CA: Arthur H. Clark, 1980.

0942. Earring, Monica F. *Prairie Legends*. Indian Culture Series. Billings: Montana Council for Indian Education, 1978.

0943. Eastman, Charles Alexander. *Red Hunters and the Animal People*. New York: Harper and Brothers, 1904.

      Sioux stories based on experiences and observations of hunters. Fables, songs, life stories of animals according to legend.

0944. Eastman, Charles. *The Soul of an Indian: An Interpretation*. Reprint of 1911 edition, Lincoln: University of Nebraska Press, 1980.

0945. Eastman, Charles A. and Eastman, Elaine Goodale. *Smokey Days Wigwam Evenings: Indian Stories Retold*. Boston: Little Brown and Co., 1924.

      Short tales focusing on animals each of which ends with a moral (in Italics).

0946. Eastman, Charles A., and Eastman, Elaine Goodale. *Wigwam Evenings: Animal Tales*. Boston: Little Brown and Co., 1930.

0947. Easton, Robert. "Humor of the American Indian." *Mankind* 2 (September 1970): 37-41, 72-73.

      Some examples of Indian humor from history and literature.

0948. Eberman, Willis. *Clatsop Drumbeats: Poetry*. Indian

Culture Series.   Billings: Montana Council for Indian
Education, 1973.

0949. Eddy, Lewis H. "A Navajo Myth." Arizona Magazine n.v.
(August 1893).

0950. Edminster,   Grace   Thompson. Four American Indian
Songs. New York: Independent Music Publishers, 1946.

0951. Ehanni   Ohunkakan.   Curriculum Materials Resource
Unit. Bethesda, MD: EDRS, ED 073 860, n.d.

        197 p. Oglala Sioux stories for ninth
    graders. ERIC source indicated this was not
    available from EDRS, but was available for
    loan from ERIC/CRESS, Box 3AP, Las Cruces,
    New Mexico 88003.

0952. Ehrlich, Clara Hilderman. "Tribal Culture in Crow
Mythology."   Ph.   D.   Diss.   New   York: Columbia
University, 1939.

        "Compares life of Crow as reflected in
    myths with that reported in ethnographies."

0953. Espey, David B.   "Endings in Contemorary American
Indian Fiction." Western American Literature 13
(Summer 1978): 133-139.

0954. Espinosa,   Aurelio   M. "Pueblo Indian Folktales."
Journal of American Folklore (January-June 1936):
69-133.

0955. Essene, Frank J., Jr. "A Comparative Study of Eskimo
Mythology." Ph. D. Diss. Berkeley: University of
California, 1947.

        "Compares east, west and central Eskimo
    with Indians of interior Canada, Northwest
    Coast tribes and northeast Asiatic peoples."

0956. Evans, Cecelia Marie. "Comparative Indian Mythology."
MA Thesis. Denver: University of Denver, 1937.

0957. Evers, Larry. "A Response: Going along with the
Story." American Indian Quarterly 5:1 (February 1979)
: 71-75.

        According to Evers, Leslie Marmon Silko
    "demonstrates that writing American Indian
    and being American Indian is a matter of
    process rather than ethnographic and
    historical fact." Claims members of Indian
    communities are shaped by the telling of
    stories and shape others by telling stories.

0958. Evers, Larry, ed. The South Corner of Time: Hopi, Navajo, Papago, and Yaqui Tribal Literature. Sun Tracks: An American Indian Literary Magazine, 6. Tucson, AZ: Suntracks, 1980; Tucson: University of Arizona Press, 1981.

> 240 p. Includes translations from Hopi, Navajo, Papago and Yaqui languages as well as first language texts in each.

0959. Evers, Lawrence J. "Further Survivals of Coyote." Western American Literature 10 (1975):233-236.

0960. Evers, Lawrence J. "The Literature of the Omaha." Ph. D. Dissertation. Lincoln: University of Nebraska, 1972.

0961. Evers, Lawrence J. "Native American Oral Literatures in the College English Classroom: An Omaha Example." College English 36 (February 1975):649-662.

0962. Farb, Peter. "Review of Literature of the American Indian by Thomas E. Sanders and Walter W. Peck." Natural History 82:8 (October 1973) : 88-92.

0963. Federal Writers' Project, South Dakota. Legends of the Mighty Sioux. Reprint of 1941 edition, New York: AMS Press, n.d.

0964. Feldman, Susan. The Story Telling Stone: Myths and Tales of the American Indians. New York: Dell Publishing Co., 1965.

> Groups 52 tales by type in three categories: In the Days of creation; trickster; tales heroes, supernatural journeys and other folktales. Each tale identified by tribe; 29 tribes represented. Bibliography.

0965. Felling, Mary E. "History of Legends of the Indians of Northwest Missouri." MA Thesis. Greeley: University of Northern Colorado (Colorado State College of Education), 1938.

> Sac-Fox, Iowa.

0966. Field, Edward. Eskimo Songs and Stories. New York: Delacorte, 1973.

0967. Fields, Kenneth. "Seventh Wells: Native American Harmonies." Parnassus 2 (Spring-Summer 1974):172-198.

0968. Filmore, John C. "Songs of the Navajos." Land of Sunshine 5:5 (1896) : 238-241.

0969. Finger, Charles J. <u>Tales from Silver Lands</u>. Reprint
      of 1924 edition, Garden City, NY: Doubleday, 1970.

0970. Fisher, Alice Poindexter.   "The   Transportation of
      Tradition: A Study of Zitkala Sa and Mourning Dove,
      Two Transitional American Indian Writers."   Ph. D.
      Diss. New York: City University of New York, 1979.

0971. Fisher, Anne B. <u>Stories California Indians Told</u>.
      Berkeley, CA: Parnassus Press, 1957; Sacramento:
      California State Department of Education, 1965.

            Grades 4-6.

0972. Fishler,   Stanley A. <u>In the Beginning: A Navaho
      Creation   Myth</u>.   Utah Anthropological Papers, 13.
      Reprint of 1953 edition, New York: AMS Press, n.d.

0973. Fletcher, Alice C. <u>Indian Story and Song from North
      America</u>.   Reprint of 1900 edition. New York: Johnson
      Reprint Corporation, 1970.

0974. Fontana, Bernard L.,ed. <u>Look to the Mountain Top</u>.
      n.p., n.d.

0975. Forbes, Jack D., ed. <u>Nevada Indians Speak</u>. Reno:
      University of Nevada Press, 1967; Bethesda, MD: EDRS,
      ED 048 966, n.d.

            Anthology   of Indian works reflecting
      attitudes of Nevada Indians, commencing 1820.

0976. Forbes, Jack D. "Voices from Native America." <u>The
      Indian   in America's Past</u>.   Englewood Cliffs, NJ:
      Prentice-Hall, 1964, pp. 54-73.

            Excerpts from speeches and statements by
      American Indians from 1609-1963 on various
      subjects.

0977. Fox, Hugh. "Mythology of the Ancient Tlingit." <u>Indian
      Historian</u> 4 (Winter 1971) : 12-15.

0978. Frachtenberg, Leo J. <u>Alsea Myths and Texts</u>. Bureau
      of American Ethnology Bulletin 67 (1920).

0979. Frachtenberg, Leo J. <u>Coos Texts</u>. Columbia University
      Contributions to Anthropology, 1. New York: Columbia
      University Press, 1913; reprint edition, New York: AMS
      Press, 1969.

            Coos mythology narrated by Coos Indian
      Jim Buchanan presented in Coos and English
      texts.

0980. Frachtenberg, Leo J. <u>Lower Umpqua Texts and Notes on</u>

Kusan Dialects. Columbia University Contributions to Anthropology Series, 4. New York: Columbia University Press, 1914; reprint edition New York: AMS Press, Inc., 1969.

0981. Frachtenberg, Leo, and Farrand, Livingston. "Shasta and Athapascan Myths from Oregon." Journal of American Folklore 28 (1915):207-242.

0982. Fraser, F. The Bear Who Stole the Chinook. n.p.: Macmillan of Canada, 1967.

Grades 5-8. Legends and folktales of Blackfoot.

0983. Freed, Ruth Helen Anderson. "An Analysis of the Literary Significance of Certain Legends of the Yosimite Indians." MA Thesis. Los Angeles: University of Southern California, 1948.

Southern Miwok.

0984. Freeman, Robert. For Indians Only. Escondido, CA: Brinck Lithography Co., n.d.

Indian joke book; cited at least once as "the first Indian joke book."

0985. Funk and Wagnalls Standard Dictionary of Folklore, Mythology and Legend. Leach, Maria, ed. New York: Funk and Wagnalls, 1949-50, 2 vols.

Includes terms and phrases relating to American Indian folklore and mythology.

0986. Gaddis, Vincent H. American Indian Myths and Mysteries. Radnor, PA: Chilton Book Co., 1977.

0987. Garber, Clark M. Stories and Legends of the Bering Strait Eskimos. Reprint of 1940 edition, New York: AMS Press, n.d.

0988. Garrett, Roland. "The Nature of Language in Some Kiowa Folktales." Indian Historian 5:2 (Summer 1972) : 32-37, 42.

Expounds the idea that folk literature "sometimes expresses a profound sensitivity to the powers, subtleties, and varieties of language itself." Author says his aim "is to illustrate this principle through a detailed analysis of some folktales of the Kiowa Indians."

0989. Gatschet, A. S. "An Isleta Myth." American Philosophical Society Proceedings Vol. 29 (1891): 208.

0990. Gatschet, A. S. "A Migration Legend of the Creeks." *Library of Aboriginal American Literature* (1884) no. 4; reprint edition, New York: AMS Press, n.d.

> The title of the AMS Press edition is slightly different: *A Migration Legend of the Creek Indians*. Kraus Reprint offers a 2 vol. reprint of an 1888 edition called *Migration Legend of the Creek Indians with a Linguistic Historical and Ethnographic Introduction* (n.d.), possibly the same work.

0991. Geiogamah, Hanay. *New Native American Drama: Three Plays*. Huntsman, Jeffrey, ed. Norman: University of Oklahoma Press, 1980.

0992. Gerber, Will. *The Rings on West-Kew's Tail: Indian Legends of the Origin of the Sun, Moon, and Stars*. Indian Culture Series. Billings: Montana Council for Indian Education, 1973.

> Grades 3-9.

0993. Gerow, Bert Alfred. "Bloodclot Boy: An Historical and Stylistic Study of a North American Indian Hero Tale." Ph. D. Diss. Berkeley: University of California, 1950.

0994. Giddings, Ruth Warner. "Folk Literature of the Yaqui Indians." MA Thesis. Tucson: University of Arizona, 1945.

> Yaqui of Potam [Sonora], Pasqua and Barrio Libre [Arizona]. 64 tales; alien influence examined.

0995. Giddings, Ruth Warner. *Yaqui Myths and Legends*. Tucson: University of Arizona Press, 1959.

> 61 tales.

0996. Gillham, Charles E. *Medicine Men of Hooper Bay: More Tales from the Clapping Mountains of Alaska*. New York: The Macmillan Co., 1955.

> Intermediate grades.

0997. Gilmore, Melvin R. *Prairie Smoke*. Reprint of 1929 edition. New York: AMS Press, Inc., 1978.

0998. Gingras, Louis and Rainboldt, Jo. *Coyote and Kootenai*. Billings: Montana Council for Indian Education, 1977.

> Grades 2-6.

0999. Glass,   Paul. Songs and Stories of the North American
       Indians: With   Rhythm   Indications   for   Drum
       Accompaniment. New York: Grosset and Dunlap, 1968.

              Grades   1-3.   Yuma,   Mandan,   Sioux,
       Pawnee, Papago; songs, games, legends.

1000. Goddard,   Pliny E. Myths and Tales from the San Carlos
       Apache.   Reprint   of   1918   edition.   New   York: AMS
       Press, Inc., 1976.

1001. Gooderham, Kent, ed. I Am an Indian. n.p.: Dent,
       1969.

              Collection   of   Canadian   Indian
       writings--fiction, poetry, biography.

1002. Goodwin,   Grenville,   ed. Myths and Tales of the White
       Mountain Apache. Reprint of 1939 edition. Millwood,
       NY: Kraus Reprint, n.d.

1003. Gordon,   (no   first   name).   "Legends   of   Kitselas."
       University of Pennsylvania Museum Journal 9:1 (1918) :
       39.

1004. Gorman,   Howard.   Materials Prepared All or in Part as
       Result of Office of Education Small Research Grant OEG
       - 9-9-120076-0050 (057) to Navajo Community College.
       Bethesda, MD: EDRS, ED 062 053, 1971.

              Contains Navajo origin story variations.

1005. Graves,   Charles   Sumner.   Lore   and   Legends   of the
       Klamath River Indians.   Yreka, California: Press of
       the Times, 1929.

1006. Greasybear,   Charley   J. Songs. Trusky, A. Thomas and
       Crews, Judson, eds. Modern and Contemporary Poets of
       the West. Boise: Ahsahta Press, 1979.

1007. Gregory,   Jack and Strickland, Rennard. Creek Seminole
       Spirit   Tales.   Pensacola,   FL: Indian   Heritage
       Association, 1971.

1008. Grey,   Herman.   Tales from the Mohaves.   Norman:
       University of Oklahoma Press, 1971.

              A telling of tribal dreams.

1009. Gridley,   Marion E. Pawnee Hero Stories and Folktales.
       Lincoln: University of Nebraska Press, 1961.

1010. Griffis,   Joseph K. (Chief Tahan). Indian Story Circle
       Stories. Burlington, VT: Free Press Printing Co.,
       1928.

Stories heard by author (Osage) as he was growing up--Kiowa, Cherokee, Choctaw, Malecite.

1011. Gringhuis, Dirk. <u>Lore of the Great Turtle: Indian Legends of Mackinac Retold</u>. Mackinac Island, Maine: Mackinac Island State Park Commission, 1970.

1012. Grinnell, George Bird. <u>Blackfoot Lodge Tales</u>. Reprint of 1892 edition, Williamstown, MA: Corner House Publishers, 1972.

Also published as <u>Blackfoot Lodge Tales: The Story of a Native People</u>. Lincoln, University of Nebraska Press, 1962. Piegan, Siksika, Kainah.

1013. Grinnell, George Bird. <u>By Cheyenne Campfires</u>. New Haven: Yale University Press, 1926, 1962; Lincoln: University of Nebraska Press, 1972.

66 tales arranged in the major classes of "War Stories," "Stories of Mystery," "Hero Myths," and "Stories about Wihio, the Cheyenne trickster."

1014. Grinnell, George Bird. <u>Pawnee Hero Stories and Folk-Tales with Notes on the Origins, Customs and Character of the Pawnee People</u>. Lincoln: University of Nebraska Press, 1961.

1015. Gunn, Hubert. "How Rabbit Brought Fire." <u>Tawow</u> 1 (Summer 1970) : 22-23.

1016. Gunn, Hubert. "A Lamp to Read by." <u>Tawow</u> 1 (Summer 1970) : 18-20.

1017. Gunn, Hubert. "The Wolverine and the Rock." <u>Tawow</u> 1 (Summer 1970) : 21-22.

1018. Gunther, (no first name). "Klallem Folk Tales." University of Washington <u>Publications in Anthropology</u> 1:4 (1925).

1019. Gustafson, Anita and Kriney, Marilyn. <u>Monster Rolling Skull and Other Native American Tales</u>. New York: Harper and Row Publishers, Inc., 1980.

Grades 4-6.

1020. Hagner, Dorothy Childs. <u>Navajo Winter Nights</u>. New York: E. M. Hale and Co., 1938.

Grade 5. Stories told by Navajos, including folktales and myths.

1021. Haile, Rev. Berard, O.F.M. Legend of the Ghostway
Ritual.   Reprint of 1950 edition, New York: AMS Press,
n.d.

1022. Haile, Rev. Berard, O.F.M. Love-Magic and Butterfly
People: The Slim Curly version of the Ajjee and
Mothway Myths. Flagstaff: Museum of Northern Arizona,
1980.

1023. Haile,   Rev. Berard, O.F.M. Origin Legend of the
Navaho Enemy Way. (Yale University Publications in
Anthropology: No. 17). Reprint of 1938 edition. New
York: AMS Press, Inc., 1983.

1024. Haile, Rev. Berard, O.F.M. Origin Legend of the
Navajo Flintway. Reprint of 1943 edition. New York:
AMS Press, Inc., 1974.

1025. Haile, Rev. Berard, O.F.M. Short Coyote Stories.
Package 4, Folders A-D. n.p., n.d.

        Since Rev. Haile's works appear to have
    been initially published by the Museum of
    Northern Arizona, perhaps the description of
    this item refers to some method of cataloging
    their holdings of his works.

1026. Haile,   Rev.   Berard,   O.F.M. Waterway.   Lincoln:
University of Nebraska Press, 1981.

1027. Hakes, Judith Ann. "Elements of Social Culture in
Teton   Sioux Folk Tales." Ph. D. Diss.   Boulder:
University of Colorado, 1974.

1028. Hale, Janet Campbell. The Owl's Song. New York:
Doubleday, 1974.

        Novel.   Protagonist is 14 year-old boy
    in cultural conflict.

1029. Hamilton,   Charles   Everett,   ed. Cry of the
Thunderbird: The American Indian's Own Story. New
York: Macmillan, 1950.

        One to four-page excerpts from about
    100 speeches and writings of about 50
    American Indians.   The bibliography includes
    sections   entitled,   "Books and Pamphlets
    Written or Dictated by American Indians," and
    "American Indian Periodicals."

1030. Hansen, L. Taylor. He Walked the Americas. Amherst,
Wisconsin: Amherst Press, 1963.

1031. Hanson, Virginia. "Alabama in Legend and Lore." MA

Thesis. West Birmingham, Alabama: Birmingham-Southern
College, 1937.

Largely   concerned   with   place   names,
sources, poetry of Indian names. Section on
Indian legends.

1032. Harkey, Ira B., Jr. "Wolves, Kuspuks and 70 Below:
Alaskans and Alaska as Seen by Eskimo and Indian
Writers." The Indian Historian 5 (Fall 1972) : 13-17.

1033. Harrington, Isis. Told in the Twilight. New York: E.
P. Dutton, 1938.

Collection of Pueblo and Navajo stories.

1034. Harrington, John. Karuk Indian Myths. Smithsoian
Institution Bureau of American Ethnology Bulletin 107.
Washington, D.C.: U. S. Government Printing Office,
1932; reprint edition, East St. Clair Shore MI:
Scholarly Press, Inc., n.d.

Bilingual   Indian myths of California
Indian tribe with phonetic key.

1035. Harrington, Mark R. Religion and Ceremonies of the
Lenape. Reprint of 1921 edition, New York: AMS Press,
n.d.

1036. Harrington, (no first name). "Hopi Myth 'The
Good-bringing' from Oraibi-Isis." New Mexico
Historical Review 6:2 (1931):227.

1037. Harrington, (no first name). "Zuni Ruins and
Legends." Southwest Museum The Masterkey 3:1 (1929):5.

1038. Harris, Christie. Once Upon a Totem. Toronto,
Ontario: McClelland and Stewart, Ltd., 1963; New York:
Atheneum, 1963.

Grade 6. Five legends of Indians of the
Northwest.

1039. Harris, Christie. Once More Upon a Totem. New York:
Atheneum, 1973.

Grades 4-7.

1040. Harris, Christie. Raven's Cry. New York: Atheneum
Publishers Co.,1966.

Haidas.

1041. Harris, Christie. Sky Man on the Totem Pole. New
York: Atheneum Publishers, Co., 1975.

1042. Harrison, Amelia W. American Indian Fairy Tales.
      New York: Dodd, Mead and Co., 1971.

1043. Harrison, Edith Swan. "Women in Navajo Myth." Ph. D.
      Diss. Boston: University of Massachusetts, 1973.

1044. Harvey, Joy. Antelope Boy: A Navajo Indian Play for
      Children. n.p.: Arequipa Press, 1968.

1045. Haslam, Gerald. "American Indians: Poets of the
      Cosmos." Western American Literature 5 (Spring
      1970):15-29.

1046. Haslam, Gerald. "American Oral Literature: Our
      Forgotten Heritage." English Journal 60 (September
      1971):709-723.

1047. Haslam, Gerald. Forgotten Pages of American
      Literature. Boston: Houghton Mifflin Co., 1970.

              Literature of Indians, Asians, Chicanos
          and Blacks.

1048. Haslam, Gerald. "The Light that Fills the World:
      Native American Literature." South Dakota Review 11
      (Spring 1973):27-41.

1049. Haslam, Gerald. "Literature of The People: Native
      American Voices." CLA Journal 15, No. 2 (December
      1971) : 153-170.

              A survey of oral poetry and prose.
          Describes characteristics of both. Also looks
          at contemporary Indian prose and poetry and
          some novels about Indians by non-Indians.

1050. Hatheway, Flora. The Little People. Billings, MT:
      Montana Reading Publications, 1971.

              Crow legends of creation for grades 3-4.

1051. Hatheway, Flora. Old Man Coyote. Billings, MT:
      Montana Reading Publications, 1970.

              Crow legends of creation for grade 3.

1052. Hausman, Gerald. Sitting on the Blue-Eyed Bear:
      Navajo Myths and Legends. Westport, CT: Hill,
      Lawrence, and Co., Inc., 1976.

              Grade 7 up.

1053. Hayes, William. Indian Tales of the Desert People.
      New York: David McKay Co., 1957.

Grades 4-6.   Pima, Papago stories.
Explains when stories were gotten and why
changes were made in some.

1054. Hays, James Robert. "The Creation Narrative of the
Native Iviatim of Southern California: An Ethnopoetic
Study." Ph. D. Diss.   Santa Cruz, CA: University of
California, 1974.

From the abstract: "The cardinal problem
in Native American literature is contextual
understanding of oral narrative. . . . The
method chosen herein supports each event with
relevant cultural data, illuminating as much
as possible its contextual meaning. . . .
Focusing upon the creation narratives of the
Iviatim, the basic plot was divided into
fifty events. . . . From the sequence of
events and commentary, the distinctive themes
of the Iviatim world view emerge."

1055. Heath, Virginia S. <u>Dramatic Elements in American
Indian Ceremonials</u>. American History and Americana
Series, No. 47.   Brooklyn, NY: Haskell Booksellers,
Inc., 1970.

1056. Helm, Mike. <u>Oregon Country Indian Legends</u>. Oregon
Country Library, 5. Eugene, OR: Rainy Day Press, 1982.

1057. Henley, Joan Asher.   "Native American Life Stories:
Problems and Opportunities for Literary Study." Ph.
D. Dissertation.   Washington,   D.C.: American
University, 1976.

1058. Henry, Jeanette, ed. <u>American Indian Reader:
Literature</u>. San Francisco: Indian Historian Press,
1973.

Samplings of ancient and modern poets,
old stories, contemporary writing, native
columnists.   Includes   "The   Walum Olum."
Includes a condensed translation of Herman
Ten Kate's, "The Indian in Literature," and
other essays on treatment of Indian in
literature and Indian literature.

1059. Herbert, J. Landar. "Four Navaho Summer Tales."
<u>Journal of American Folklore</u>, Part 1 (April-June 1959)
: 161-164; Part 2 (July-September 1959) : 248-251;
Part 3 (October-December 1959) : 298-309.

1060. Highwater, Jamake. <u>ANPAO: An American Indian Odyssey</u>.
New York: Harper and Row Publishers, Inc., 1977.

Grades 5-9.

1061. Hill, Elbert Ray. "Tales and Trials: Children's Stories and Cultural Alienation among the Winnebago." Ph. D. Diss. Lincoln: University of Nebraska, 1973.

> See _Dissertation Abstracts International_ 34/12-A, p. 7706.

1062. Hill, Kay. _More Gloosecap Stories: Legends of the Wabanaki Indians_. New York: Dodd, Mead and Co., 1970.

1063. Hill, Willard W. "Navaho Humor." _General Series in Anthropology_ 9 (1943) : 1-28.

1064. Hill, Willard W. "Two Navaho Myths." _New Mexico Anthropologist_ 6-7 (1943): 111-14.

1065. Hill, Willard W., and Hill, D. W. "Navaho Coyote Tales and Their Position in the Southern Athabascan Group." _Journal of American Folklore_ 5:58 (1945): 317-343.

1066. Hill-Tout, Charles. "Okanagan Myths." _Journal_ Royal Anthropological Institute, 41 (1911) : 130.

1067. Hines, Donald M., ed. _Tales of the Okanogans_. Fairfield, WA: Ye Galleon Press, 1976.

1068. Hinton, Leanne and Watahomigie, Lucille, eds. _Spirit Mountain: An Anthology of Yuman Story and Song_. Tucson: University of Arizona Press, n.d.

> A new Sun Tracks Book.

1069. Hobson, Geary. _The Remembered Earth: An Anthology of Native American Literature_. Albuquerque: Red Earth Press, 1979.

1070. Hodge, Gene M. _Four Winds, Poems from Indian Rituals_. Santa Fe, New Mexico: The Sunstone Press, 1979.

1071. Hodge, Gene M. _The Kachinas Are Coming_. Flagstaff: Northland Press, 1967.

> Pueblo folktales and myths.

1072. Hogan, Linda. "The Nineteenth Century Native American Poets." _Wassaja/The Indian Historian_ 13 (November 1980): 24-29.

1073. Holthaus, Mary. _The Hunter and the Ravens_. (Indian Culture Series). Billings, Montana: Montana Council for Indian Education, 1976.

> For grades 1-6.

1074. Holtuman, Jack. "Seven Blackfeet Stories." Indian Historian 3 (Fall 1970) : 39-43.

1075. House, Kay Seymour. "James Fenimore Cooper's American Characters." Ph. D. Diss. Stanford, CA: Stanford University, 1963.

1076. Houston, James. Songs of the Dream People: Chants and Images from the Indians of North America. New York: Atheneum, 1972.

1077. Howard, Helen A. American Indian Poetry. United States Authors Series, No. 334. Boston: Twayne Publishers, 1979.

1078. Howard, Helen A. "Literary Translators and Interpreters of Indian Songs." Journal of the West 12 (April 1973):212-228.

1079. Huffman, Bert. "Legend of Wallowa Lake." in Echoes of the Grand Ronde. La Grande, OR: Eldridge Huffman, 1934, pp. 71-73.

1080. Hulpach, Vladimir, comp. American Indian Tales and Legends. n.p.: n.p., 1965.

1081. Hymes, Dell. "Comment: Problem of Versions." Journal of the American Folklore Institute 18, Nos. 2-3 (1981):144-150.

1082. Hymes, Dell. "Discovering Oral Performance and Measured Verse in American Indian Narrative [with Discussion]." New Literary History 8 (Spring 1977): 431-457, 521-534.

1083. Hymes, Dell. "In Vain I Tried to Tell You." Essays in Native American Ethnopoetics. Philadelphia: University of Pennsylvania Press, 1981.

1084. Hymes, Dell. "Myths and Tale Titles of the Lower Chinook." Journal of American Folklore 72:284 (April-June 1959): 139-145.

1085. Hymes, Dell. "Particle, Pause and Pattern in American Indian Narrative Verse." American Indian Culture and Research Journal 4, No. 4 (1980):7-51.

1086. Hymes, Dell. "Some North Pacific Coast Poems: A Problem in Anthropological Philology." American Anthropologist 67, No. 2 (April 1965):316-341.

Structural functions of poems, problems in translation. Gives literal and literary translations of six poems plus comments. Encourages use of linguistics. Bibliography.

1087. "Images and Counterimages: Ohiyesa, Standing Bear and American Literature." _American Indian Culture and Research Journal_ 5:2 (1981): 37-62.

1088. "The Importance of Native American Authors." _American Indian Culture and Research Journal_ 5:3 (1981): 1-12.

1089. "Indian Legends of the Mammoth." _El Palacio_ 28:1-4 (1930) : 21.

1090. "Indian Legends of Oregon." _Oregon Teacher's Monthly_ (October 1903-April 1912).

1091. Insley, Bernice. _Indian Folklore Tales_. New York: Exposition Press, 1961.

        Legends from various tribes.

1092. "Integrity in Teaching Native American Literature." _English Journal_ 72:2 (February 1983): 46-48.

1093. Interracial Books for Children, The Council on. _Chronicles of Indian Protest_. Greenwich, CT: Fawcett Publishing, Inc., 1971.

        Indian orations 1622-1971. American Indian political thought and literature.

1094. Jacobs, Elizabeth. _Nehalem Tillamook Tales_. Eugene: University of Oregon Books, 1959.

1095. Jacobs, J. _Indian Folk and Fairy Tales_. New York: G. P. Putnam's Sons, n.d.

1096. Jacobs, Melville. _Clackamas Chinook Texts_, pts. 1 and 2. Research Center in Anthropology, Folklore, and Linguistics, Publications 8 and 11, International Journal of American Linguistics 24, No. 1, pt. 2; 25, No. 2, pt. 2.

1097. Jacobs, Melville. _Content and Style of an Oral Literature: Clackamas Chinook Myths and Tales_. Chicago: University of Chicago Press, 1959.

1098. Jacobs, Melville. _Coos Ethnographic and Narrative Texts_. University of Washington Publications in Anthropology, vol. 8, No. 1 (1939).

1099. Jacobs, Melville. _Coos Myth Texts_. University of Washington Publications in Anthropology, vol. 8, No. 2 (1940).

1100. Jacobs, Melville. _Kalapuya Texts_. University of Washington Publications in Anthropology, vol. 11 (1945).

1101. Jacobs, Melville. <u>Northwest Sahaptin Texts</u>.
Columbia University Contributions to Anthropology,
vol. 19 (1934).

1102. Jacobs, Melville. <u>The People Are Coming Soon:
Analyses of Clackamas Chinook Myths and Tales</u>.
Seattle: University of Washington Press, 1960.

1103. Jacobs, Melville. "Titles in an Oral Literature."
<u>Journal of American Folklore</u> 70, No. 276 (April-June
1957):157-172.

1104. Jacobs, Melville, ed. <u>Nehalem Tillamook Tales</u>.
Eugene: University of Oregon Books, 1959.

          A collection of Nehalem-Tillamook-Salish
     myths and anecdotes dictated to Elizabeth D.
     Jacobs by a Nehalem speaker in 1934.

1105. Jacobs, Melville, ed. <u>Northwest Sahaptin Texts</u>.
University of Washington Publications in Anthropology
2:6. Seattle: University of Washington Press, 1929.

          Thirteen folktales narrated by Joe Hunt,
     Klikitat Indian, recall customs and mythology
     of Klikitat culture in both English and
     Klikitat.

1106. Jahner, Elaine. "An Act of Attention: Event Structure
in <u>Ceremony</u>." <u>American Indian Quarterly</u> 5:1 (February
1979) : 37-46.

          Offers the idea that the Mythic (stated
     in poetic form) and Contemporary (stated in
     prose) narrative shapes the events of L. M.
     Silko's novel.

1107. Jahner, Elaine, ed. <u>American Indians Today: Thought,
Literature, Art</u>. New York: Horizon Press Publishers,
1982.

1108. "James Welch's Poetry." <u>American Indian Culture and
Research Journal</u> 3:1 (1979): 19-38.

1109. Jamison, Blanche Norma Miller. "The Western American
Indian: Cross-Cultural Literary Attitudes."   Ph. D.
Dissertation.   Commerce, Texas: East Texas State
University, 1978.

1110. Jaskoski, Helen. "A Word Has Power: Poetry and
Healing in American Indian Cultures." Paper presented
at annual meeting of the Modern Language Association.
Bethesda, MD: ED 193 660, December 1979.

1111. Jenness, Diamond. <u>The Indians of Canada</u>. National
Museum of Canada Bulletin 65, Anthropological Series

No. 15.   Ottawa: National Museum of Canada, 1960.

Languages,   folklore,   religion, oratory,
drama, music.   Includes bibliography.

1112. Jenness,   Diamond. "Myths and Traditions from Northern
Alaska, The Mackenzie Delta and Coronation Gulf."
Reports, Canadian Arctic Expedition, Vol. 13, Part A,
1924.

1113. Johnson,   Broderick H., ed. Navajo Stories of the Long
Walk Period. Tsaile, AZ: Navajo Community College
Press, 1975.

1114. Johnson,   Donald   and Johnson, Jean E.   Through Indian
Eyes, Vol. I: The Wheel of Life. Rev. ed.   Clark,
Leon E., ed.   United Nations Plaza, NY: Center for
International Training and Education, 1981.

Grades 9-12.

1115. Johnson,   F.   Roy.   North Carolina Indian Legends and
Myths. Murfreesboro, NC: Johnson Publishing Co., 1981.

1116. Jones,   Charles,   ed.   Look to the Mountain Top.   San
Jose, CA: H. M. Gausha, 1972.

Articles   on   various   aspects   of Indian
life   including   literature,   oratory.
Discussion   of   stereotypes.   Includes
bibliography.

1117. Jones,   Hettie,   ed.   The Trees Stand Shining: Poetry
of the North American Indian. Illus. by Robert Andrew
Parker. New York: Dial Press, 1971.

32 pages.   Several tribes.

1118. Jones,   James   A.   Traditions of the North American
Indians.   Upper   Saddle   River,   New   Jersey: Gregg
Press, 1970.

Legends   from   east   of   the   Mississippi
River in the early 1800's.

1119. Jones,   Louis T.   Aboriginal American Indian Oratory:
the Tradition of Elogence Among Indians.   Los Angeles:
Southwest Museum, 1965.

1120. Jones,   Louis   T. "Indian Speech Arts." Masterkey 37:3
(1963) : 91-97.

1121. Jones,   William.   Fox Texts.   (American Ethnological
Society,   Publications: No. 1).   Reprint of 1907
edition.   New York: AMS Press, Inc., 1973.

1122. Jones, William, compiler. <u>Kickapoo Tales</u>. Michelson, Truman, translator. (American Ethnological Society, Publications: No. 7). Reprint of 1915 edition. New York: AMS Press, Inc., 1973.

1123. Judd, M. C. <u>Wigwam Stories</u>. New York: Gordon Press Publishers, 1977.

1124. Judson, Katherine Berry. <u>Myths and Legends of Alaska</u>. Chicago: Chicago University Press, 1911.

1125. Judson, Katherine Berry. <u>Myths and Legends: California and the Old Southwest</u>. Chicago: A. C. McClurg and Co., 1912.

1126. Judson, Katherine Berry. <u>Myths and Legends of the Great Plains</u>. n.p.: n.p., 1913.

1127. Judson, Katherine Berry. <u>Myths and Legends of the Pacific Northwest, Especially of Washington and Oregon</u>. Third ed. Chicago: A. C. McClurg, 1910; facsimile reproduction Seattle: Shorey Bookstore, 1967.

1128. Keithahn, Edward L. <u>Igloo Tales</u>. U.S. Bureau of Indian Affairs, Marshall Institute, 1950; Seattle: Craftsman Press, A Robert D. Seal Publication, 1958.

1129. Kelly, Isabel. "Northern Paiute Tales." <u>Journal of American Folklore</u> 51 (1938):363-437.

1130. Kendall, Martha B. <u>Coyote Stories, No. 11</u>. International Journal of American Linguistics Native American Texts Series Monograph No. 6, 1980. Ann Arbor, MI: University Microfilms International, 1981.

1131. Kerr, B. "Novel as Sacred Text: N. Scott Momaday's Myth-Making Ethic." <u>Southwest Review</u> 63 (Spring 1978): 172-179.

1132. Kilpatrick, Jack Frederick. <u>Muskogean Charm Songs Among the Oklahoma Cherokees</u>. Washington, D. C.: U. S. Government Printing Office, 1967.

1133. Kilpatrick, Jack Frederick, and Kilpatrick, Anna G. <u>Friends of Thunder: Folktales of the Oklahoma Cherokees</u>. Dallas: Southern Methodist University Press, 1964.

1134. Kilpatrick, Jack Frederick, and Kilpatrick, Anna G. <u>Walk in Your Soul: Love Incantations of the Oklahoma Cherokees</u>. Dallas: Southern Methodist University Press, 1965.

1135. Klah, Hasteen. <u>Navajo Creation Myth: The Story of Emergence</u>. Museum of Navajo Ceremonial Art and

Religion Series, No. 1. Reprint of 1942 edition, New York, AMS Press, Inc., n.d.

1136. Krenov, J. "Legends from Alaska." Journal de la Societe des Americanistes, 40:n.s. (1951)n : 173-195.

1137. Kroeber, A. L. Indian Myths of Southcentral California. Publications in American Archaeology and Ethnology 7:4. Berkeley: The University Press, 1907.

1138. Kroeber, A. L. "Gros Ventre Myths and Tales." American Museum of Natural History Anthropological Papers 1:3 (1907).

1139. Kroeber, Alfred L. More Mojave Myths. University of California Publications in Anthropological Records 27. Berkeley: University of California Press, 1972.

1140. Kroeber, Alfred L. Yunek Myths. Berkeley: University of California Press, 1976.

1141. Kroeber, Karl. "Deconstructionist Criticism and American Indian Literature." Boundary 2, Vol. 7, No. 3 (Spring 1979):73-92.

1142. Kroeber, Karl. "Scarface vs. Scar-face: The Problem of Versions." Journal of the Folklore Institute. 18, Nos. 1-3 (1981): 99-124.

1143. Kroeber, Karl, ed. Traditional Literatures of the American Indian: Texts and Interpretations. Lincoln: University of Nebraska Press, 1981.

1144. Kroeber, Theodora. The Inland Whale: Nine Stories Retold from California Indian Legends. Berkeley: University of California Press, 1959.

1145. Kroeber, (no first name). "Yuki Myths." Anthropos Vol. 27 (1932): 905.

1146. Krupat, A. "Approach to Native American Texts." Critical Inquiry 9 (December 1982): 323-338.

1147. Krupat, A. "Indian Autobiography: Origins, Type and Function." American Literature 53 (March 1981): 22-42.

1148. Kunz, D. "Lost in the Distance of Winter: James Welch's Winter in the Blood." Critique 20:1 (1978): 93-99.

1149. Kuykendall, G. B. "Myths of the Columbia River Indians." West Shore 13:4 (April 1887) : 273-283; 13:5 (May 1887) : 370-378.

1150. Lander, Herbert J. "Four Navajo Summer Tales."

Journal of American Folklore 5:72 (1959): 161-164, 248-251, 298-309.

1151. LaPointe, James. *Legends of the Lakota*. San Francisco: Indian Historian Press, 1976.

   Author is Lakota. Stories are those told to him 60 years ago put into modern context.

1152. Larned, W. T. *American Indian Fairy Tales*. 9th ed. New York: P. F. Volland Co., 1921.

   Larned retells stories adapted from the legends of Henry R. Schoolcraft.

1153. Larson, Charles R. *American Indian Fiction*. Albuquerque: University of New Mexico Press, 1978.

   A critical classification, comparison and evaluation of novels by American Indians, according to the publisher, "the first critical and historical account of novels by American Indians." In the opening section, "The Emergence of American Indian Fiction," Larson discusses the problems of developing criteria for his study such as determining Indian identity, defining "Indian fiction," evaluating the relationship between art and culture. Beginning with Chief Simon Pokagon's *Queen of the Woods* (1889), Larson discusses each of several works in detail. Larson examines the works of Pokagon, John Milton Oskison, John Joseph Mathews, D'Arcy McNickle, N. Scott Momaday, Dallas Chief Eagle, Hyemeyohsts Storm, Denton R. Bedford, George Pierre, James Welch, Leslie Marmon Silko, Nasnaga. Includes footnotes, bibliography, index.

1154. Larson, Charles R. "Indian Fiction: A Tribal Vision." *Saturday Review* 5 (November 25, 1978) : 28.

1155. Larson, C. "*Seven Arrows*: Saga of the American Indian." *Books Abroad* 47 (Winter 1973) : 88-92.

   A review of the book claimed to be the first novel written by an American Indian, later discredited by the Indian newspaper, *Wassaja*. See H.S. McAllistor's article on "Our Indian Heritage" (*English Journal* 64 (October 1975) : 80-82) for more on *Seven Arrows*.

1156. Lattin, V. E. "Quest for Mythic Vision in Contemporary Native American and Chicano Fiction."

American Literature 50 (January 1979): 625-640.

1157. Law, Katherine. <u>Legends of the Bitterroot Valley</u>. Indian Culture Series. Billings: Montana Council for Indian Education, 1971.

> Grades 1-4.   Salish folk stories about Coyote.

1158. Law, Katheryn. <u>Salish Folk Tales</u>. (Indian Culture Series).   Billings, Montana: Montana Council for Indian Education, 1972.

> For grades 1-6. Stories of the Flathead Indians.

1159. Leeper, Vera. <u>Indian Legends Live in Puppetry</u>. Happy Camp, CA: Naturegraph Publishers, Inc., 1973.

1160. <u>Legends of the Yosemite Miwok</u>. Yosemite National Park, CA: Yosemite Natural History Association, 1981.

1161. Leland, Charles G. <u>Algonquin Legends of New England</u>. Reprint of 1884 edition. Detroit: Gale Research Co., 1968.

1162. Lerman, Norman Hart. "An Analysis of the Folktales of the Lower Fraser Indians, British Columbia." MA Thesis. Seattle: University of Washington, 1952.

1163. Levin, Beatrice. <u>Indian Myths from the Southeast</u>. (Indian Culture Series). Billings, Montana: Montana Council for Indian Education, 1974.

> Grades 4-12.

1164. Levitas, Gloria; Vivelo, Frank R; and Vivelo, Jacqueline J. <u>American Indian Prose and Poetry: We Wait in Darkness</u>. New York: G. P. Putnam's Sons, 1974.

> Anthology of songs and prose, representative samples from prehistory to present. Many tribes.

1165. Lewis, Richard. <u>I Breathe a New Song: Poems of the Eskimo</u>. New York: Simon and Schuster, 1971.

> Primary.

1166. Lewis, Virginia, ed. <u>The Zunis: Self-Portrayals</u>. Albuquerque: University of New Mexico Press, 1972.

> Stories told by the Zuni people and translated by Alvina Quam.

1167. Lincoln,   Kenneth.   "Native   American   Poetries."
Southwest Review 63 (Autumn 1978):367-384.

1168. Lincoln,   Kenneth.   Native   American   Renaissance.
Berkeley: University of California Press, 1983.

        Index.   Bibliography.

1169. Lincoln,   Kenneth.   "Native American Tribal Poetics."
Southwest Review 60 (Spring 1975):101-116.

1170. Linderman,   Frank Bird.   Indian Old-Man Stories: More
Sparks   from   War Eagle's Lodge Fire.   New   York:
Charles Scribner's Sons, 1920.

        Chippewa (?).

1171. Linderman,   Frank   Bird.   Indian Why Stories: Sparks
from   War Eagle's Lodge Fire.   New   York: Charles
Scribner's Sons, 1915; Reprint edition, Milwood, New
York: Kraus Reprint, 1975.

        Blackfoot (?).

1172. Linderman,   Frank   Bird.   Kootenai   Why Stories.   New
York: Blue Ribbon Books, 1926.

1173. Linderman,   Frank   Bird.   Old Man Coyote. New York:
The John Day Co., 1931.

        Crow.

1174. Link,   Margaret   S.,   retold   by.   The Pollen Path: A
Collection of Navajo Myths.   Stanford, CA: Stanford
University Press, 1956.

1175. "Literature."   American Indian Journal. 6:1 (January
1980): 32-35.

1176. Littlejohn, Flavius J. Legends of Michigan and the
Old Northwest. n.p.: Singing Tree, 1969.

1177. Lockett, Hattie G. The Unwritten Literature on the
Hopi.   Arizona University Social Sciences Bulletin No.
2.   Reprint of 1933 edition, New York: AMS Press, n.d.

1178. Lloyd,   John   W.   Aw-Aw-Tam Indian Nights: Being the
Myths and Legends of the Pimas of Arizona. Westfield,
New Jersey: The Lloyd Group, 1911.

1179. Lockett, Hattie G.   The Unwritten Literature of the
Hopi.   Arizona University Social Sciences Bulletin No.
2.   Tucson: University of Arizona, 1933; reprint
edition, New York, AMS Press, Inc., n.d.

1180. Lookly, Thomas B. World of the Manabozno: Tales of

the Chippewa   Indians.   New   York: Vanguard   Press,
Inc., n.d.

　　　　Grades 4-7.

1181. Lord, Albert. The Singer of Tales. Harvard Studies
      in Comparative Literature, No. 24. Cambridge: Harvard
      University Press, 1960.

1182. Lotz, M. Marvin, and Monahan, Douglas. Twenty Tepee
      Tales. n.p.: Association Press, 1950.

1183. Lourie,   Dick,   ed. Come to Power: Writings by
      American   Indians. Trumansburg, NY: The Crossing
      Press, 1973.

1184. Lowerfels, Walter, ed. From the Belly of the Shark:
      A New Anthology of Native Americans. New York:
      Vantage Press, Inc., 1973.

1185. Lowie, Robert. "Chipewyan Tales." American Museum
      of Natural History Anthropological Papers 10:3 (1912).

1186. Lowie, Robert.   "Crow Myths and Traditions."
      American Museum of Natural History Anthropological
      Papers 25:1 (1918); reprint edition, New York: AMS
      Press, Inc., n.d.

　　　　Also appears under the title Myths and
      Traditions of the Crow Indians.

1187. Lowie, Robert H. "Myths and Traditions of the Crow."
      Anthropological Papers of the American Museum of
      Natural History. Vol. 25 (1918): 30-31.

1188. Lowie, Robert H. "The Test-Theme in North American
      Mythology." Ph. D. Diss. New York: Columbia
      University, 1908.

1189. Lowie, Robert H. "The Test Theme in North American
      Mythology." Journal of American Folklore 21: 82
      (April-September 1908): 97-148.

1190. Luce, Carol Jean. "A Comparative Study of the 'Popol
      Vuh' and myths of the Southeastern American Indians."
      Ed. D. Diss. Commerce, TX: East Texas State
      University, 1975.

1191. Luckert, Karl W. A Navajo Bringing-Home Ceremony: The
      Claus Chee Sonny Version of Deerway Ajilee.
      Flagstaff: Museum of Northern Arizona, 1980.

1192. Luckert, Karl W. Navajo Mountain and Rainbow Bridge
      Religion. Flagstaff: Museum of Northern Arizona, 1980.

　　　　Also listed as: Luckert, Karl W. Navajo
      Mountain and Rainbow Bridge Religion.

Goossen, Irvy W. and Bilagoody, Harry, Jr. trs. from Navajo.   American   Tribal   Religion   Series   No.   1. Flagstaff: Museum of Northern Arizona, 1977.

1193. Ludovici,   Paola.   "The   Struggle   for   an   Ending: Ritual and Plot in Recent American Indian Literature." Ph. D. Dissertation.   Washington,   D.   C.:   American University, 1979.

1194. Lummis,   Charles   F.   The Man Who Married the Moon and Other   Pueblo   Indian   Folk   Stories.   Reprint of 1894 edition.   New York: AMS Press, Inc., 1974.

1195. Luomala,   K.   Oceanic,   American   Indian   and   African Myths   of   Snaring   the   Sun.   Reprint of 1940 edition, Millwood, NY: Kraus Reprint, n.d.

1196. Lyback,   Johanna   R.   M.   Indian   Legends   of   Eastern America.   Chicago: Lyons and Carnahan, 1963.

1197. Lyback,   Johanna   R.   M.   Indian   Legends of the Great West.   Chicago: Lyons and Carnahan, 1963.

1198. Lyman,   Wiliam   D.   "Indian   Myths   of the Northwest." American   Antiquarian   Society   Proceedings 25 (October 1915): 375-395.

1199. McAllister,   H.   S.   "'The Language of Shamans':   Jerome Rothenberg's   Contributions   to   American   Indian Literature."   Western American Literature 10 (February 1976):293-309.

1200. McClintock,   (no   first   name).   "Blackfoot Legends." Southwest Museum, The Masterkey 7:2 (1933): 41.

1201. McClintock,   (no   first   name).   "Blackfoot   Legends." Southwest museum, The Masterkey 7:3 (1933): 70.

1202. McClintock,   Walter.   Old Indian Trails.   n.p.:   n.p., 1923.

1203. McClintock,   Walter.   The Old North Trail: Or, Life, Legends   and   Religion   of   the   Blackfeet   Indians. Lincoln: University of Nebraska Press, 1968.

1204. McDonald,   Louise.   "Folklore of the Flathead Indians of   Idaho."   Journal   of American Folklore.   14 (1901): 250-251.

1205. McDonald,   W.   H.   Creation   Tales   from   the   Salish. Billings: Montana Council for Indian Education, 1973.

            Grades 3-9.

1206. Macfarlan, Allan A., ed. Heritage Book of American

Indian Legends.   Forest   Park,   Georgia: Heritage
Press, Inc., 1970.

1207. Mackenzie, Donald. _Indian Myth and Legend_. Reprint
of 1913 edition, West Newfield, ME: Longwood Press,
Ltd., 1978.

1208. Mackenzie, Donald A. _Myths of Pre-Columbian America_.
Reprint of 1923 edition, West Newfield, ME: Longwood
Press, Ltd., 1978.

1209. McKern, (no first name). "Winnebago Dog Myths."
Milwaukee Public Museum _Yearbook_ (1930) : 317.

1210. McKern, (no first name). "A Winnebago Myth."
Milwaukee Public Museum _Yearbook_ (1929) : 215.

1211. McLaughlin, Marie.   _Myths and Legends of the Sioux_.
Bismarck, North Dakota: Bismarck Tribune Co., 1976.

1212. McLuhan, T. C. _Touch the Earth_.   New York:
Outerbridge and Bientstfrey, 1971.

1213. MacMillan, Cyrus.   _Gloskap's Country_.   New York:
Oxford University Press, 1955.

        Tales of Micmas retold.

1214. McNickle, D'Arcy. _Runner in the Sun; a Story of
Indian Maize_. New York: Holt, 1954.

        Novel.   Protagonist is 16 years old,
    male.

1215. McNickle, D'Arcy. _The Surrounded_.   New York: Dodd,
Mead and Co, 1936.

        Novel set on Western Montana
    reservation. Focuses on the conflict between
    a boy's desire for a wider life and the
    traditions of his tribe.

1216. McNickle, D'Arcy. _Wind from an Enemy Sky_. New York:
Harper and Row, 1978.

        Novel.

1217. McTaggart, Fred.   "American Indian Literature:
Contexts for Understanding." In _The Worlds between
Two Rivers: Perspectives on American Indians in Iowa_,
edited by Bataille, Gretchen M. and others, pp. 2-9.
Ames: Iowa State University Press, 1978.

1218. McTaggart, Fred.   "Native American Literature:
Teaching for the Self." _English Education_ 6:1
(October-November 1974) : 3-10.

The study of Indian literature can lead
us to a better understanding of American
literature and of ourselves.

1219. Magic World: American Indian Songs and Poems. New
York: William Morrow and Co., 1971.

1220. Magnarella, Paul J. "Structural Analysis of a Koryak
Incest Myth." Artic Anthropology 6:2 (1970) 21-28.

1221. Malotki, Ekkehart. Hopi Tales. Malokti, Ekkehart,
tr. Reprint of 1900 edition, New York: Johnson
Reprint Corp., n.d.

1222. Malotki, Ekkehart. Hopiutuwutsi or Hopi Tales: A
Bilingual Collection of Hopi Indian Stories. (Sun
Tracks Series). Tucson: University of Arizona Press,
1983.

1223. Marriott, Alice M. The Potter of San Ildefonso. Rev.
ed. Reprint of 1948 ed., Norman: University of
Oklahoma Press, 1976.

1224. Marriott, Alice M. Saynday's People: The Kiowa
Indians and the Stories They Told. Lincoln:
University of Nebraska Press, 1963.

1225. Marriott, Alice M. Ten Grandmothers. Civilization of
the American Indian Series, No.26. Reprint of 1945
edition, Norman: University of Oklahoma Press, 1977.

Historical sketches (personal
narratives) gathered from Kiowas, translated,
and organized in such a way as to give an
historical account of the Kiowa from
1847-1944, but reflecting Kiowa story-telling
traditions and legends, and readable as much
as literature as history.

1226. Marriott, Alice M. Winter Telling Stories. New York:
Thomas Y. Crowell Co., 1947; New York: Harper and
Row, 1969.

Stories told by Kiowa Indians about how
things got started and came to be. Suitable
for grades 3-7.

1227. Marriott, Alice and Rachlin, Carol K. American
Indian Mythology. New York: Thomas Y. Crowell Co.,
1968.

1228. Marriott, Alice, and Rachlin, Carol. Plains Indian
Mythology. New York: Thomas Y. Crowell, Co., 1975.

31 tales told by 11 tribes.

1229. Marsh, Jessie. Indian Folk Tales from Coast to Coast.
Indian Culture Series. Billings: Montana Council for
Indian Education, 1978.

1230. Martin, Francis G. Nine Tales of Raven. New York:
Harper and Row, 1950.

Northwest Indian tales told to author.

1231. Martin, Fran. Nine Tales of Coyote. New York: Harper
and Row, 1950.

Legends of Nez Perce.

1232. Martino, Bill. The Dreamer: A Tale of the Sioux.
Boston: Branden Press, Inc., 1975.

1233. Marvin, M., and Monahan, Douglas. Twenty Tepee
Tales. n.p.: Association Press, 1950.

1234. Mary-Rousseliere, Guy. Beyond the High Walls: A Book
of Eskimo Poems. New York: World Publishing Co.,
1961.

1235. Mason, Bernard S. Dances and Stories of the American
Indian. Cranbury, NJ: A. S. Barnes and Co., 1944.

1236. Masson, Marcelle. A Bag of Bones. Happy Camp, CA:
Naturegraph, 1966.

Also listed as A Bag of Bones: Legends
of the Wintu Indians of Northern California.
Winter myths told by Grant Towendolly, a
Trinity River Wintu.

1237. Mathur, Mary E. Fleming. "The Tale of the Lazy
Indian." Indian Historian 3:3 (Summer 1970) : 14-18.

1238. Mathews, Cornelius, ed. Enchanted Moccasins and
Other Legends of the American Indians. Reprint of
1877 edition. New York: AMS Press, Inc., 1973.

1239. Mathews, John Joseph. Sundown. New York: Longmans,
Green and Co., 1934.

Novel. Fictional life of a mixed blood
Indian set during Great Depression.

1240. Matson, Emerson. Legends of the Great Chiefs.
Nashville, Tennessee: Thomas Nelson, Inc., 1972.

Grades 5-8.

1241. Matson, Emerson. Longhouse Legends. Camden, New
Jersey: Thomas Nelson, Inc., n.d.

1242. Matthews, Washington. _Navaho Legends_. (American Folklore Society Memoirs Series). Reprint of 1897 edition. Millwood, NY: Kraus Reprint, n.d.

1243. Matthews, Washington. "Navaho Mythology." _American Antiquarian Magazine_ Vol. 5 (1883): 208.

1244. Matthews, Washington. _Navaho Myths, Prayers and Song_. P. E. Goddard, ed. Publications in Anthology and Archaeology Vol. 2, pp. 21-63. Berkeley: University of California Press, 1907.

1245. Matthews, Washington. _Navaho Myths, Prayers and Song, with Texts and Translations_. Publications in American Archaeology and Ethnology 5:1; 5:2. Berkeley: University of California Press, 1907.

1246. Matthiessen, Peter. _Indian Country_. New York: Viking Press, Inc., 1984.

1247. Mays, John Bentley. "The Flying Serpent: Contemporary Imaginations of the American Indian." _Canadian Review of American Studies_ 4, No. 1 (Spring 1973) : 32-47.

    Discusses translations of Indian literature since Schoolcraft and Brinton, and criticizes some anthologies of Indian poetry.

1248. Melancon, Claude. _Indian Legends of Canada_. Ellis, David, tr. from French. New York: Vanguard Press, Inc., 1975.

1249. Melody, Michael E. "Lakota Myths and Government: The Cosmos as the State." _American Indian Culture and Research Journal_ 4:3 (1980) : 1-19.

    Analysis of several accounts of White Buffalo Calf Woman's appearance among the Lakota and of her teachings illustrates how aboriginal Indian government rests upon myths of the god(s) which symbolically insert the people into the larger cosmic order.

1250. Melzack, Ronald. _The Day Tuk Became a Hunter and Other Eskimo Stories_. Toronto: McClelland and Stewart Ltd., 1967.

    Stories from Eskimo legend.

1251. Miller, Juaquin. _True Bear Stories_. Portland: Binford and Mort Publishers, n.d.

1252. Miller, Wick R. _Newe Natekwinappeh: Shoshoni Stories and Dictionary_. (Utah Anthropological Papers:

No. 94). Reprint of 1972 edition. New York: AMS Press, Inc., nd.

1253. Milspaw, Yvonne. "An Analysis of Folklore theories as Applied to Great Basin Oral Narratives." Ph. D. Diss. Bloomington: Indiana University, 1975.

1254. Milton, John R., ed. The American Indian Speaks. Vermillion, SD: Dakota Press, 1969, 1974.

　　　　　　Anthology of contemporary poetry, fiction, art by 36 American Indians.

1255. Milton, John R., ed. American Indian II. Vermillion, SD: Dakota Press, 1971.

　　　　　　Prose and poetry by 10 American Indian contributors.

1256. "The Minnesota Story, American Indian Legends." Bethesda, MD: EDRS, ED 075 307, April 5, 1971.

　　　　　　9 Indian folktales. Includes bibliography.

1257. Mitchell, Carol. "Ceremony as Ritual." American Indian Quarterly 5:1 (February 1979) : 27-35.

　　　　　　Argues that myth and ritual, the basis of the ceremony, are crucial to Tayo's reidentification with nature.

1258. Mitgang, Herbert. "By American Indians." (column) New York Times Book Review 84:1 (December 30, 1979) : 27.

1259. Mithun, Marianne and Woodbury, Hanni, eds. Northern Iroquoian Texts. International Journal of American Linguistics--Native American Texts Series: Monograph, No. 4. (pub by University of Chicago) Ann Arbor, MI: University Microfilms International, 1980.

1260. Momaday, Al and Momaday, Natachie Scott. Indian Legends Indian Life. n.p.: Gallup, 1960.

1261. Momaday, N. Scott. House Made of Dawn. New York: Harper and Row, 1969.

　　　　　　Pulitzer Prize-winning novel of American Indian veteran of World War II who finds himself in cultural conflict.

1262. Momaday, N. Scott. "The Man Made of Words." In Indian Voices: The First Convocation of American Indian Scholars, pp. 49-84. San Francisco: Indian Historian Press, 1970.

Discusses the relationship of ecology, storytelling and the imagination also the narrative and the device of the journey in The Way to Rainy Mountain. A transcript of a discussion between Momaday and other members of the convocation about oral tradition follows the essay.

1263. Momaday, N. Scott. The Names: A Memoir. New York: Harper and Row, 1976.

Tales of the author's ancestors and of his early years.

1264. Momaday, N. Scott. The Way to Rainy Mountain. Albuquerque: University of New Mexico Press, 1969.

Personal narrative: reminiscences of his childhood lived with his grandmother. Relates legends of his people (Kiowa), reviews Kiowa history. Retells story of migration of the Kiowas from headwaters of Yellowstone River to Rainy Mountain in three voices: legendary, historical, and contemporary.

1265. Momaday, N. S. Owl in the Cedar Tree. n.p.: Ginn and Co., n.d.

1266. Momaday, Natachie Scott, ed. American Indian Authors. Boston: Houghton Mifflin, 1972.

Created as a classroom text for secondary schools. Samples various types of literature: 26 selections by 15 contemporary American Indian authors include legends, ceremonial chants, prayers, poems and stories. Also included are topics for discussion. Pictures of and brief biographical notes on contributors. Reviewed in The Weewish Tree 1:3 (Spring 1972): 31.

1267. Monckton, E. The White Canoe and Other Legends of the Ojibways. New York: Gordon Press Publishers, 1977.

1268. Moon, G. P. and Moon, Carl. Lost Indian Magic. n.p.: n.p., 1918.

1269. Moon Grace, and Moon Carl. Indian Legends in Rhyme. New York: n.p., 1917.

1270. Moon, Sheila. A Magic Dwells: A Poetic and Psychological Study of the Navaho Emergence Myth. New York: Columbia University Press, 1970.

1271. Mooney, James. <u>Myths of the Cherokee</u>. (American Indian History Series). Reprint of 1900 edition. East St. Clair Shores, Michigan: Scholarly Press, Inc., 1970.

1272. Morgan, W. and Young, R. W. <u>Coyote Tales</u>. Washington: n.p., 1949.

1273. Morris, Clyde Patrick. "An Analysis of Upland Yuman Myths with the Dying God and Monster Slayer Stories." Ph. D. Diss. Tempe: Arizona State University, 1974.

1274. Morrisseau, Norvel. <u>Legends of My People the Great Ojibway</u>. Selwyn, Dewdney, ed. Toronto: The Ryerson Press, 1965.

        Chippewa.

1275. Mourning Dove. <u>Coyote Stories</u>. Guie, Heister D., ed. and illus. Reprint of 1933 edition. New York: AMS Press, Inc., 1976.

1276. Munoz, Braulio. <u>Sons of the Wind: The Search for Identity in Spanish American Indian Literature</u>. New Brunswick, New Jersey: Rutgers University Press, 1982.

1277. "Myth and Legend Number." <u>Junior Historical Journal</u> 4:3 (January 1944) : 99-136.

1278. Nasnaga [Roger Russell]. <u>Indians' Summer</u>. New York: Harper and Row, 1975.

        Novel.

1279. "Native American Literature in an Ethnohistorical Context." <u>College English</u> 41:2 (October 1979): 147-162.

1280. "Native American Poets: The Nineteenth Century." <u>Indian Historian</u> Vol. 13:4 (November 1980): 24-29.

1281. Navajo Curriculum Center. <u>Coyote Stories of the Navajo People</u>. Chinle: Rough Rock Demonstration School, 1968.

        Grades 2-5; 14 tales.

1282. Navajo Curriculum Center. <u>Grandfather Stories of the Navajo</u>. Chinle: Rough Rock Demonstration School, 1968.

        11 narratives.

1283. "Navaho Legend of the Petrified Forest." <u>El Palacio</u> 25:8-11 (1928) : 177.

1284. Nequatewa, Edmund. _Truth of a Hopi and Other Clan Stories of Shungopovi_. Mary Russell F. Colton, ed. Museum of Northern Arizona, Bulletin No. 8. Flagstaff: Northern Arizona Society of Science and Art, 1936; second edition, 1947; reprint edition (paper) Flagstaff: Northland Press, 1967.

1285. Newcomb, Franc Johnson. _Navajo Bird Tales_. Lillian Harve, ed. Wheaton, Illinois: The Theosophical Publishing House, a Quest Book for Children, 1970.

1286. Newcomb, Franc Johnson. _Navajo Folk Tales_. Santa Fe: Navajo Museum of Ceremonial Art, 1967.

1287. Newcomb, Franc Johnson. _A Study of Navajo Symbolism_. Cambridge: The Museum, 1965.

1288. Newell, Edythe W. _The Rescue of the Sun and Other Tales from the Far North_. Chicago: Albert Whitman and Co., 1970

1289. Newell, Gordon and Sherwood, Don. _Totem Tales of Old Seattle_. Sausalito, California: Comstock Editions, 1974.

1290. Newell, W. W. "Navaho Legends." _Journal of American Folklore_ 5:9 (1896): 211-218.

1291. Niatum, Duane. _Songs for the Harvester of Dreams_. Seattle: University of Washington Press, 1981.

        Niatum is a Native American poet.

1292. Nicholson, Irene. _Mexican and Central American Mythology_. n.p.:n.p., n.d.

        Maya, Olmec, Zapotec, Mixtec, Totonac, Toltec, Aztec.

1293. "North American Indian Myths and Legends for Classroom Use." _Journal of Reading_ 24:6 (March 1981): 494-496.

1294. "North American Mythology." in _The Mythology of All Races_. 13 vols. MacCullock, John A. and Gray, Louis, eds. New York: Cooper Square Publications, Inc., 1922.

1295. Nye, Wilbur S. _Bad Medicine and Good: Tales of the Kiowas_. Norman: University of Oklahoma Press, 1969.

        44 stories 1700's-1930's.

1296. Oaks, Priscilla. "The First Generation of Native American Novelists." _MELUS_ 5 (1978):57-65.

1297. O'Brien, Aileen. <u>The Dine Origin Myths of the Navaho Indians</u>. Reprint of 1956 edition. East St. Clair Shores, Michigan: Scholarly Press, n.d.

1298. Odjig, Daphne. <u>The Nanabush Series</u>. New York: Ginn and Co., 1970.

    Teaching stories for children. Lessons on cheating, stealing, meanness, etc. For early childhood—fourth grade.

1299. Old Coyote, Sally and Yellow Tail, Joy. <u>Indian Tales</u>. Billings: Montana Reading Publications, n.d.

1300. Old Coyote, Sally and Toineeta, Joy Yellow Tail. <u>Indian Tales of the Northern Plains</u>. (Indian Culture Series). Billings, Montana: Montana Council for Indian Education, 1972.

    Grades 2-5.

1301. Olin, Caroline and Olin, D. <u>Myths and Legends of the Indian Southwest</u>. Santa Barbara, CA: Bellerophon Books, 1978.

1302. Oman, Lela. <u>Eskimo Legends</u>. Nome, Alaska: Nome Press, 1966.

1303. Opler, Morris E. <u>Dirty Boy: A Jicarilla Tale o Raid and War</u>. (American Authors Association Memoir Series). Reprint of 1938 edition. Millwood, NY Kraus Reprint, n.d.

1304. Opler, Morris E. "Humor and Wisdom of Some American Indian Tribes." <u>New Mexico Anthropologist</u> 3:1 (1938) : 75-79.

1305. Opler, Morris E. <u>Myths and Legends of the Lipan Apache Indians</u>. (American Folklore Society Memoirs Series). Reprint of 1940 edition. Millwood, NY: Kraus Reprint, n.d.

1306. Opler, Morris E. <u>Myths and Tales of the Chiricahua Apache Indians</u>. (American Folklore Society Memoirs Series). Reprint of 1942 edition. Millwood, NY: Kraus Reprint, n.d.

1307. Opler, Morris E. <u>Myths and Tales of the Jicarilla Apache Indians</u>. (American Folklore Society Memoirs Series). Reprint of 1938 edition. Millwood, NY: Kraus Reprint, n.d.

1308. Ortiz, Simon J. "Literature." <u>American Indian Journal</u> 6 (January 1980): 32-35.

1309. Oskison, John Milton. <u>Black Jack Davy</u>. New York: D.

Appleton & Co., 1926.

Novel with romantic focus set in frontier town in Cherokee Indian (Oklahoma) Territory. Author is Cherokee.

1310. Oskison, John Milton. _Brothers Three_. New York: Macmillan Co., 1935.

This novel is story of 1873 Oklahoma farm family.

1311. Oskison, John Milton. _Wild Harvest_. New York: D. Appleton & Co., 1925.

Novel with romantic focus set in Cherokee Indian Territory.

1312. Oswalt, Robert L., ed. _Kashaya Texts_. University of California Publications in Linguistics, Vol. 36. Berkeley: University of California Press, 1964.

Traditional stories, myths, tales of the supernatural, and folk history narrated by James Herman, Essie Parrish and others. Both Kashaya and English texts.

1313. Overholt, Thomas W. and Callicott, J. Baird. _Clothed-in-Fur and Other Tales: An Introduction to an Ojibway World View_. Lanham, MD: University Press of America, 1982.

1314. Paige, Harry W. _Songs of the Teton Sioux_. Los Angeles: Westernlore Press, 1970.

1315. Palmer, William R. _Why the North Star Stands Still_. Springdale, UT: Zion Natural History Association, 1978.

1316. Parker, Arthur C. _Seneca Myths and Folk Tales_. (Buffalo Historical Society. Publication: Vol. 27). Reprint of 1923 edition. New York: AMS Press, Inc., 1976.

1317. Parker, Arthur C. _Skunny Wundy, Seneca Indian Tales_. Chicago: Albert Whitman and Co., 1970.

Grades 4-6.

1318. Parker, Everett, and Ryan, Kenida (Oledeska). _The Secret of No Face_. Santa Clara, CA: Native American Publishing Co., 1972.

1319. Parsons, Elsie W., ed. _Kiowa Tales_. Reprint of 1929 edition. Millwood, NY: Kraus Reprint, n.d.

1320. Parsons, Elsie W., ed. Taos Tales. Reprint of 1940
      edition. Millwood, NY: Kraus Reprint, n.d.

1321. Parsons, Elsie W., ed. Tewa Tales. Reprint of 1926
      edition. Millwood, NY: Kraus Reprint, n.d.

1322. "Particle, Pause and Pattern in American Indian
      Narrative Verse." American Indian Culture and Research
      Journal 4:4 (1980): 7-51.

1323. Patronella, (no first name). Tales of Nokomis.
      Toronto: Mussen, 1970.

1324. Payne, E. G. and Driggs, H. R. Red Feather's
      Homecoming. Chicago: Lyons and Carnahan, 1940.

            Stories of plains and forest Indians.

1325. Peet, (no first name). "Creation Legends." American
      Antiquarian Magazine Vol. 17 (1895): 128.

1326. Peet, (no first name). "Transformation Myths."
      American Antiquarian Magazine Vol 16 (1894): 275.

1327. Penny, (no first name). Tales of the Cheyennes. Palo
      Alto, CA: Houghton Mifflin Co., 1953.

            Grades 5-8.

1328. Peterson, Bonnie, ed. Dawn of the World, Stories of
      the Coast Miwok Indians. Fairfax, CA: Tamal Land,
      1976.

1329. Peyer, B. "Samson Occom: Mohegan Missionary and
      Writer of the 18th Century." American Indian Quarterly
      6 (Fall-Winter 1982): 208-217.

1330. Phillips, Yvonne Elizabeth. "A Study of the
      Distribution of Wishram Indian Myths." BA Thesis.
      Portland, OR: Reed College, 1955.

1331. Phinney, Archie. Nez Perce Texts. Columbia
      University Contributions to Anthropology Series: Vol.
      25. New York: Columbia University Press, 1934;
      reprint edition, New York: AMS Press, n.d.

            Tales narrated by author's mother (Nez
      Perce) in Nez Perce and English.

1332. Pierre, Chief George. Autumn's Bounty. San Antonio:
      Naylor Co., 1972.

            Novel. An old Indian leader opposes
      reservation termination and loss of a way of
      life.

1333. Pietroforte, Alfred. Songs of the Yokuts and Paiutes. Healdsburg, CA: Naturegraph Publishers, 1965.

Grades 4-6.

1334. "Poetry, Fiction, Art, Music, Religion by the American Indian." South Dakota Review 7:2. (1969) : entire issue.

1335. Poetry Society of Alaska, Inc. One Hundred Years of Alaska Poetry. Alaska: Big Mountain Press, n.d.

1336. Pohlmann, John Ogden. "California's Mission Myth." Ph. D. Diss. Los Angeles: University of California, 1974.

1337. Porter, Kenneth W. "A Legend of the Biloxi." Journal of American Folklore (April-June 1946): 168-173.

1338. Povey, John. "My Proud Headdress: New Indian Writing." Southwest Review 57 (Autumn 1972):265-280.

1339. Povey, John. "A New Second-Language Indian Literature." Alaska Review 4 (Fall-Winter 1969):73-78.

1340. Price, John A. "Stereotyping by Indians." in Native Studies: American and Canadian Indians. Toronto: McGraw-Hill Ryerson, Ltd., 1978, pp. 217-225.

Stereotpyes of whites by Indians; Indian jokes about whites.

1341. "Pueblo Portraits." Seventeen 39 (November 1980) 150+.

Student poetry from New Mexico.

1342. Rachlin, Carol K. and Marriott, Alice. Plains Indians Mythology. New York: New American Library, 1977.

1343. Radin, Paul. The Evolution of an American Indian Prose Epic: A Study in Comparative Literature. 2 Parts. Special Publications of the Bollingen Foundation, Nos. 3, 5. Baltimore: Waverly Press, 1954-56.

Analyzes a prose tale of the Winnebagos, The Two Boys.

1344. Radin, Paul. Literary Aspects of North American Mythology. Canada Geological Survey Museum Bulletin 16 and Anthrpological Series 6. Ottawa: Government Printing Bureau, 1915; reprint edition, Norwood, PA: Norwood Editions, 1973.

          Makes a case for the existence of two
types of myth: the folklore variety and the
literary variety. Contends folklore myths,
similar to fairy tales, pass on more or less
unchanged while other myths, which originated
sometime in the past, are subject to literary
modification   by   their   tellers.   He
demonstrates his belief with several North
American Indian myths of both varieties. He
also suggests this might be an explanation of
why some myths have unaccountable elements in
them.

1345. Radin, Paul. <u>Primitive Man as Philosopher</u>. New York:
Dover Publications, 1957.

          Philosophies of Winnebago, Oglala Sioux,
Zuni, and others.

1346. Radin, Paul.   <u>Road of Life and Death</u>. (Bollingen
Series: Vol. 5). Princeton: Princeton University
Press, 1945.

          Drama.

1347. Radin, Paul.   <u>The Trickster: A Study in American
Indian Mythology</u>. London: Routledge & Kegan Paul,
1956.

1348. Ramsey, Jarold.   "The   Bible in Western Indian
Mythology." <u>Journal of American Folklore</u> 90, No. 358
(October-December 1977):442-454.

1349. Ramsey, Jarold. "Coyote Goes Upriver: A Cycle for
Story Theater and Mime." <u>Georgia Review</u> 35, No. 3
(Fall 1981): 524-551.

1350. Ramsey, Jarold.   "Crow: Or   the   Trickster
Transformed." <u>Massachusetts Review</u> 19, No. 1 (Spring
1978): 111-127.

1351. Ramsey, Jarold.   "Fish-Hawk's Raid against the
Sioux." <u>Alcheringa</u>, n.s., Vol. 3, No. 1 (1977):
96-99.

1352. Ramsey, Jarold. "From 'Mythic' to 'Fictive' in a Nez
Perce Orpheus Myth." <u>Western American Literature</u> 13
(Summer 1978):119-131.

1353. Ramsey, Jarold. "The Indian Literature of Oregon."
<u>Northwest Perspectives: Essays on the Culture of the
Pacific Northwest</u>. Edwin R. Bingham and Glen A. Love,
eds. Seattle: University of Washington Press, 1979,
pp. 2-19.

1354. Ramsey, Jarold. <u>Reading the Fire: Essays in the</u>

Traditional Indian   Literatures   of   the   Far   West.
Lincoln: University of Nebraska Press, 1983.

Among other points that Ramsey argues
convincingly in these eleven essays, he makes
a case for the "pluralistic" functioning of
traditional Indian literatures (which are as
various as the tribes producing them)--that
is, that a given myth or tale or song or poem
may serve several cultural, literary, and
perhaps psychological purposes at the same
time. He urges a broader interpretation of
traditional Indian literature as literature
and acceptance of it as part of the heritage
of American literature. Ramsey explores
various aspects of the literature in each
essay and draws upon numerous examples.
Footnotes by chapter at end of book.
Bibliography. Index.

1355. Ramsey,   Jarold. "The Teacher of Modern American
      Indian Writing as Ethnographer and Critic." College
      English 41:2 (October 1979) : 163-169.

Discusses the fusion of culture and
imagination in Indian writings and urges
scholars not to consider such works solely
from an ethnographic viewpoint.

1356. Ramsey,   Jarold.   The Trickster. New York: Schocken
      Books, 1972.

1357. Ramsey,   Jarold.   "The Wife Who Goes Out Like a Man
      Comes Back as a Hero: The art of Two Oregon Indian
      narratives." PMLA 92 (January 1977):9-18.

1358. Ramsey,   Jarold.   "Word Magic: Indian Poetry."
      Parnassus 4, No. 1 (Fall-Winter 1975): 165-175.

1359. Ramsey,   Jarold, ed. Coyote Was Going There: Indian
      Literature of the Oregon Country. Seattle: University
      of Washington Press, 1977.

1360. Rand, Silas T. Legends of the Micmacs. Reprint of
      1894 edition. New York: Johnson Reprint Corp., 1971.

1361. Rand, (no first name). "Glooscap Myths." American
      Antiquarian Magazine Vol. 12 (1890): 283.

1362. Raskin, Joseph and Raskin, Edith. Indian Tales. New
      York: Random House, Inc., 1969.

Grades 1-6. Legends of the Hudson
Valley.

1363. Reed, E. H. The Silver Arrow and Other Indian

Romances of the Dune Country. New York: Gordon Press
Publishers, 1977.

1364. Reichard, Gladys A. An Analysis of Coeur d'Alene
Indian Myths. Philadelphia: American Folklore, 1947;
reprint edition New York: Kraus Reprint, n.d.

1365. Reid, Dorothy M. Tales of Nanabozho. New York: Henry
Z. Walck, Inc., 1963.

Grade 6. Chippewa.

1366. Reveles, (no first name). Indian Campfire Tales.
n.p.:n.d.

1367. Ressler, (no first name). Treasury of American Indian
Tales. New York: Association Press, 1957.

Indian tales for pre-teens.

1368. Rhodes, Geri Marlane. "Shared Fire: Reciprocity in
Contemporary American Indian and Related Literature."
Ph. D. Diss. Albuquerque: University of New Mexico,
1976.

Dissertation   Abstracts   International
37/10-A, p. 6488.

1369. Richardson, B. E. "A Wind is Rising." Library Journal
95 (February 1, 1970) : 463-467.

1370. Ridge, John Rollin (Yellow Bird). Cherokee Poems.
San Francisco: Henry Payot and Co. Publishers, 1868.

1371. Riggs, S. R. Dakota Grammar, Texts and Ethnography.
Contributions to North American Ethnology, Vol. 9.
Washington, D. C.: U. S. Geological and Geographical
Survey, 1893.

1372. Riggs, S. R. "Dakota Mythology." American
Antiquarian Magazine Vol. 5 1889): 89.

1373. Rink, (no first name). "Comparative Study of two
Eskimo and Indian Legends." American International
Congress of Americanists Proceedings 1:13 (1902) :
279.

1374. Robertson, Marion. Red Earth: Tales of the Micmacs
with an Introduction to the Customs and Beliefs of the
Micmac Indians. Halifax, Nova Scotia: The Nova
Scotia Museum, 1969.

1375. Roemer, Kenneth M. "Bear and Elk: The Nature(s) of
Contemporary Indian Poetry." Journal of Ethnic
Studies 5 (Summer 1977): 69-79.

1376. Roessel, Robert A., Jr. and Platero, Dillon, eds. Coyote Stories. Rough Rock, AZ: Navajo Curriculum Center Press, 1975.

        Grades 3-12.

1377. Roessel, Ruth, ed. Navajo Studies at Navajo Community College. Chinle, AZ: Navajo Community College Library, 1971; Bethesda, MD: EDRS, ED 062 028, 1971.

        Contains origin myths of Navajos.

1378. Rosen, Kenneth. "American Indian Literature: Current Condition and Suggested Research." American Indian Culture and Research Journal 2, No. 2 (1979):57-66.

        Discusses Indian writings of the last 10 years, particulary poems, short stories and novels. Suggests needs and opportunties for research. Analyzes work of Bedford, McNickle, Momaday, Nasnaga, Pierre, Silko and Storm.

1379. Rosen, Kenneth, ed. and intro. The Man to Send Rain Clouds: Contemporary Poetry by American Indians. New York: Vintage Books, 1975.

1380. Rosen, Kenneth, ed. Voices of the Rainbow: Contemporary Poetry by American Indians. New York: Viking, 1975.

1381. Rothenberg, Jerome. "American Indian Workings." Poetry Review 63 (1972):17-29.

1382. Rothenberg, Jerome, ed. Shaking the Pumpkin: Traditional Poetry of the Indian North Americas. Garden City, NY: Doubleday, 1972.

1383. Roulet, (no first name). Indian Folk Tales. n.p.: American Book Co., 1911; New York: Van Nostrand Reinhold, n.d.

1384. Running, Corinne. When Coyote Walked the Earth: Indian Tales of the Pacific Northwest. New York: Holt, Rinehart, and Winston, Inc., 1949.

1385. Ruoff, LaVonne. "History in Winter in the Blood: Background and Bibliography." American Indian Quarterly 4 (No. 2, 1978): 169-172.

1386. Ruoff, LaVonne. "Ritual and Renewal in Kares Traditions in the Short Fiction of Leslie Silko." MELUS 5, (1978): 2-17.

1387. Rupert, James. "The Uses of Oral Tradition in Six

Contemporary Native American Poets." _American Indian Culture and Research Journal_ 4:4 (1980) : 87-110.

1388. Rush, Emmy Matt. "Indian Legends." _El Palacio_ 32:n.s. (1932) : 137-54.

1389. Rushmore, Helen. _The Dancing Horses of Acoma_. n.p.: n.p., n.d.

Twelve legends of the Pueblo.

1390. Russell, J. A. "Indian Oratory: An Interpretation of the Indian in His Own Words." _Dartmouth Magazine_ n.v.:n.s. (January 1930) : n.p.n.

1391. Sanders, Ruth Manning. _Red Indian Folk and Fairy Tales_. London: Oxford University Press, 1960; n.p.: Roy Publishers, 1962.

Grades 5-9.

1392. Sanders, Thomas E. and Peck, Walter W., comps. _Literature of the American Indian_. New York: Glencoe Press/Macmillan, 1973.

Designed as a textbook, this anthology includes summary of historical development; religious literature, folklore, hero myths, poetry (including pre-Columbian and Eskimo). An abridged edition was published by Macmillan in 1976.

Reviews:
Natural History 82 (October 1973) : 88.
Library Journal 98 (August 1973) : 2301.
Choice 10 (January 1974) : 1720.
Booklist 70 (September 1, 1973) : 24.

1393. Sands, Kathleen M. "A Man of Words: The Life and Letters of a Yaqui Poet." _American Indian Culture and Research Journal_ 4:1-2 (1980) : 143-159.

Discussion of life and work of Refugio Savala. Includes analyses of selected poems and tales.

1394. Sands, Kathleen M. "Preface: A Symposium Issue." _American Indian Quarterly_ 5:1 (February 1979) : 1-5.

Introduces issue devoted to discussion of Leslie Marmon Silko's _Ceremony_.

1395. Sands, Kathleen M. and Ruoff, A. Lavonne, eds. "A Discussion of _Ceremony_." _American Indian Quarterly_ 5:1 (February 1979) : 63-70.

> Seminar participants discuss novel,
> *Ceremony*, as a curing ceremony, the function
> of memory in the novel, and the distinctly
> American Indian aspects of the novel.

1396. Sapir, [Edward?]. "Two Paiute Texts." University of Pennsylvania *Museum Journal* 1:1 (1910): 15.

1397. Sapir, Edward. *Wishram Texts*. Publications of the American Ethnological Society, Vol. 2. Leydon, New Jersey: E. J. Brill, 1909.

1398. Sapir, Edward, and Dixon, Roland B. *Yana Texts* bound with *Yana Myths*. Reprint of 1910 edition, New York: AMS Press, Inc., n.d.

1399. Sasse, Mary Hawley. "Teaching Native American Literature in the High School: Theory and Practice." Ph. D. Diss. Carbondale, Illinois: Southern Illinois University, 1979.

1400. Saunders, Thomas E. "Tribal Literature: Individual Identity and the Collective Unconscious." *College Composition and Communication* 24 (October 1973):256-266.

1401. Saunders, Thomas E., and Peck, Walter W., eds. *Literature of the American Indian*. Abr. ed. Beverly Hills, CA: Glencoe; London: Collier Macmillan, 1976.

1402. Saxton, Dean and Saxton, Lucille. *Legends and Lore of the Papago and Pima Indians*. Tucson: University of Arizona Press, 1973.

1403. Scarberry, Susan J. "Memory as Medicine: The Power of Recollection in *Ceremony*." *American Indian Quarterly* 5:1 (February 1979): 19-26.

> Tayo's recollection of old stories is
> instrumental in effecting his healing.

1404. Sayre, Robert F. "Vision and Experience in *Black Elk Speaks*." *College English* 32:5 (February 1971) : 509-535.

1405. Scharback, Alexander. "Aspects of Existentialism in Clackamas Chinook Myths." *Journal of American Folklore* 75:295 (January-March 1962): 15-22.

1406. Schevill, Margaret E. "Navajo Ritual Poetry." MA Thesis. Tucson: University of Arizona, 1942.

1407. Schneider, Jack W. "The New Indian: Alienation and the Rise of the Indian Novel." *South Dakota Review* 17 (Winter 1979-1980): 67-76.

1408. Schneider, Jack W. "Patterns of Cultural Conflict in
      Southwestern Indian Fiction." Ph. D. Diss. Lubbock:
      Texas Tech University, 1977.

1409. Schoolcraft, Henry R. Myth of Hiawatha, and Other
      Oral Legends, Mythologic and Allegoric, of the North
      American Indians. Reprint of 1856 edition. Millwood,
      NY: Kraus Reprint, n.d.

1410. Schoolcraft, Henry R.   Schoolcraft's Indian Legends
      from Algic Researches. Williams, Mentor L., ed. East
      Lansing: Michigan University Press, 1956; reprint
      edition Westport, CT: Greenwood Press, 1974.

            Williams   has   selected   the   principal
      legends from Schoolcraft's major works. He
      provides   a   short   critical   history   of
      Schoolcraft's life and writings, and supplies
      a few footnotes to the tales.

1411. Schultz, James Willard.   Blackfeet Tales of Glacier
      National Park. Boston: Houghton Mifflin Co., 1916.

1412. Schultz, James W. Why Gone Those Times? Silliman,
      Lee, ed. Civilization of the American Indian Series:
      Vol. 127.   Norman: University of Oklahoma Press,
      1974.

            Blackfoot tales.

1413. Schwarz, Herbert T.   Windigo and other Tales of the
      Ojibway. Toronto: McClellend and Stewart, Ltd., 1969.

            Eight legends told by Normal Morrisseau,
      Ojibway.

1414. Scribner, Sarah. "Resume of the Indigenous Novel and
      Ciro Alegria." Pacific Historian 14:2 (Spring 1970) :
      12-14.

1415. Sears, Priscilla F.   A Pillar of Fire to Follow:
      American Indian Dramas, 1808-1859. Bowling Green,
      Ohio: Bowling Green University Popular Press, 1982.

1416. Seton, Julia M. Indian Creation Stories. Hollywood,
      CA: House-Warven, Publishers, 1952.

            Grades 5-6.

1417. "Several Mayo Myths and Rituals." Journal of American
      Folklore 83:327 (January-March 1970) : 69-76.

1418. Severance, Elsie Elliott. "Life and Legends of the
      Navajos." MA Thesis. Whittier, CA: Whittier College,
      1935.

1419. Shaw, Anna M. _Pima Indian Legends_. Tucson: University of Arizona Press, 1968.

Stories heard from author's parents and grandparents.

1420. Shor, Pekay. _When the Corn is Red_. Nashville, TN: Abingdon Press, 1973.

Grades 4-6.

1421. Shotridge, (no first name). "Tlinkit Myth: Ghost of Courageous Adventurer." University of Pennsylvania _Museum Journal_ 11:1 (1920) : 11.

1422. Shows, Harry B. and Gilliland, Hap. _Legends of Chief Bald Eagle_. Billings: Montana Council for Indian Education, 1977.

Grades 2-10.

1423. Shutz, Noel William, Jr. "The Study of Shawnee Myth in an Ethnographic and Ethnohistorical Perspective." Ph. D. Diss. Bloomington: Indiana University, 1975.

Dissertation Abstracts International 36/05-A, p. 2946.

1424. Silko, Leslie Marmon. _Ceremony_. New York: Viking Press, 1977.

Novel. A World War II veteran has difficulty readjusting to life on the reservation, but the problems are deeper than a culture conflict or a social dilemma: they involve his basic perception of the world.

1425. Silko, Leslie Marmon. _Storyteller_. New York: Seaver, 1981.

1426. Simeon, Anne. _The She-Wolf of Tsla-a-Wat: Indian Stories from British Columbia_. n.p.: Douglas and McIntyre, n.d.; avail. from International Scholarly Book Services, Inc., Beaverton, OR 97075.

1427. Skeels, Dell. "A Classification of Humor in Nez Perce Mythology." _Journal of American Folklore_ 67:263 (January-March 1954): 57-63.

1428. Skeels, Dell. "The Function of Humor in Three Nez Perce Indian Myths." _American Imago_ 11 (1954): 249-261.

1429. Skeels, Dell. "Style in the Unwritten Literature of the Nez Perce Indians." 2 vols. Ph. D. Diss. Seattle: University of Washington, 1949.

1430. Skinner, Charles M. Myths and Legends of Our Own Land. Philadelphia: Lipincott, 1896.

1431. Skinner, (no first name). "Mascouten Mythology and Folklore." Milwaukee Public Museum Bulletin Vol. 6, Art. 3 (1927).

1432. Skinner and Satterlee (no first names). "Menomini Folklore." American Museum of Natural History Anthropological Papers 13:3 (1915).

1433. Slickpoo, Allen, Sr., et al. Nu-Mee-Poom Tit-Wah-Tit: Nez Perce Tales. Nez Perce Tribe, 1972.

1434. Smith, E. [Erminnie?] "Animal Myths." American Association for the Advancement of Science Proceedings 30: n.s. (1881) : 321.

1435. Smith, Erminnie. "Iroquois Myths." American Antiquarian Magazine Vol. 4 (1880): 31.

1436. Smith, Erminnie. "Myths of the Iroquois." Bureau of American Ethnology Annual Reports Vol. 2 (1880-1881): 47.

1437. Smith, Rose Marie. "A Critical Study of the Literature of N. Scott Momaday as Intercultural Communication." Ph. D. Diss. Los Angeles: University of Southern California, 1975.

1438. Smith, William F., Jr. "American Indian Autobiographies." American Indian Quarterly 2 (1975): 237-245.

1439. Smith, William F., Jr. "American Indian Literature." English Journal 63 (January 1974):68-72.

1440. Smith, William F., Jr. "Modern Masterpiece: Seven Arrows." Midwest Quarterly 24 (Spring 1983): 229-247.

1441. Snake, Reuben A., Jr. Being Indian is . . . Macy, NE: Indian Press, 1972.

1442. Snelling, William J. Tales of the Northwest. Reprint. Wayzata, MN: Ross and Haines Old Books Co., n.d.

1443. Sneve, Virginia Driving Hawk. Betrayed. New York: Holiday House, Inc., 1974.

        Grade 7 up.

1444. Sneve, Virginia Driving Hawk. When Thunders Spoke. New York: Holiday House, Inc. 1974.

        Novel. Story of a 10 year-old boy's

growing awareness of his own culture.

1445. "The Song Remembers: Native American Voices and Visions." Language Arts 60:4 (April 1983): 439-446.

1446. Speck, Frank G. Catawba Texts. (Columbia University Contributions to Anthropology Series: Vol. 24). Reprint of 1934 edition. New York: AMS Press, Inc., 1977.

1447. Speck, [Frank G.?]. "A Malecite Myth." University of Pennsylvania Museum Journal 6:3 (1910): 49.

1448. Speck, [Frank G.?]. "Wawenock Myth Texts from Maine." Bureau of American Ethnology Annual Reports Vol. 43 (1925-1926): 165.

1449. Spence, Ahab. "The Little Bird's Arrow." Tawow 1:3 (Autumn-Winter 1970) : 19.

1450. Spence, Lewis. Myths of the North American Indians. Reprint of 1914 edition, Milwood, New York: Kraus Reprint, n.d.

1451. Spence, L. [Lewis?]. Myths and Legends of the North American Indians. Blauvelt, New York: Steinerbooks, 1975.

1452. Spencer, Katherine. Mythology and Values: An Analysis of Navajo Chantway Myths. Philadelphia: American Folklore Society, 1957.

1453. Spinden, [Herbert Joseph?]. "Spider Myths of the American Indian." American Museum of Natural History Natural History Journal 21:4 (1921): 382.

1454. Spinden, Herbert Joseph. Songs of the Tewa. New York: Exposition of the Indian Tribal Arts, Inc., 1933; Santa Fe, New Mexico: The Sunstone Press, 1976.

1455. Squier, Emma-Lindsay. Children of the Twilight: Folktales of Indian Tribes. New York: Gordon Press Publishers, 1977.

1456. Squire, Roger. Wizards and Wampum: Legends of the Iroquois. New York: Abelard-Schuman, 1971.

1457. Standiford, Lester A. "Worlds Made of Dawn: Characteristic Image and Incident in Native American Imaginative Literature." Proceedings of the Comparative Literature Symposium (Lubbock, Texas) 9 (1978): 327-352.

1458. Stands-in-Timber, John and Liberty, Margot. Cheyenne Memories. Lincoln: University of Nebraska Press, 1972.

The work which is listed only under the
name of John Stands-in-Timber, published by
Yale University Press (New Haven, 1967), is
probably the same work. In any event,
Cheyenne Memories is one of the few
Indian-organized tribal histories.

1459. Steiner, Stan, and Witt, Shirley Hill. The Way: An
Indian Anthology of American Indian Literature. New
York: Vintage Books, 1970.

Speeches ancient and modern, poetry,
prophecy.

1460. Stephens, Alexander M. "Hopi Tales." Journal of
American Folklore Vol 42 (1929): 1-72.

1461. Stephens, Alexander M. "Navajo Origin Legend."
Journal of American Folklore. (January-March 1930):
88-104.

1462. Stensland, Anna Lee. "American Indian Culture:
Promises, Problems, and Possibilities. English
Journal 60 (December 1971):1195-1200.

1463. Stensland, Anna Lee. "Integrity in Teaching Native
American Literature." Paper presented to the annual
meeting of the Conference on English Education.
Bethesda, MD: ED 199 765, March 1981.

1464. Stensland, Anna Lee. "Traditional Poetry of the
American Indian." English Journal 64 (September
1975):41-47.

1465. Stevens, James R. Sacred Legends of the Sandy Lake
Cree. Toronto: McClelland and Stewart, Ltd., 1971.

1466. Stewart, Mary Ida. "Legends of the Mississippi
Indians in Prose and Fiction." MA Thesis. Nashville,
TN: George Peabody College for Teachers, 1931.

Choctaw, Chickasaw, Natchez,
Pascagoiula, Biloxi--original material said
never to have been collected before.

1467. Storm, Hyemeyohsts. Seven Arrows. New York: Harper
and Row, 1972.

Novel. Cheyenne.

1468. Swann, Brian, intro by. Smoothing the Ground:
Essays on the Native American Oral Literature.
Berkeley: University of California Press, 1983.

1469. Swann, Brian, tr. & introd.; Allen, Paula Gunn,
foreword; Hays, Doris, musical scores. Song of the

Sky: Versions of Native American Songs and Poetry.
Ashuelot, New Hampshire: Four Zoas Night House, 1982.

1470. Swanton, [John R.?]. Haida Songs. Publications of
the American Ethnological Society 3 (1912).

1471. Swanton, John R. Haida Texts and Myths: Skidegate
Dialect. (Landmarks in Anthropology Series). Reprint
of 1905 edition. New York: Johnson Reprint
Corporation.

1472. Swanton, John R. Myths and Tales of the Southeastern
Indians Bureau of American Ethnology Bulletin, No. 88
(1929); reprint edition, New York: AMS Press, Inc.,
n.d.

1473. Swanton, John R. Myths and Tales of the Southwestern
Indians. n.p.: n.p., n.d.

        Creek, Natchez.

1474. Swanton, John R. Tlingit Myths and Texts. Bureau of
American Ethnology Bulletin 39 (1909).

1475. Tall Bull, Henry and Weist, Tom. Cheyenne Legends of
Creation. (Indian Culture Series). Billings, Montana:
Montana Council for Indian Education, 1972.

        Grades 4-9.

1476. Tall Bull, Henry and Weist, Tom. Mista!. Billings:
Montana Reading Publications, 1971.

        Cheyenne ghost stories for grades 3-8.

1477. Tall Bull, Henry and Weist, Tom. The Rolling Head:
Cheyenne Tales. (Indian Culture Series). Billings,
Montana: Montana Council for Indian Education, 1971.

        Grades 3-9.

1478. Tall Bull, Henry and Weist, Tom. The Turtle Went to
War. Billings: Montana Reading Publications, 1971.

        Northern Cheyenne folk tales for grades
    2-4.

1479. Tall Bull, Henry and Weist, Tom. Ve-Ho. Billings:
Montana Reading Publications, 1971.

        Cheyenne. For grades 2-6.

1480. "The Teacher of Modern American Indian Writing as
Ethnographer and Critic." College English 41:2
(October 1979): 163-169.

1481. "Teaching   Native   American   Authors,   1772-1968."
Association   of   Departments   of   English   (New   York)
Bulletin No. 75 (Summer 1983): 43-46.

1482. Tebbel,   John. The Conqueror.   New York: E. P. Dutton,
1951.

Novel.   Set   in   what   is   now   New York
before   French and Indian War. Protagonist   is
Irish.

1483. Tedlock,   Dennis.   "On   the   Translation   of Style in
Oral   Narrative." Journal of American Folklore 84, No.
331 (January-March 1971):114-133.

Examines Zuni narratives.

1484. Tedlock,   Dennis.   "Oral History as Poetry." Boundary
2, 23 (1975): 707-726.

1485. Tedlock,   Dennis,   translator. Finding   the   Center:
Narrative   Poetry   of   the   Zuni   Indians.   Lincoln:
University of Nebraska Press, 1978.

1486. Tehanetorens. Tales of the Iroquois. n.p.:n.p., n.d.

Author is Mohawk.

1487. Teit,   James.   "Folktales   of   Salishan   Tribes."
Memoirs   of   the   American   Museum   of Natural History,
Vol. 11 (1917): 82 ff.

1488. Teit,   James A. Tahltan Myths.   Boas Memorial Volume
1906. n.p.: n.p., 1906.

1489. Teit,   Gould,   Ferrant,   Spinder   (no   first   names).
Folktales   of   Salishan   and Sahaptin Tribes.   American
Folklore   Society   (1917).   Reprint edition, New York:
Kraus Reprint, n.d.

1490. Teit,   Gould,   Ferrant,   Spinder   (no   first   names).
Salishan   and   Sahaptin   Folktales.   American Folklore
Society Memoirs, Vol. 11 (1917).

1491. Terpening,   Lucy   Lee. "Educational   Value   of   the
Contributions   of   the   American   Indian   to   American
Literature." MA Thesis.   Albany: State University of
New York at Albany, 1933.

1492. Theisz,   R.   D. Perspectives   on   Teaching   American
Indian   Literature. Spearfish, South Dakota: Center of
Indian Studies, Black Hills State College, 1977.

1493. "To   Think   Anew: Native   American   Literature   and
Children's   Attitudes." Reading   Teacher 36:8   (April
1983): 790-794.

1494. Thomas, Darlene K. "Time Concept in North American Indian Mythology." Ph. D. Diss. Boulder: University of Colorado, 1972.

        Dissertation   Abstracts   International 33/08-B, p. 3438.

1495. Thompson, Stith. European Tales among the North American Indians. Colorado College Publications in Language, Vol. 2 (1919).

1496. Thompson, Stith. "Sunday School Stories among Savages." Texas Review 3 (1917): 109-116.

1497. Thompson, Stith. Tales of the North American Indians. Cambridge: Harvard University Press, 1929; reprint edition, Bloomington: Indiana University Press, 1966.

        Comparative notes identify themes occurring in each myth and cite sources discussing these themes. Notes give the distribution of each myth and discuss additional examples. Arrangement of tales is by story content following the idea that there are many recurrent patterns or types of tales which transcend geographical and linguistic boundaries.

1498. Thorne, J. Frederic. In the Time That Was: Being Legends of the Klingits. (Shorey Indian Series). Reprint of 1900 edition. Seattle, WA: Shorey Publications, n.d.

1499. Threepersons, Lorene. Navajo Legend Accounts for Rabbit's Long Ears. Silver City, New Mexico: Silver City Daily Press, 1945.

        Source did not make it clear whether this was article (which seems likely from subject) or book (which the nature of the source listing suggested).

1500. Titiev, Mischa. "Two Hopi Myths and Rites." Journal of American Folklore (January-March 1948): 31-43.

1501. Toelken, J. Barre. "The 'Pretty Language' of Yellowman: Genre, Mode, and Texture in Navaho Coyote Narratives." Genre 2, No.3: 211-235.

1502. Towegishig, Larry. "The Great Bear." Tawow 1:3 (Autumn-Winter 1970) : 21.

1503. Towegishig, Larry. "The Wolf Cry." Tawow 1:3 (Autumn-Winter 1970) : 20.

1504. Towendolly, Grant. A Bag of Bones. Healdsburg, CA: Naturegraph Publishers, 1965.

       Wintu.

1505. Townsend, M. J. "Taking Off the War Bonnet: American Indian Literature." Language Arts 53 (March 1976) : 236-244.

1506. Toye, William, retold by. The Mountain Goats of Temlaham. Toronto: Oxford University Press, 1969.

       Primary.

1507. Trask, Willard R. The Unwritten Song. 2 vols. New York: n.p., 1966.

       World-wide anthology includes Indian and Eskimo expression.

1508. Traveller Bird. The Path to Snowbird Mountain: Cherokee Legends. New York: Farrar, Straus and Giroux, Inc., 1972.

1509. Trejo, Judy. "Coyote Tales: A Paiute Commentary." In Readings in American Folklore, Brunvand, Jan, ed. New York: Norton, 1979.

1510. Trimble, Charles. Shove it, Buster. We'd Rather Have Our Land Denver: American Indian Press Association, 1971.

       A joke book by Indians for Indians.

1511. Trimmer, Joseph F. "Native Americans and the American Mix: N. Scott Momaday's House Made of Dawn." Indiana Social Studies Quarterly 28:2 (Autumn 1975) : 75-91.

1512. Turner, Frederick W. III, ed. The Portable North American Indian Reader. (Viking Portable Library: No. 77). New York: Viking Press, Inc., 1974; New York: Penguin Books, Inc., 1977.

1513. Turpin, Thomas Jerry. "The Cheyenne World View as Reflected in the Stories of Their Culture Heroes, Erect Horns and Sweet Medicine." Ph. D. Diss. Los Angeles: University of Southern California, 1975.

1514. Tvedten, Benet, comp. An American Indian Anthology Marvin, SD: Blue Cloud Abbey, 1971; Bethesda, MD: EDRS, ED 069 457, 1971.

       A collection of contemporary writings, some professional, some not.

1515. Tyler, Hamilton A. Pueblo Animals and Myths.

Norman: University of Oklahoma Press, 1975.

Bibliography included.

1516. Tyler, Hamilton A.   Pueblo Gods and Myths. Norman:
University of Oklahoma Press, 1964.

1517. Tyree, Donald W. "Northwest Indian Poets." Portland
Review Magazine 20 (March 1974):39-56.

1518. Underhill, Ruth. Singing for Power: The Song of the
Papago Indians of Southern Arizona. Reprint of 1938
edition, Berkeley: University of California Press,
1968.

1519. "The Uses of Oral Tradition in Six Contemporary North
American Poets." American Indian Culture and Research
Journal 4:4 (1980): 87-110.

1520. "Ute Creation Legend." El Palacio 14:7 (1923) : 104.

1521. Vallejos, Thomas. "Mestizaje: The Transformation of
Ancient   Indian   Religious Thought in Contemporary
Chicano Fiction." Ph. D. Diss. Boulder: University
of Colorado, 1980.

1522. Vanderworth, W. C. Indian Oratory: Famous Speeches
by Noted Indian Chieftans. Norman: University of
Oklahoma Press, 1971.

1523. Vaudrin, Bill. Tanaina Tales from Alaska.
Civilization of the American Indian Series, No. 96.
Norman: University of Oklahoma Press, 1969.

Author is Chippewa, lives and teaches in
Alaska.

1524. Velarde, Pablita. Old Father, the Story Teller.
Globe, Arizona: Dale Stuart King, 1960.

An Indian painter tells stories and
legends she heard froom her grandfather and
great grandfather.

1525. Velie, Alan R. "Cain and Abel in N. Scott Momaday's
House Made of Dawn." Journal of the West 17 (April
1978): 55-62.

1526. Velie, Alan R. Four American Indian Literary
Masters: N. Scott Momaday, James Welch, Leslie Marmon
Silko, and Gerald Vizenor. Norman: University of
Oklahoma Press, 1981.

Introductory chapter traces development
of Indian literature, identifying common

themes   and   pointing   out   misconceptions.
Bibliography.

1527. Velie,   Alan   R.   "James   Welch's   Poetry."   <u>American</u>
<u>Indian   Culture   and   Research   Journal</u>   3:1   (1979)   :
19-38.

1528. Velie,   Alan   R.,   ed.   <u>American Indian Literature: An</u>
<u>Anthology</u>.   Norman: University   of   Oklahoma   Press,
1979.

> Reviews:
> <u>Journal   of   American   Folklore</u> 94 (April
> 1981) : 251.
> <u>New   York   Times   Book   Review</u> (December 30,
> 1979) : 27.
> <u>Choice</u> 17 (April 1980) : 216.
> <u>Library   Journal</u>   104 (September 1, 1979)
> : 1700.
> <u>Booklist</u> 76 (October 1, 1979) : 209.

1529. Vizenor,   Gerald.   <u>Anishinabe   Adisokan; Tales of the</u>
<u>People</u>. Minneapolis: Nodin Press, 1970.

1530. Vlahos,   Olivia. <u>New World Beginnings: Indian Cultures</u>
<u>in the Americas</u>. New York: Viking Press, 1970.

1531. Wagner,   (no   first   name).   <u>Yuchi   Tales</u>.   American
Ethnological Society Publications, No. 13 (1931).

1532. Wah-Be-Gwo-Nese   [Pseud.].   <u>Ojibwa   Indian   Legends</u>.
Marquette,   MI: Northern   Michigan   University   Press,
1972.

1533. Walker,   Deward E.,   Jr.   <u>Myths of Idaho Indians</u>.   Rev.
ed.   (Gem   Book   and   Anthropological   Monograph).
Moscow: University Press of Idaho, 1980.

1534. Walker,   Louise   Jean.   <u>Legends   of   Green   Sky   Hill</u>.
Grand Rapids, Michigan: William B. Eerdmans, 1961.

1535. Wallis,   W.   D.   "Folktales   from   Shumopovi,   Second
Mesa."   <u>Journal   of   American   Folklore</u> Vol.(?) 49
(n.d.): 191-192.

1536. Walsh,   Anna   C.,   and   Adams,   Caryl   L.   "A Critical
Analysis   of   Selected   Native   American   Literature for
Juvenile Readers." Bethesda, MD: ED 219 780, 1979.

1537. Walton,   Eda   Lou.   "Navaho Poetry."   <u>Texas Review</u> V,
No. 7 (1922):198-210.

1538. Walton,   Eda   Lou. "Navaho Songs." <u>Nation</u> 110 (1920) :
517.

1539. Walton, Eda Lou. "Navaho Traditional Poetry." Ph. D. Thesis. Berkeley: University of California, 1921.

1540. Walton, Eda Lou, and T. T. Waterman. "American Indian Poetry." American Anthropologist 27, No. 1 (January-March 1925):25-52.

        Discusses   forms,   tribal   patterns,
    influences   of   culture,   problems   of
    translations. Includes bibliography.

1541. Warburton, Austen D. Indian Lore of the North California Coast Santa Clara, CA: Pacific Pueblo Press, 1966.

    Myths, stories, customs, anecdotes.

1542. Washburne, Marion (Foster) Indian Legends. Chicago: n.p., 1915.

1543. Wasuchope, Robert. Lost Tribes and Sunken Continents: Myth Method in the Study of American Indians. Chicago: University of Chicago Press, 1962.

1544. Waterman, T. T. "The Explanatory Element in the Folk-Tales of the North American Indians." Journal of American Folklore 27, No. 103 (January-March 1914):1-54.

    Contains bibliography.

1545. Waters, Frank. Book of the Hopi. New York: Ballantine Books, Inc., 1969.

1546. Waters, Frank. Masked Gods: Navaho and Pueblo Ceremonialism. Athens, OH: Swallow Press, 1950; reprint edition, New York: Ballantine Books, 1975.

1547. Waters, Frank. Pumpkin Seed Point: Being Within the Hopi. Athens, OH: Swallow Press, 1973.

1548. Weatherby, H. Tales the Totems Tell. Toronto: Macmillan Co. of Canada, 1962.

        Grades 5-8. Tales which the totem poles
    of British Columbia represent.

1549. Webb, George. A Pima Remembers. Tucson: University of Arizona Press, 1959.

        Author, a Pima, relates Pima history and
    traditions in form of short stories--designed
    to teach young Pimas and whites.

1550. Webster, Loraine and Schleif, Mabel. "The Creation of Stories and Beginning Reading Material for

Pre-School Indian Children in South Dakota." Bethesda,
MD: ED 062 080, n.d.

Sioux stories for pre-readers and poor
readers.

1551. Webster, Loraine and Schleif, Mabel. "Read Aloud
Stories Series: A Product of a Project to Create
Stories and Beginning Reading Materials for Pre-school
Indian Children in South Dakota." Bethesda, MD: ED
062 081, March 31, 1972.

Sioux stories.

1552. Webster, Loraine and Schleif, Mabel. "Rebus Reading
Book Series: A Product of a Project to Create Stories
and Beginning Reading Material for Pre-school Indian
Children in South Dakota." Bethesda, MD: ED 062 082,
March 31, 1972.

Sioux stories.

1553. Weeks, Rupert. <u>Pachee Goyo: History and Legends from
the Shoshone</u>. Laramie, WY: Jelm Mountain Publications,
1981.

1554. Welch, James. <u>The Death of Jim Loney</u>. New York:
Harper and Row Publishers, Inc., 1979.

Novel.

1555. Welch, James. <u>Winter in the Blood</u>. New York: Harper
and Row, 1974.

Novel. Nameless reservation Indian
caught in a spiral of losing that can end
only in death, ignorant of the old ways and
tormented rather than relieved by memories
from his own past.

1556. Welch, James. <u>Riding the Earthboy 40</u>. New York:
World Publishing, 1971.

Collection of poems.

1557. Welsch, Roger. <u>Omaha Indian Myths and Trickster
Tales</u>. Athens, Ohio: Swallow Press, 1975.

1558. Weltfish, Gene. <u>Caddoan Texts, Pawnee, South Band
Dialect</u>. (American Ethnological Society Publications.
No. 17). Reprint of 1937 edition. New York: AMS
Press, Inc., 1973.

1559. Wetherill, Hilda (told by Cha-La-Pi, Navajo). <u>Navajo
Indian Poems: Translations from the Navajo and Other
Poems</u>. New York: Vantage Press, 1952.

1560. Wetherill, Louisa Wade. "A Navaho Folktale of Pueblo Bonito." Art and Archaeology 5:14 (1922): 132-136.

1561. Wetherill, Louisa Wade. "Navaho Stories." The Kiva Arizona State Museum, Tucson, AZ 12:5-6 (1947) : 39-40.

1562. Wheelwright, Mary C. Atsah and Yohe. Museum of Navaho Ceremonial Art Bulletin No. 3 (n.d.) : 1-16.

1563. Wheelwright, Mary C. Coyote Chant. Museum of Navaho Ceremonial Art n.v. (1946).

1564. Wheelwright, Mary C., de Johly, Hasteen and BiYash, Estsan Hatrali. Myth of Willa-Chee-Ji Deginnh Keygo Hatral and Myth of Natohe Bajaki Hatral. Museum of Navaho Ceremonial Art Bulletin No. 7 (1958).

1565. Wheelwright, Mary C. Male Shooting Chant. Museum of Navaho Ceremonial Art Bulletin No. 7 (1958).

1566. Wheelwright, Mary C. and McAllester, David. Texts of the Navajo Creation Chants. Cambridge: Peabody Museum, Harvard University, 1961.

1567. Wheelwright,Mary C. and Newcomb, Franc J. Navaho Myths and Ceremonies of the Blessing Chant, Water Chant and Hail Chant. New York: n.p., 1940.

1568. Wherry, Joseph. Indian Masks and Myths of the West. New York: Funk and Wagnalls Publishing Co., 1969.

     Considers similarities between Indian legends and Christianity.

1569. White, John. "A Story from the Lenape." Weewish Tree 2:5 (March 1974) : 3-5.

1570. Whitman, William, 3rd. Navaho Tales. Boston: Houghton Mifflin, 1925.

1571. Whitney, Blair. "American Indian Literature of the Great Lakes." Great Lakes Review 11 (Winter 1976): 43-53.

1572. Wiget, Andrew. "The Oral Literature of Native North America: A Critical Anthology." 2 vols. Ph. D. Diss. Salt Lake City: University of Utah, 1977.

1573. Wiget, Andrew. "Saytasha's Night Chant: A Literary Textual Analysis of a Zuni Ritual Poem." American Indian Culture and Research Journal 4:1-2 (1980) : 99-140.

     After describing the poem's cultural

context, the article addresses its shape,
structure, language and style. Includes
English language text of poem.

1574. Wilbert, Johannes. Folk Literature of the Warao
Indians: Narrative Material and Motif Content.
Berkeley: University of California Press, 1970.

1575. Wilbert, Johannes, ed. Folk Literature of the Yamaha
Indians: Martin Gusinde's Collection of Yamaha
Narratives. Berkeley: University of California
Press, 1977.

1576. Wilkie, Raymond. Navajo Folktales. Societies around
the World. New York: The Dryden Press, 1956.

1577. Williams, Mentor L., ed. Schoolcraft's Indian Legends
from Algic Researches. East Lansing, MI: Michigan
State University Press, 1957; reprint edition,
Westport, CT: Greenwood Press, 1974.

Williams has selected the principal
legends from Schoolcraft's major works. He
provides a short critical history of
Schoolcraft's life and writings and supplies
a few footnotes to the tales.

1578. Williams, Ted. The Reservation. New York: Syracuse
University Press, 1976.

Novel.

1579. Willoya, William and Brown, Vinson. Strange and
Prophetic Dreams of the Indian Peoples. Happy Camp,
CA: Naturegraph, 1962.

Grade 4 up.

1580. Wilson, Blanche N. Minnetonka Story. Wayzata, MN:
Ross and Haines Old Books Co., n.d.

1581. Wilson, Norma Jean Clark. "The Spirit of Place in
Contemporary American Indian Poetry." Ph. D. Diss.
Norman: University of Oklahoma, 1978.

1582. Wilson, (no first name). Indian Hero Tales. n.p.:
American Book Co., 1916; reprint [?] edition New York:
Van-Nostrand-Reinhold Books, n.d.

1583. Wissler, Clark. Mythology of the Blackfoot Indians.
Reprint of 1908 edition, New York: AMS Press, Inc.,
n.d.

This work may be the same as that
attributed to Wissler and Duvall below.

1584. Wissler, Clark, and Duvall, D. _Mythology of the Blackfoot Indians_. Anthropological Papers of the American Museum of Natural History, Vol. 2, Part 1 (1909); reprint edition, New York: AMS Press, Inc., n.d.

1585. Witt, Shirley H. and Steiner, Stan, eds. _The Way: An Anthology of American Indian Literature_. New York: Alfred A. Knopf, 1972.

   More than 100 selections: tales, poems, oratory, humor, letters, articles.

1586. Wood, Charles E. _A Book of Tales, Being Myths of the North American Indians_. New York: Gordon Press Publishers, n.d.; reprint of 1929 edition, New York: Vanguard Press, 1971.

   BIP 82-83 lists only the Gordon Press edition, n.d.

1587. Wood, Nancy. _Many Waters_. Limited edition. Garden City, NY: Doubleday and Co., Inc., 1974.

   Grade 6 up.

1588. Wood, Nancy. _War Cry on a Prayer Feather: Prose and Poetry of the Ute Indians_. Garden City, NY: Doubleday, 1979.

1589. Wood, Nancy. _When Buffalo Free the Mountains_. Garden City, NY: Doubleday and Co., Inc., 1980.

1590. Woodyard, Darrel. _Dakota Indian Lore_. San Antonio, TX: Naylor Co., 1968.

   Legends portraying history and customs.

1591. Woolgar, Jack and Rudnicki, Barbara J. _Hopi Mysteries_. Indian Culture Series. Billings: Montana Council for Indian Education, 1974.

   Grades 5-9.

1592. Wright, Harold Bell. _Long Ago Told: Legends of the Papago Indians_. New York: Appleton-Century-Crofts, Division of Merideth Publishing Co., 1929.

1593. Wyss, Thelma H. _Star Girl_. New York: Viking Press, 1967.

   Grades 4-7.

1594. Yellow Robe, Rosebud. _Tonweya and the Eagles and Other Lakota Indian Tales_. New York: Dial Press, 1979.

Grades 2-6.   BIP 81-82 lists name as
"Robe, Rosebud Y."

1595. Young, Eggerton R. _Stories from Indian Wigwams and Northern Campfires_. Reprint of 1893 edition, Detroit: Gale Research, 1970; New York: Gordon Press Publishers, 1977.

1596. Zachrau, Thelka. "N. Scott Momaday: Towards and Indian Identity." _American Indian Culture and Research Journal_ 3 (No. 1, 1979): 39-56.

1597. "Zitkala Sa: The Evolution of a Writer." _American Indian Quarterly_ 5:3 (August 1979): 229-238.

1598. Zepeda, Ofelia, ed. _When It Rains: Papago and Pima Poetry_. Sun Tracks Series. Tucson: University of Arizona Press, 1982.

1599. Zolla, Elemire. _The Writer and the Shaman: A Morphology of the American Indian_. New York: Harcourt Brace Jovanovich, 1969, 1973.

Author Index

Subject Index

871 877, 881, 916,
923, 924, 925, 926,
927, 943, 957, 966,
971, 973, 987, 999,
1010 1020, 1033,
1053, 1068, 1074,
1113, 1123, 1130
1166, 1170, 1171,
1172, 1194, 1224,
1235, 1282, 1284,
1295, 1312 1328,
1349, 1351, 1363,
1419, 1426 1524,
1541, 1551, 1561,
1595
Storm, Hyemeyohsts 895, 1153
Storyteller 1425
Storytelling 1262
Structure 717
Student poetry 1341
Studies 759, 0
Studies in Native American
  literature 718
Study 1378
Study guides 171, 265
Style 1429, 1483
Sunday School stories 1496
Sundown 486, 487
Sweet Grass Cree 798
Symbol 717
Symbolism 830, 868, 1287
Tahltan 1488
Tales 42, 179, 257, 708, 730,
  734, 741, 744, 751, 756,
  760, 761, 763, 773, 777,
  785, 796, 799, 800, 804,
  805, 808, 809, 810, 815,
  834, 838, 850, 884, 892,
  897, 900, 914, 915, 933,
  935, 945, 946, 964, 969,
  993, 994, 996, 1002, 1007,
  1012, 1013, 1019, 1053,
  1059, 1061, 1067, 1080,
  1084, 1091, 1094, 1097,
  1102, 1104, 1129, 1133,
  1138, 1150, 1180, 1181,
  1182, 1185, 1202, 1221,
  1230, 1231, 1233, 1237,
  1263, 1272, 1285, 1288,
  1289, 1299, 1300, 1303,
  1307, 1312, 1313, 1317,
  1319, 1320, 1321, 1323,
  1327, 1331, 1343, 1362,
  1365, 1366, 1367, 1374,
  1384, 1393, 1411,

1412, 1433, 1442,
1460, 1472, 1473,
1477, 1486, 1495,
1497, 1523, 1529,
1531, 1548, 1557,
1576, 1582, 1585,
1586, 1594
Tales of the Northwest 632
Tanaina 1523
Taos 902, 903, 904, 906,
  908, 912, 1320
Teachers' guides 194,
  707, 855, 1092, 1266,
  1399
Teaching 1355, 1399,
  1463, 1480, 1481,
  1492, 1493
Teaching Native American
  literature 1092, 1218
Tebbel, John 1482
Television programs 338
Tell Them Willie Boy is
  Here 447
Terror 464
Test theme 1188, 1189
Teton 914, 915
Teton Sioux 1027, 1314
Tewa 913, 1321, 1454
Textbooks 68, 111, 1392
Texts 833, 958, 978, 979,
  980, 1096, 1143, 1146,
  1371, 1396
Theatre 315, 614, 1349
Theme 769
Themes 1497
Theses 49, 85, 183, 203, 220
Thlinget 793
Thoreau, Henry D. 330,
  450, 504, 505, 514,
  623, 629
Tillamook 1094, 1104
Time 1494
Tlingit 764, 977
Tlingit texts 1474
Tlinkit 1421
Toltec 1291
Totem tales 1289
Totems 764, 1548
Totonac 1291
Tour on the Prairie, A 653
Toys 338
Traditional poetry 1382
Traditions 1118

About the Compiler

ROGER O. ROCK teaches high school English in Nashua, Montana.